JONATHAN PATRICK

CHECKMATE

BOOK ONE

Palmetto Publishing Group, LLC
Charleston, SC

For more information regarding special discounts for bulk purchases, please contact Palmetto Publishing Group at Info@PalmettoPublishingGroup.com.

ISBN-13: 978-1-944313-51-7
ISBN-10: 1-944313-51-6

For my boys…

Red is gray and

yellow white

But we decide

which is right...

And which is an illusion

—Moody Blues

CHAPTER 1

Grand Hyatt Taipei

TAIPEI, TAIWAN

It was a real shame they would only be using the room for two hours. Located on the top floor of the luxurious Hyatt Taipei, the room had been designed for occupants with very discriminating tastes, an extreme desire for privacy and very deep pockets. At $2,500 US dollars per night, the suite consisted of a spacious main room in the center of which rested a large, highly-polished teak conference table. The table was surrounded by ten of the most comfortable leather chairs money could buy. Off this main room was an enormous master bedroom suite with a king sized bed, its own marble bathroom, sauna and jetted tub. The men surveyed their temporary surroundings and smiled, fully understanding what, and for whom, this suite had been designed. They all agreed that if they survived the events of the next year, they would return to this very room and use it for its intended purpose.

The five Iranian men had come to Taiwan with only one purpose in mind, to get very, very rich. Taiwan was not chosen as the meeting place by pure happenstance. The Iranians were here to meet with several senior ranking Chinese officials whom they had met last fall while in Pyongyang, North Korea. The Chinese men had expressed interest in the Iranian's rather unique proposal at the Pyongyang symposium several months earlier.

The Chinese officials included General Zhao from China's Army and his two cohorts, Admiral Feng from the navy, and a man with a face that closely resembled that of a desert shrew, who went by the name "Chen," from the Chinese Ministry of State Security. The Chinese also brought along a small security detail, which the Iranians assumed were there as money couriers. The Chinese had come to Taiwan under the auspices of some business meetings at the nearby Chinese embassy earlier in the week and had simply extended their visits. The meeting's location was close enough to the Chinese officials' bases that a day or two away wouldn't raise any red flags.

The Iranians simply wanted to see Taiwan and were here as tourists, or so they said to anyone who asked. They were not concerned with world chaos, destruction, or dishonor. All five of the Iranian men had grown up poor, made important contacts young in life, and found power. The men all felt they had better things to do in their lives than live in the nicest houses on the nicest streets in Tehran. Despite being friends since their youth, they hadn't always agreed on everything in life. In their mid-thirties now, they did agree on at least one important thing; the men hated living in the sand. They had traveled the world and enjoyed themselves when out from under the watchful eyes of their Imams. From the decadence of Rio de Janeiro, and both the Mexican and French Rivera, to the beaches of southern Florida, the men liked to party. Although they wore the trappings of Islam, they were hypocrites of a magnitude yet to be fully discovered.

The leader of the group from Tehran was Mehrak Kazemi. A consummate Oliver Twist character, he lived his youth on the streets of Tehran and learned to survive by any means possible. Mehrak met Atash Rahbar when they were nine; they had been friends on and off since then. Atash caught a break when he learned to read and eventually, through luck and being at the right place at the right time, managed to get himself through the University of Tehran. He graduated near the top of his class with a bachelor's degree in Social Sciences. It was in the pursuit of his degree that Atash realized there were many different people in the world and many more places to live than the hot deserts of Iran.

The three other men traveling in their company had educations received on the streets. In larger, more legitimate organizations, they would have titles such as management facilitator or logistics expediter. In reality, these guys were the guys that got whatever needed to be done, done.

Each man wanted it all and no risk was too great to achieve their objectives. It had taken significant planning and connections, but they believed they had figured out a way to accomplish their goals. The men were here to present their plan and receive an initial cash payment of two million dollars each. They would also be discussing the one percent commission on projected oil and gas sales as payment for their devised nefarious scheme. The Iranian men hoped to gain the wealth they sought from the actions of North Korea, an unwitting country with proven nuclear weapons knowledge and just enough technology to almost be dangerous. They would con their own country, Iran, a country with great technology and a little nuclear knowledge, and get rich from yet a third party, China. All they felt they would need to do was topple the first domino; the rest of them should fall on their own. Today's meeting was called to show the other key players of the game exactly how to set up and perfectly align the dominoes.

The Chinese officials had little patience for the Iranians as a whole but decided to attend today's meeting when they were told that, with very little work on their behalf, they could be rich beyond their wildest dreams. Who wouldn't agree to a meeting like that? The best part, of course, was that the meeting was being held in Taipei, Taiwan. With their wives back home in China, the men intended to take full advantage of the numerous Western vices available in Taiwan.

The Chinese visitors knocked on the door of the luxury penthouse suite at exactly 2 p.m. Mehrak let them in and, noticing that the normal pleasantries of meet and greet simply weren't going to happen, had showed the men to their luxurious seats around the large teak conference table. The security detail, carrying what Atash presumed was the agreed payment for his plan, was shown into an adjoining room and the door had been secured with a deadbolt from both sides. Atash joined the other men at the table, introduced himself and opened the meeting.

"Gentlemen, thank you for coming today. My partners and I want to assure you this room is soundproof and we have taken the precaution of sweeping it for both audio and video surveillance equipment. It is important that you know we are risking our lives to bring you this idea and hope you will treat the information in such a way that we will all live long enough to enjoy our wealth."

Atash continued, "Our idea has everything to do with the world's oil and gas reserves and the expanding problem of who has those resources compared to those who need them. My country, Iran, has the potential and resources to develop itself as a nation, feed and clothe its entire population, and make something of itself, yet instead, it has chosen a dangerous path that will almost certainly get a third of my people killed."

Atash checked the faces of the men who sat before him. Their faces registered no emotion of any kind. Was that a good sign? He cautiously continued, "As we all saw several months ago, in Pyongyang, the North Korean leadership continues its policies as it has for the past twenty years, ravaging its own people for the sake of their nuclear ambitions. They are ahead of my country in the weapons race but apparently lack the technology needed to pursue their ambitions of not just having nuclear power; they want to have the potential to engage in war with the west. Even a country as mighty as yours hesitates to take on American might." Upon hearing some throats being cleared, he quickly added, "And rightly so."

Atash thought he detected a glance of distain from the man the others called General Zhao, from the Chinese Army. At least now he knew they were listening. "Our plan is designed to ignite the passion of the young leader from North Korea, who, as a boy, probably liked to play with matches and pull the wings off of insects with the religious zealots of my government, who believe a war with the west is not only inevitable, but necessary. The best part of our plan from your perspective would be that you and your country will become very, very wealthy."

He watched their faces. These men would make excellent card players as each wore a face of stone. Atash went on, "In order to proceed, we will need some assurances from you that you will be operating in good faith. As you were advised in Pyongyang, listening to our proposal will cost you ten million dollars. I'll assume you brought the money?"

General Zhao rose and walked to the door of the adjoining room, slid back the deadbolt, knocked two times, paused, and knocked once again. He returned to his seat on the opposite side of the conference table from the Iranians. Responding quickly to Zhao's knock, the deadbolt on the other side of the door could be heard sliding back and the three large men from the security detail entered, bringing in five identical black Pelican waterproof cases. They placed the heavy cases on the table and then each man took his respective position behind their Chinese charge.

Atash watched the generals and the man without the uniform smirk as the heavy black cases were placed on the table.

The Iranians had decided that the risks of presenting a plan so bold and fraught with danger would require that they receive enough money from the Chinese, today, for them to drop off the grid, potentially indefinitely, if the ambitious plan suddenly went sideways.

Atash had studied his counterpart's culture years ago, and was about to tell his friends what was to happen next, when all four of his partners suddenly reached across the table and pulled the briefcases toward them. Before Atash could warn them, Mehrak spoke. "Due to the nature of today's business, you gentlemen understand that we have to count the money."

Only Atash left his briefcase across the table. Each man to Atash's left subsequently opened their brief cases and counted the numerous bundles of money. The Chinese men watched in silence. Atash continued, "Very well. Is everyone sure they want to be involved?" The Chinese men slowly nodded without smiling.

Atash was getting concerned. He hadn't been exactly sure how this meeting was going to go but certainly had thought he would have been able to read these men better than he was. He feigned a smile and continued. "Very good, let's proceed. If you gentlemen will kindly direct your attention to the monitors in front of you, I will bring up my presentation."

Atash smiled and carefully typed in the fourteen-character code that unlocked his laptop. He turned, nodded at Mehrak, who in turn typed in a separate code to unlock the specific file that contained the presentation.

Atash thought to himself, *deep breath, ready, go*!

"As you gentlemen will recall, the salient points briefed at the conclusion of the conference last fall were that there are three targets the North Koreans deem as the key elements of the American's Ground-Based Midcourse Defense (GMD) system, and that this system and its various components are the very backbone of America's defense against missile strikes."

The first PowerPoint slide was a brief overview of what the North Koreans felt was a major concern last fall, the American's relatively new Sea-Based X-band radar system or SBX. He tabbed forward through the slides and stopped on a slide of the base of the SBX platform. "By looking at schematics, foolishly provided to us by the program's lead contractor and several other sources, my team has determined that the weakness of this system is that it is inherently slow, difficult to maneuver and vulnerable at several points above and below the waterline. I'll spare you gentlemen the finer details for both time and operational security reasons. Sufficed to say, we have plans in place to remove the SBX from operational use."

The Chinese men had no questions, made no sound and never made eye contact with Atash. Atash furrowed his brow and nodded at Mehrak. Mehrak used his remote to advance the briefing slides to the second concern voiced by the North Koreans. He quickly advanced through the preliminary slides and settled on a Goggle Earth image of Fort Greeley Army Base in Alaska. "According to the North Koreans, the missile fields at Fort Greeley are perhaps the greatest threat and deterrent to any potential missile attack on the United States. It is the missiles at Fort Greely that are controlled by the various radars of the American defense system. Although the missiles themselves will be nearly impossible to get to in their buried and hardened silos, we feel that interfering with the various communication systems of the missiles will render them useless."

Mehrak scrolled through several images from various websites showing the construction of the missile fields themselves, as well as pictures from the general contractor showing related support buildings such as the missile sites satellite communications arrays and related power systems.

Atash, Mehrak and the three other Iranians briefly exchanged glances. With what could best be described as butterflies in his stomach, and perhaps even a slightly nauseous feeling, Atash resumed the briefing.

The next series of slides were of the Cobra Dane radar system on Shemya Island, Alaska. Although he knew the Chinese men knew as much as he did about the system, Atash hit the points of concern raised by the Koreans again as well as what he and his team had determined to be the system's vulnerabilities.

Atash quickly wrapped up the presentation and turned off the lap top. "Do any of you have any questions?"

The Chinese men sat back in their respective chairs and, in perfect unison, shook their heads, no. Atash thought quickly to himself as he turned briefly away from the men's gazes, *no point in stopping now*, took a long, shallow breath and went on.

"Step one, gentlemen, will be for you to convince your young North Korean neighbor, Kang Dae, that he should construct and deliver a very large nuclear weapon to the shores of America as a sort of hedge against any future sanctions, and to encourage the cancellation of all sanctions currently in force. We believe he is weak enough to be manipulated into doing as you suggest."

Atash looked for some type of feedback from the Chinese men, but they didn't nod in agreement or shake their heads in disapproval. He found it slightly unnerving but he pressed on.

"Step two, you must convince the Iranian High Council that it's in their best interest to assist with the outfitting of a ship to deliver the North Korean weapon to the shores of America and detonate it on the west coast of America in a mighty stroke for Jihad to avenge the deaths of all Muslims murdered by the Americans in the past twenty or so years. This shouldn't be a hard sell, as they still consider America "The Great Satin." We can work out all the details in the coming months. We will also need the use of an Iranian submarine to deliver some items up north to the Aleutians."

"Is everyone clear on the plan so far?" Atash anticipated a little more engagement on the officials' parts. Positive *or* negative feedback at this point would be great, so Atash would know that he wasn't talking to soldiers from Emperor Qin Shi Huan's Terracotta Army. Finally, the little man from state security, with the face of a shrew, nodded for the group.

Relieved for receiving at least some acknowledgement that the man was listening, Atash finished by saying, "I have mentioned these preliminary steps first, as we believe they will take the longest amount of time to complete. The most important aspect to this operation is to get the North Koreans and my Iranian countrymen to believe they are each in charge of this operation. Their egos alone will inspire great things. Every action that is taken will be relayed to you but not connected to you. You must remain as far away as possible for deniability. What is the American expression so widely used these days, plausible deniability?"

As if on cue, two of the Chinese men looked at their watches. Atash glanced at Mehrak who had also noticed the men check their watches. These men actually seemed bored!

Sensing he had only moments before they were walking out of the suite, Atash rushed to the final part of the presentation.

"This leads us to our end game, gentlemen. How would China like to drill for oil and natural gas, unhindered or challenged by other countries in the South China Sea, specifically the Spratly Islands?"

"Impossible!" shouted General Zhao. "I've had enough, you're obviously quite mad." He pounded his hand on the table. "The American Navy would never allow it!"

"Good point, General Zhao, and we are getting to that next. Can I ask you gentlemen to briefly play the role of the Americans?" Now all three men were definitely paying attention.

Atash continued, "As American generals, what do you believe the North Koreans are trying to do with their nuclear program as we speak here today?"

General Zhao spoke first, "I would think they are putting all their efforts into building a small nuclear device to go on top of their lousy rockets."

"Correct, general! What if we wanted to be sure the Americans would narrow their intelligence gathering to all things small and mobile?"

Eyes narrowed and looks were exchanged between the officials. Now he seemed to have their full attention.

"What if you supplied the Americans with details outlining the progress North Korea was making in their miniaturization efforts? If you were the Americans, how hard would it be to convince you that the North Koreans were gearing up to conduct a series of long range missile tests?" Atash continued, "What if we could convince Al Qaeda to attack several strategic targets, convincing the Americans that someone was going to launch a missile attack on the west coast of the United States?" Atash smiled. Now, at least, he had them leaning forward in their chairs.

The little man with no military insignia looked directly at Atash. "How would you intend to do that?" he asked.

Atash leaned forward slightly, "Our plan is to create such a diversion west of Alaska, in the Aleutians, and in Alaska proper, that America will have no choice but to expect a missile attack." General Zhao looked directly at Atash. "You mentioned handling the American Navy; how do you expect to accomplish that feat with one outdated Iranian diesel submarine?" Again, the question appeared to be directed toward Atash.

"An excellent point, general, you will recall I said both of these countries need to believe they are in charge?"

The general slowly nodded.

"It is imperative the North Koreans believe that the weapon they think they are sending to the port of Los Angeles is strictly for black mail purposes. At this point, although he talks a good game, I think Kang Dae and his generals would do anything to get the West off their backs, especially if they can do it with their favorite toy. What they won't know is the Iranians will actually be in control of two key parts of this plan. An Iranian submarine, with a Chinese advisor on board, will be in charge of delivering high explosives to the Aleutians for a coordinated diversion we've already discussed. They will also be in control of a uniquely modified freighter carrying the nuclear device. The Iranians will put the freighter into the port of San Diego and detonate the device in the name of Allah." Each of the Chinese officials' faces dropped a shade of color.

Atash went on, "With all of the economic chaos in the United States in the past few years, they have retracted their navy back home with over seventy-five percent of the Pacific fleet moored in the waters immediately surrounding San Diego, as well as the port itself. All you gentlemen need to focus on is that these actions, in conjunction with some other events, will virtually eliminate the threat of America's Navy in the Pacific. With the American Navy's teeth all but removed, you will have free reign in both the Pacific and regional waters of Southeast Asia for the foreseeable future." Whereas before, Atash had not been able to discern the men's emotions, it was suddenly very clear. They appeared genuinely pleased with the plan.

The officials rose and were shaking hands across the table when General Zhao looked at Atash, "It would appear to me you know all the complexities of the plan being discussed this afternoon." Atash smiled, perhaps a bit too broadly and nodded yes.

With that, the most unassuming man in the security detail pulled out his sound suppressed pistol, reached across the table and promptly shot and killed Mehrak and the other three Iranians.

Atash was too stunned to move and waited for the inevitable shot that never came. General Zhao came around the table and walked up in front of him, adjusted his tunic, and said, "Two things spared your life today, Atash. The one thing that made our decision not to kill you, specifically, was that you did not dishonor us by counting your money."

As the officials were walking away, Atash hesitated briefly, then asked, "What was the other?" General Zhao smiled a thin, almost unperceivable, smile. "We like your plan."

Atash asked his last question and immediately regretted it. "Why did you feel you needed to kill them all?"

The Chinese officials and their escorts stopped, turned and looked at Atash. Mr. Chen from the Chinese state security spoke for the group. "Atash," he began, before glancing briefly to his left at the Chinese naval officer, "we don't like loose ends."

"Enjoy your money, Atash. It would be unwise to let us down."

With that, the Chinese left the hotel suite, leaving Atash staring at the four dead bodies of his associates and all five of the black briefcases.

Over the coming year, the intricate planning and implementation of the dangerous plan was put into motion. As predicted, once the seeds of the plan were planted in the minds of the key players, the egos of the two rogue leaders had done the rest.

CHAPTER 2

BOATSS

Over at the newly created, yet not fully operational or fully funded, Broad Ocean Area Transit and Smuggling Surveillance (BOATSS) desk, Julie Folk, "Jewels" to her friends, was just starting her shift and was reviewing the BOATSS computer logs from the weekend.

It was Monday morning and the BOATSS computer had been programmed to generate reports on demand based on several variables. These included, but were not limited to, particular ports of interest, a particular vessel's time of arrival or departure, etc. These variables were both fluid and flexible by design, and could potentially look back on months of stored information.

"Jewels" stood at five foot eleven in flats, had emerald green eyes, long deep chestnut brown hair and a shape like she had walked off the pages of Maxim magazine. She was strikingly beautiful. If you were to throw in her one hundred thirty point IQ and magnetic personality, she was the whole package. Miss Julie Folk was not, however, without her minor flaws. She was first and foremost a self-confessed coffee-junkie. Everywhere Jewels went, she had a coffee in her hand. It didn't seem to matter where she was or what time of day, she always had her coffee.

Jewels would tease her friends that the coffee was just to keep her hands warm in the ice-box cold computer vault she worked in. Several spurned men in her office disagreed and believed that she was a frigid "ice queen" and held the coffee so as not to drop below the required temperature to function as a human. Jewels' other minor flaw was that she was stubborn. Unfortunately for others, with her smarts, Jewels was usually right.

The problem facing Jewels was that being right all the time often led to people feeling intimidated by her. This bothered Jewels; she often sought solace through the only activity she enjoyed outside of work, other than drinking coffee at the Firehook Bakery; running. She was almost fanatical about her running. Unless the forecast called for heavy snow, Jewels would be out after work running the loop from her apartment down to the Washington Monument and back. On nice days she could run farther, down 14th and around the Jefferson Memorial, expanding the loop to five miles. Jewels would tell you she ran to keep herself mentally sharp. It also didn't hurt her ability to maintain her killer looks.

Over time, Jewels heard the whispered derogatory comments about her in some shape or form, either directly from her coworkers or through her best friend and coworker, Gina. Jewels didn't care much for the things people said about her. She was smart and confident in her job and enjoyed her life. She just wasn't into anything trendy.

Gina Hughes, or as Jewels teasingly liked to call her, "Gina Who?" on the other hand, was into *whatever* was trending today. She was on Facebook, Twitter, Skype, Snapchat, LinkedIn, and whatever else she could think of. Gina was attractive but in an athletic way. She was only five foot six, but lean, strong and very much in shape. She was a very busy girl with an active social life, often times she disappeared a bit early on a Friday afternoon and would drop back into town bright and early on a Monday morning.

The girls had been friends since they met at Stanford almost seven years ago. Both graduated magna cum laude in computer science and both attained their Masters at MIT's School of Computer Engineering. They maintained their friendship after college but drew the line at being roommates. Although scholastically they could be twins, their social lives differed greatly. By their own admissions, they embraced the inner "Nerd." It was the company they kept, while the "Nerd" rested that was so much different.

The girls' relationship was often more like sisters and they had seen each other through both thick and thin. Gina was there when Jewels' mom suffered through the last four months of inoperable ovarian cancer and likewise, Jewels was there for Gina when her twin brother had been killed in Iraq. They had no secrets from each other.

After both girls graduated with their doctorates from MIT, Gina bid on, and won, a contract from a software startup firm in Silver Springs, Maryland, to develop a tracking program. She needed help with the project and hired Jewels to help her. They negotiated the contract whereby in lieu of one large fixed payment, the girls received a more moderate initial payment and royalties from any future sale or use of the product.

The "*Confero*" software, which they named after the Greek phrase, "to gather," was hugely successful and was purchased from the software company by a national telecommunications firm. It had been almost four years now and a check for $1,856 came to each of them like clockwork on the first of each month. The girls had cleverly both copy written and secured proprietary rights for the software.

Rent for nice apartments in downtown D.C. were not for the faint of heart and the "magic checks" as they referred to them, allowed the girls to live far above the current wages they received working as freelance computer programmers. Both girls lived in two of Washington's most sought after areas. Jewels lived one block west of DuPont Circle and her seventh floor apartment was just high enough that she could see the northern edge of the circle from her front window. Several foreign embassies were located in or around the circle and it was viewed as a very cosmopolitan neighborhood. Jewels enjoyed the easy walk to several of her favorite weekend haunts, including Pizzeria Paradiso and The Firehook Bakery and Coffee House. When she was in a hurry, she could throw on almost anything and walk across the street to one of the many restaurants on her block.

Gina's apartment was just over a mile and a half away in what is referred to as the Mount Vernon Triangle. Her apartment was just south of the US Immigration & Customs Enforcement office, and about a half mile from Union Station. Her favorite haunts were the Sixth Engine pub across the street from her apartment and the fitness center about a quarter mile away. Gina was always on the go; enjoying both her freedom and the numerous benefits that being single and attractive in the nation's capital had to offer.

The week that the CIA conjured up the idea of using the BOATSS program, the senior plans and program director at CIA, Roger Batsly, was having lunch at Kinkead's with an old buddy from college. They caught up on all the things that two old friends talk about; kids, grandkids, wives and golf, although usually not in that order, the two settled into talking about work.

Roger loved his job but was not a bureaucrat by nature. He liked to fix things the right way the first time and then be off to the next problem. Over the years as he moved up in the agency, he was asked to handle more and more of the daily minutia that flowed in a giant organization like the CIA. The theory of doing more with less had been the rule for the past ten years. He understood the theory and in most circumstances it was a laudable goal. Lately, he had been nurturing a program that would automate data collection and free up personnel to do tasks that computers, at this point in time, still couldn't do.

The problem he was having with launching his latest project was funding. In all programs, time is money, and the longer it took to develop a program and successfully launch it meant more money. This morning he'd received the news that his funding was being cut by a third. It was notably out of character for him to blow off some steam but he was tired of the B.S. being shoveled at his desk. He was bemoaning the situation facing him and the fact that it would take his agency forever to get their newest program off the ground. Without divulging any classified secrets, more than the usual half-truths and the usual "talk around" done every day in the beltway, he explained to his friend, Steve Kensington, what they were looking for.

Steve had been with the agency for almost fifteen years and watched it change from an agency of power and worldwide respect to the current administration's lapdog. Steve bailed on the agency a few years back and used his numerous connections and their resources to start his own telecommunication company.

As it turns out, Roger's friend had done very well for himself and told him about some tracking software he just sold to the NSA not six months earlier. It was very user friendly, adaptable, and the government already owned it. They would have to work out some licensing agreements but that should be the easy part.

Roger had been elated but was still faced with finding someone who could not only be a user for the system, but also program it to suit the agency's special needs. Steve laughed and said that for the cost of today's lunch he would solve that problem as well. Roger readily agreed. They even shook hands on it. Steve leaned over the table and said to his friend, "I've got two women you've just got to meet."

Roger reached out to Gina and Jewels and they agreed to an interview. After the initial interview, the two parties agreed, in writing, on two things. The first was that both Gina and Jewels would start at the highest civil service wage Roger could push through, and second, nobody but the three of them would ever know that the girls had written the *Confero* software. Roger agreed and put them into the system for background checks the following day. The girls couldn't believe they were now going to get paid to work on the very software they had written.

The government background check took almost six weeks to get them cleared into the building. During that time, they spent their days scrubbing the software of the specific requirements for the previous user and leaving a clean slate for them to build whatever it was the CIA wanted. It took another four weeks for them to get their initial agency specific Top Secret clearances and find out what they would be doing.

As it was explained to them by Ramón Rodriquez, the BOATSS system was a new and emerging system global acoustic array that had been designed to identify ships over twenty-five tons by their unique sound characteristics or "acoustic" signature. This information would be cross referenced against any other information gathered on the vessel, such as photographs of the vessels in port, at sea, or by satellite imagery. With this information, a profile could then be created for the particular vessel.

The emerging concept was that by documenting and tracking the ships, you could identify which ports they visited and potentially predict not only where they were traveling to, but potentially what they were transporting. This was the system the United Nations had wanted and partially funded.

The system's hardware technology was a significant upgrade from the navy's current Sound Surveillance System (SOSUS) array that had begun to show signs of wear and tear due in some part to age but funding issues as well.

Although upgraded and combined with other systems, and now called the Integrated Undersea Surveillance System (IUSS), the system had not been designed for the overwhelming amount of data now being demanded from it. The new "BOATSS" system was marketed as a standalone system whose information would be released to the UN for treaty and embargo enforcement.

Like many other programs in D.C., the reality and scope of the program was somewhat different than what was publicly announced or revealed. The reality of the project was that the CIA pushed some much needed funding over to the navy's side of the ledger for some projects for which the navy had been unable to acquire funding. They did this in exchange for the navy's complete acoustical libraries on all foreign ships, and some trained personnel. The CIA's plan was to piggy back the information gathered with old SOSUS sensors onto the new, more robust, system and be able to track whatever it wanted, where ever and whenever it saw fit.

Jewels, Gina, and several other new program staff members listened intently to the new employee presentation. The man giving them their briefing said he realized that all this information was a lot to digest on their first day. He addressed his next comments in the direction of Jewels and Gina. He let them know he understood the magnitude of the task at hand and that he would understand if it took some time to get the new software figured out. Ramón Rodriquez explained, in what both Jewels and Gina later described as a most condescending manner, that this was very complex software unlike any he had ever seen.

It had been quite obvious during the presentation that Ramón Rodriquez was a pig of a man. He gave Jewels the once over, twice, and appeared to be smitten the moment Jewels walked in. He was so obvious that even the other people in the room were uncomfortable.

At the conclusion of his presentation, Ramón asked them if they had any questions. Jewels found him very annoying and noticed his rather poor attempts at hiding his desire for her. With as dry a wit as she could muster, and in an obvious attempt to embarrass him, she looked him in the eye and said, "I've seen this type of program before and it's actually very simple to use. Are you sure this is all they need us to do?"

Several people snickered.

Ramón Rodriquez, his face red as a beet, replied, "Yes."

Jewels was very pleased with herself. As they walked out the door, she turned and nonchalantly asked Ramón, "What is it you do around here?"

He looked at her with what could best be described as pure detestation and said, "I'm your boss."

In a combination of poor planning, budget cuts and ineptitude, the building housing the BOATSS program was not well suited for its human inhabitants. The architect that designed the space had "under heated" their suite of offices by fifteen degrees. The BOATSS office was on sub-basement level three and had originally been slated for some very robust mainframe computer servers. Computer servers are renowned for putting off a tremendous amount of heat. Architects always took this into account when designing a particular building's Heating Ventilation and Air Conditioning (HVAC) system. To alleviate the potential for an overheating situation, this floor had been given its own air conditioning system. Since the space was originally designed with the thought the computer servers would never be shut down, the warmest the rooms were ever allowed to get was sixty degrees. Since spending money to add heating coils that would never be used was considered a waste of money, they hadn't. When funding dried up and the server farm project chopped, they didn't have the money to re-engineer the offices with heat.

So here they sat, every day, cold and miserable. To make matters worse, both the building superintendent and the IT guy said no to coffee at the new workstations. Those guidelines lasted for the first week. No heat *and* no coffee meant no work. The "Ice Queen" won her first battle.

Both girls had been working in recent weeks to set up a new matrix to track ships to and from ports of interest. In the past, ships could opt out of being tracked and many had. Several ships from ports in the Indian Ocean were always on the watch list. The navy accommodated the BOATSS operation by placing thirty of the new sensors in those areas first. A few dozen multisensory buoys were added to the surface in the major shipping lanes of the region and several dozen others in areas deemed "High Interest Areas" and an immediate concern to the agency.

What the girls were working on was the creation of a hydro acoustic data map of all commercial shipping in the world. Although the plan was ambitious, both the technology and funding were there. The agency started eight months ago recording the sounds of the propellers and power plants of all the large transportation ships that volunteered to participate in the program. The program recorded almost all of them at different speeds and conditions. Some ships transited the area so often that they had programmed the computer that ran the system to ignore those ships' specific acoustic signatures all together. Once the voluntary signatures were collected, the agency moved forward with the collection of the non-volunteers. The only significant difference was that for most of the non-voluntary vessels, the agency had very few pictures to correlate with the collected acoustic signatures. Once the data base was complete, they would turn them back on and begin tracking them. They reasoned that by being able to tell what ship's signature they weren't listening to would act as a discriminator and help identify the remaining ships.

Monday mornings were tough enough but were always the worst temperature wise in the office. Only a skeleton crew worked over the weekend and they did nothing to lift the temperature in the offices. It wasn't in Vogue but both girls had taken to keeping cardigan sweaters in their offices. They were now a staple Monday morning accessory.

Gina walked over to Jewels' cubicle to have her first cup of coffee of the morning. Jewels' cubicle looked very much like a Wall Street stock trader's office. Each of her four computer systems: Military Network (MILNET) for Unclassified traffic, Defense Secure Network One (DSNET 1) for Secret traffic, Defense Secure Network Two (DSNET 2) for Top Secret traffic, had two monitors which enabled her to multi-task and more efficiently spread her work out. Her Defense Secure Network Three (DSNET 3) for Top Secret/Sensitive Compartmented Information (TS/SCI) only had one monitor. Jewels didn't do very much work on the "high side" system and quite frankly didn't have the room in her cubicle.

Gina brought with her a stack of reports in order to give the rest of the folks in the office the impression they were working. This week, Gina had agreed to review both the Friday night and Sunday night log entries. Jewels would do Saturday's and they would switch next weekend. It really didn't matter because they reviewed everything together, every day.

This was one of those parts of the job that both girls found so very annoying. Their boss, Ramón, was an overbearing, horse's ass of a boss. Both girls were of the opinion that although he was a GS14 it could not have been by anything more than luck. It wasn't his smarts; he'd proven that much already. Ramón was in charge of this fledgling outfit and he found it important to let everyone know that fact, as often as possible.

The girls couldn't just have an agreement to review the logs together, that would have been viewed as against policy. The policy and published "metrics" for the office required that each person look at their own assigned areas of responsibility individually. Everything that was done in the BOATSS office was in the Operations Plan. If it wasn't in "the plan," it wasn't getting done.

After a bit of catching up on Gina's weekend exploits, some blushing, and suppressed giggles, the girls got down to work. Unlike Jewels, Gina had a new boy toy. They met at the gym a month ago and had been going hot and heavy since then. Monday mornings were by far the most interesting mornings to catch up.

Gina, unfortunately for Jewels, believed in kissing and telling everything. Twice in the past month, both girls had damn near peed themselves laughing at Gina's weekend exploits. It had been agreed that Gina would warn Jewels ahead of time to "go pee" before she'd start her "telling" part.

Several ships of interest perked their interest this morning. The software took a lot of the work out of crunching the gigabytes of data that the system produced every day. Despite being a tremendous time saver, someone had to look at the data dump to insure that the *Confero* program was creating the information they were actually looking for.

By mid-morning, Gina was reviewing a report the system spit out regarding a freighter named the *Shooting Star*. The freighter pulled into the port of Dalian, China at 9:00 p.m. local time in Dalian. According to the BOATSS computer, the freighter slowed significantly between its last two acoustic buoy check points as it passed through the Yellow Sea.

The computer could only model where it "thought" a ship might be heading and when it should arrive. It was generally understood that nothing was really ever rock solid until the anchor dropped. At first glance, the report would seem to indicate that the *Shooting Star* slowed significantly for it to have arrived in port so late. Most ship captains prefer to get into a crowded port during the daylight hours whenever possible. It was merely a curiosity at this point.

Since no laws had been broken, no report needed to be generated explaining why the ship was late to port. They both found it exhilarating to see "their child" doing so well in the real world.

Since, technically, the BOATSS section wasn't yet operational, both girls agreed they shouldn't spend very much time on a ship whose only crime was that it came into port late. None the less, both techies thought it "cool" the computer could figure out that kind of stuff. With no more reason than their idle curiosities of what the system could do, Gina requested a report of all ships transiting that area for the past 72 hours. She stared at the screen that listed all of the "search parameters" some of which included speed, weather, departure, and destination ports. Gina selected "ALL" and grabbed Jewels for their second cup of coffee of the morning.

CHAPTER 3

The Spratly Islands
SOUTH CHINA SEA

The Vietnamese research ship *Bien Hoa* (Sea Flower) made its way slowly back and forth in the warm water and light swells of the South China Sea. The geologists on board were in the routine they had established for the past several weeks now, slowly working their way back and forth in a grid shaped search pattern. They were contracted to search several locations on the seabed in an area just over forty miles to the south of Nanshan Island in the Spratly Islands. The Spratly "Islands" are actually one of three archipelagos of the South China Sea, which comprise more than 30,000 islands in the South China Sea.

The crew of the *Bien Hoa* had been doing high resolution sonar mapping of the seabed between Hopps Reef and Livock Reef since their second day here. The mapping involved sending sound waves down to the ocean floor from a transmitter towed behind their boat and then collecting the reflected signals off the bottom. The reflected sound waves would indicate the depth of the water and provide an accurate and detailed image of every detail on the ocean's floor. The oil and gas exploration company funding the mapping was looking for that special geologic sweet spot that would both provide a high probability of gas and oil beneath the sea floor and a sea floor that they could safely drill into. After numerous passes and some computer magic, the computer onboard the boat would hopefully have a 3-D map of all the mountains, plains, and valleys on the sea floor.

The *Bien Hoa* had been surveying the area day and night for almost a week straight. It was boring, tedious, and hot work. Without the benefit of landmarks, it was easy to think they had been going back and forth over the same spot for days. As had several other parties interested in exploring the riches beneath the sea floor, they found several areas in which they saw exceptional potential for further exploration.

This area of the South China Sea had been rife with conflict over the past several years with China having laid claim to most of the rich oil and gas reserves beneath the waves, as well as the Spratly Islands themselves. By some geologists' estimates, the region could have as much as 28 billion barrels of oil and 266 trillion cubic feet of natural gas, and both were desperately needed by China to feed its rapidly expanding industry based economy. If China were to establish their claim to the disputed chain of small islands, it would put a strategic lock not only on the mineral reserves beneath the surface but could also, realistically, lead to the literal control of the second busiest sea-lane in the world.

When the crewmen of the *Bien Hoa* were not busy with their duties, many of them were taking full advantage of the South China Sea's more easily attainable natural resource, fish. With the region's waters still in territorial contention, even the sea's bountiful fish population was being put under strain of overfishing. Several nations including Vietnam, China, Malaysia, and the Philippines were all fishing the same waters for fish and other sea life to feed their growing populations, as well as the world market's demand for seafood.

Over the past several months, numerous sightings of both American and Chinese "research," or surveillance ships, had been a routine occurrence in this area. However, since the *Bien Hoa* started its mapping project several weeks ago, no one reported any foreign surveillance vessels in the area.

Most people involved with the mapping project agreed that only on-going international pressure from the Americans kept the Chinese from sliding in with their drilling derricks and setting up shop.

One thousand feet below the waves of the South China Sea lurked the nuclear powered Chinese attack submarine, *Great Wall*. She had now been waiting patiently for two weeks, submerged in the deep still water, just above the sea floor, on the eastern slope of Eldad Reef. The submarine was thirty miles due west of Livock Reef and close to the bottom to avoid detection. She was centered in a cluster of shallow reefs and atolls making her almost undetectable. Although the submarine's passive sonar array was always listening carefully for the threat of any approaching ships, the chief focus of the *Great Wall's* attention was the Vietnamese Geologic Research Vessel *Bien Hoa* twenty miles to her east.

The *Great Wall* was a relatively new Type 093G submarine introduced by the Chinese People's Liberation Army Navy in mid-2006. The captain of the *Great Wall* received his preliminary orders just over a month ago and had been on station just over four days now. Unfortunately for her crew, the submarine had become affectively trapped where she was. After only being on station for one day, the captain received word that a new acoustic detection array had been installed by the United Nations and was now operational in both the Palawan Trench to his east and the commercial shipping lanes to his west. If detected and identified, the UN would be notified that the Chinese had a nuclear attack submarine on station in the Spratly's. This was not something the leadership wanted to deal with. Not yet.

Although the improved Type 093G incorporated new technologies such as retractable diving planes and a modified hull for greater acoustic stealth, it was not invisible. The problem, at the moment, for the captain of the *Great Wall* really was not the acoustic arrays to his east and west. The major problem, for the moment, was the research equipment on the *Bien Hoa* itself.

The captain's orders were to keep his submarine undetected, at all costs. If this meant sinking the *Bien Hoa*, his orders were to do just that. His submarine had six bow torpedo tubes and was carrying 10 Yu-8 torpedoes.

Each torpedo had a 992-pound warhead with a maximum range of 28 miles and a top speed of 50 mph. The Yu-8 warhead utilizes sodium hydride compounds and on detonation releases a large amount of sodium powder. This powder reacts with seawater to produce large amounts of very-high-temperature hydrogen. The temperature within a radius of a few dozen yards instantly increases to over 3650°F. This type of warhead affectively sinks its target by melting it. The *Great Wall* was in a position to either defend itself against almost any foe or, if needed, swiftly attack and sink the research vessel.

The *Great Wall's* captain knew the sonar-mapping program used on the *Bien Hoa* was brand new and so state of the art that it could accurately locate something as small as an old boat anchor. With that level of detection, it would very easily find and identify his 360-foot-long submarine. His submarine, like most in the world's oceans today, had special hull coatings called anechoic tiles that absorbed an active sonar's "ping" and would therefore not give an accurate reading of his location. Under normal circumstances, he would remain undetected. His problem was that the *Bien Hoa* wasn't looking for him. The *Bien Hoa* was mapping the bottom. If it was to attempt mapping the seabed below the submarine, the picture on the screen wouldn't necessarily come back looking like a submarine, it would come back as a void. For any operator trained in underwater mapping, watching a monitor and seeing a void on the screen would definitely warrant another look. This "void" would cause them to call in a technology of even greater concern to the submarine-a remotely operated vehicle or ROV.

The *Great Wall's* sonar team kept reporting to him that it could hear the low frequency high speed motor that was characteristic of an ROV. The ROV was actually the most dangerous technology and of the most concern. The *Bien Hoa* had routinely been using its ROV to check out areas of interest on the seabed. The operator of the ROV was either very bored or very curious. Either way, his actions were a problem. Every few minutes he would send the ROV down to the bottom and presumably look at something of interest that caught his eye.

The *Great Wall's* communications officer had already determined that the ship had a live satellite and potentially a video link back to its home offices in the southern Vietnamese port city of Vung Tau. That live link could potentially spell big trouble for both the Chinese submarine and the *Bien Hoa.* The captain considered his options. He thought to himself about the old adage "curiosity killing the cat." He smiled and realized with some amusement that, today he wasn't the cat.

Last month, the People's Republic of China (PRC) finished the secret installation of two elaborate sets of underwater footings. These footings were specifically designed at the Dalian shipyard to quickly anchor two newly designed offshore drilling platforms to the sea floor. It took precision planning but they had accomplished the task in just less than two weeks.

They brought in the eight-ton steel footings suspended under two ships almost half a mile apart to hide their intentions from the air and other passing ships. By using several teams of divers and some smaller boats disguised as fishing boats they slowly lowered the platforms into place and secured them to the seabed. The 3D maps of the two sites the computers compiled had been placed into the computers at the Dalian shipyard. The software converted the 3D image of the seabed to shop plans. Using those plans, another milling machine at the site either cut or welded the four massive I-beams and legs to fit puzzle perfect over their respective spots on the seabed. Only one diver, on one of the forty-eight legs resting on the seabed, needed to use a small shovel to get his assigned steel leg to align properly.

The engineers designed the base to be held in place by welding four thirty-six-inch-wide by forty-eight-inch-tall stainless steel cylinders at the four corners of each square shaped footing. After being placed and leveled on the seabed, these cylinders were then filled with precast concrete cylinders. It was calculated that the 3200-pound weight of each cylinder would be more than adequate to keep the footings in place on the seafloor.

Unlike traditional drilling rig installations that can take several days to get into place and align, the new design allowed for the drilling platform to be towed into place and within an hour aligned and secured to the sea floor. According to the structural and petroleum engineers, drilling at the two sites could commence as early as the second day on site. The PRC had already done all the research and exploration they felt was needed and chosen these two reef beds for their oil and gas exploration project. These two promising locations had been named "Jing qi" (Prosperity) for the northern reef and "Qi Wang" (Expectation) for the southernmost reef. The potential for conflict over the location of the wells was a result of the unfortunate inconvenience that both locations were located in international waters. To compound that problem, both sites currently lay directly between the *Bien Hoa* and the *Great Wall.*

According to the Chinese leadership and subsequently the Chinese Naval command, early discovery of the sites was not considered to be a "viable" option. This translated into the somewhat tenuous operational situation that they were faced with today.

In their most recent searches, the crew of the *Bien Hoa* seemed to be focusing on several areas to the east of the *Great Wall's* location. Their latest search grid was built on a twelve nautical mile leg to the northeast and six nautical mile leg to the northwest. They started at the northeastern end of the search box two days ago and had been working their way gradually to the southwest. They were doing six-mile legs, turning around and heading in the opposite direction every fifty-five minutes.

The crew of the *Great Wall* was watching every turn of the *Bien Hoa* with great interest.

"Target's projected turn to the southeast coming up in two minutes, sir." The crew on the *Great Wall* waited.

"Sir," said the navigator. The captain patiently awaited the news of the boat's latest turn.

"Sir," said the navigator, louder this time.

"Speak!" replied the captain, seeming almost annoyed at being disturbed.

"Sonar reports that the target has not turned as projected. The target is continuing its last leg to the northwest."

The captain made a quick mental note of the fact that his navigator's voice was showing a bit of stress.

"Target is projected at its current course and speed to be above "Jing qi" in forty-seven minutes." To the captain of the *Great Wall* it appeared, for at least the moment that the "cat" named *Bien Hoa* may have indeed run out of lives.

After a tense ten minutes of watching the *Bien Hoa* approach their position, the captain of the *Great Wall* found he was growing more curious as to the boat's intentions.

"Take us to periscope depth," the captain put his fingers to his lips for added illustration and then whispered, "as quietly as a mouse." The massive sub *Great Wall* began to lift slowly and silently from the base of Eldad Reef.

Onboard the *Bien Hoa* the men could not believe their good fortune. For almost an hour now they had been pulling in some of the largest fish they had ever caught. Even the ship's captain was impressed. He marked their last position in the computers mapping program and was letting the entire crew try their hands at catching some fish. The freezer on the ship was almost empty and now seemed as good a time to fill it as any.

The captain loved his job on the *Bien Hoa,* but even he was getting bored with the constant back and forth mapping pattern. The seas were calm for a change; why not give the men a short break. As he walked down the stairs to the deck, two of the Vietnamese deckhands excitedly encouraged him to try his hand at fishing. He was not Vietnamese and spoke very little of their language but he got the general message. His translator was saying that according to the guys watching the fish finder, a school of large fish was still directly ahead of the ship.

"Alright," he agreed, laughing. "One more mile then we'll head back to work."

Ten minutes later the diving officer on the *Great Wall* announced they were at periscope depth. The captain of the *Great Wall* slid the periscope up until it just barely broke the surface. He found the *Bien Hoa* right *where* he thought it would be. It just wasn't doing *what* he thought it would be doing.

On the bow of the boat was the only white man he could see on the whole boat. He was wearing a long sleeved white linen shirt and a floppy hat to protect him from the brutal tropical sun. The man appeared to be struggling with whatever was on the end of his line. It was apparent to the Chinese submarine captain that the man on the *Bien Hoa* was quite obviously an amateur fisherman.

The captain watched his moves and determined that today might have actually been his first attempt at fishing. He adjusted the focus a bit tighter on the periscope and could see the man's face. Even at this distance he could tell that it didn't matter if the man actually landed the fish or not. The smile on the man's face meant he would remember today's experience for the rest of his life.

From what the *Great Wall's* captain could see, most of the crew of the *Bien Hoa* was offering the neophyte fisherman pointers on how to best land his catch. It was amusing as the crew would give him contradicting advice and he would dutifully try and follow their instructions to the letter.

Not being well known by his crew for his sense of humor, the sub captain laughed. Several nearby crewmen glanced warily in his direction. He had grown up in a fishing village himself and truly missed that amazing connection with the sea that only a true fisherman understands.

"Do you need a firing solution sir?" asked his rather impatient weapons officer.

Still laughing, the captain responded, "No, not yet, let's let them catch their dinner in peace. Put us back on the bottom as quietly as we came up."

The Chinese submarine began her slow silent descent back into the depths with her captain remembering a simpler life long ago, and still chuckling.

CHAPTER 4

Kesheh Research Facility

IRAN

Harem was born in the slums of Mashhad, Iran. Although the second largest city in Iran, the safety net for poor families was desperately inadequate. His family was dirt poor and he knew it. In Arabic, the name Mashhad means the place of martyrdom. Sadly, for many in Mashhad, martyrdom was also becoming a way to insure your family would be taken care of. Harem's uncle, Mahmood, had taken on the role of family patriarch since the loss of Harem's father who had been severely burned and eventually succumbed to his injuries after an Iraqi missile attack at the end of the Iran/Iraq conflict in 1989.

Mahmood worked for the Ministry of Engineering in Tehran and felt it was his duty to assist his sister-in-law and her family. Unfortunately, Tehran was 530 miles to the west of Mashhad. This adversely affected the amount of time Mahmood could spend with Harem's family. Although he visited the family as often as he could since his brother's death, today's visit would be special.

On this particular hot and miserable summer evening, Uncle Mahmood made the long trip to Mashhad to celebrate Harem's tenth birthday.

After a traditional birthday dinner and evening prayers, Mahmood gathered Harem and his brothers in the shade behind the house for what he called "life's teachings." Without a father figure in the household, Mahmood felt someone needed to guide the three boys.

Mahmood held up an old Cyprus stick and asked the brothers, "What is this that I hold in my hand? And, what shall we do with it?" Harem's younger brother Shaheen, which meant falcon, stated the obvious; "It's a stick, uncle, and we should throw it."

Harem's uncle smiled but shook his head, "A good guess Shaheen, but no."

Harem's older brother Saeed, which meant lucky, was a teenager who thought he had life all figured out, had laughed and chided his younger brother and stated that it was clearly best suited for firewood and that we should not throw it, but keep it for the fire. Harem's uncle had smiled once again but shook his head no and said, "You must open your mind to all possibilities Saeed."

Only Harem understood the reason for the question. He responded to his uncle; "It is many things to many people, Uncle. Whoever holds the stick ultimately decides the purpose and value of the stick."

His uncle was very pleased with his response and reached into his pocket awarding Harem with a piece of hard candy. This was a lesson Harem would carry with him for the rest of his life.

Earlier that afternoon, in the shadows of their very austere home, stood a man who had arrived with Uncle Mahmood. Uncle had introduced him as a business acquaintance named Shahab. Shahab watched the lesson with the stick and was very impressed. After a short time, Uncle Mahmood, Shahab and Harem's mother went up the hill a short way from the house. Harem wasn't sure what had been discussed but his mother came back from the meeting sobbing. It wasn't unusual for his mother to sob; she was a woman with three sons and no real way to support them. His uncle did send them money and would bring them food and clothes on special occasions but, times were tough and his uncle had a family of his own.

A week after his uncle's visit, life seemed to improve around Harem's house. Foods they hadn't eaten in years were on the table and all the boys had new clothes. For all the changes that Harem saw, his mother seemed to grow more upset with each passing day. Perhaps a week after his uncle's visit, Shahab returned to Harem's house.

Shahab announced that he found a job for Harem's older brother Saeed. To Harem's surprise his mother began to wail. Shahab held his mother firmly by the shoulders and said, "Allah Akbar." He sent Saeed out to his car and paused for a moment by the door. He glanced at Harem's younger brother briefly and then turned to Harem. Shahab smiled a strange and almost wicked smile. Harem thought it was perhaps the most evil expression he had ever seen. The man drove away with Saeed staring forlornly out the back window. They never saw him again. Several weeks later, they received word that Saeed had martyred himself in the name of Allah.

Harem's mother gave him the news while they walked up the rock strewn road behind their house. It was quite obvious to Harem that Shahab had taken Saeed to Hamas to do their dirty work in exchange for payment of some kind.

Before Saeed had been taken away there was never any talk of martyrdom or radical approaches to anything in life. Reflecting honestly, even though Harem loved his older brother he never thought of him as being very bright. Somebody obviously put him in an unattainable position where he felt that the martyrdom route was his only path. Harem recalled kicking the largest rock he saw in the road and thinking, "So much for having a name that meant *lucky*."

Mahmood Fallahi never spoke of Saeed again. It was awkward at times because Mahmood still visited the family from time to time. He hadn't really needed to visit as often since Hamas held up their end of the bargain by helping the family. Mahmood did remember the day of the lesson, and the answer Harem had given to the riddle he had posed to the boys. He also remembered the deal struck with Shahab Tehrani those many years ago. Shahab would leave the other boys alone, especially Harem.

When the time came, Mahmood Fallahi made sure his nephew Harem's sharp mind would not be wasted. Mahmood used his government connections to place Harem into every educational opportunity available. After college in the states, Harem had been placed in the Iranian Defense Forces Special Projects Group.

Twenty-five years later, Harem now found himself sitting deep under a mountain in central Iran. Somewhere, two hundred feet above him was the opening to the Kesheh Research Center.

Above ground, you would never have imagined what lay deep below the boulder strewn face of the mountain. The outside of the Kesheh facility was camouflaged to look like any of the hundreds of greenhouse type farms in the area. There were several entrances and exits enabling people to arrive or depart surreptitiously. It also made the facility significantly more difficult to target from the air. Like a giant shell game, the entrances and exits were moved randomly.

Once past physical security, which included a platoon of Republican Guard troops, blast doors and cipher locks, lay the elevators. The elevators were guarded and had their own electronic pass codes. Only one worker was allowed on an elevator car per trip. The floors where the major projects were being worked on were coded as well and not accessible directly. No one at the facility really could be sure what floor they worked on because the computer controlling the elevators had been programmed to never take a direct route to any given floor.

The elevators themselves were somewhat masterful in their inception. The elevators at this complex were operated using a touch pad that randomly changed the requested destination not by floor number, but by coded cipher. In any given week, your destination code could be varied. In addition, the computer recognized the workers by their biometric finger prints. Because it could keep track of the workers trips, the system would never take the same path twice to their selected floor.

Last week, everyone who worked on project "Blazing Nile" would see and select "Blazing Nile" on the touch pad and after going up and down past the floor an indeterminate amount of times, a worker would arrive at their selected project level. This week, "Blazing Nile" didn't even show up on the keypad. This week the floor was designated "Sky Fire."

To access laboratories handling even more classified projects, the elevator shafts were placed at fifty foot offsets. Every day, technicians would get on an elevator, select their specific project code and then subsequently be delivered several floors down. They would then walk fifty feet, pass through a set of blast doors, get on another elevator, select their destination, place their finger on the pad to be verified for the level they were trying to get to and then touch their project code on the screen. If everything was as it should be they would be delivered to their selected floor.

If the Kesheh facilities' personnel were required to do this on a daily basis it would have been rather time consuming and inefficient. One of the greatest perks of the facility, depending on your point of view, of course, was that assigned personnel actually lived at the Kesheh facility. Although it may have seemed overly cautious and perhaps extreme at the time of its inception, many thought it was the only reason the complex had not been penetrated by American or Israeli bunker busting bombs. The bunker busting bombs were a devastating weapon, but like most high tech weapons, had an Achilles heel. The penetrating bombs tended to be less efficient when they didn't know the actual depth of their intended target. No one working in the Kesheh complex truly knew what level they had ever worked on. It was masterful.

Major Harem Fallahi, the genius behind the clandestine complex's security systems and elevator design, was sitting at his desk on the newly designated floor "Boiling Sea." The Major was running out of time and he knew it. The daily pressure from his supervisors was unrelenting. He had been boastful several months back and now his chickens were coming home to roost.

Facing a technological hurdle he was directed to overcome by their leader himself, Harem boasted that if the military could get him an

American reconnaissance drone, he could reverse engineer it and create what they were looking for in less than a year.

Someone should have thrown a flag on the plan, but had not. When his country eventually captured the American drone last year, America suspected and had even been waiting for Iran to produce and fly a drone of their own design. Harem smiled, the Americans were still waiting. This was Harem's stick, and he was choosing how to best use it.

Now Harem was in the race of his life, literally, to complete his task. He didn't dare offer excuses at this point, for the plan had been set in motion and would succeed or fail on his ability to deliver what he had so confidently promised. His laboratory had everything he'd requested and was as technologically advanced as any in the west. The computers were lightning fast, the room had been designed by him, and for him, for one task.

Harem received his Master's in Engineering Degree from MIT and then stayed on and completed his PhD as well. The study and work load of the program had been bearable. What he found grueling was the mandatory requirement to teach for a term. He figured that for many, teaching was the next step. What he really didn't understand was why you would spend almost two hundred thousand dollars on an education which you could only parley into a job that paid you so little. It was just another one of those American things that puzzled him. The other side of the coin was equally as puzzling to him; why would you pay those who formulate and teach the future generations so little for their efforts?

What was going to help his plan was that the Americans who he knew so well had lost an important ingredient for success-imagination. He spent nine years in the States and was well versed in all nuances and idiosyncrasies of the Americans. He noticed, even in his short stay in the States, a profound drop in creativity was taking place. It was as if the nation was in a constant state of "waiting for the next big thing" but not willing to be the creator of that next big thing.

Over the years he studied in America, he noticed that Americans were tending to be more literal in their thought. Fewer and fewer of them thought "outside the box." It was this line of thought and lack of creativity coupled with the misconception that every other country in the world had idiots working in their labs, which would give him the edge. Most of these so called "idiots" had been schooled in the very same schools as their American counterparts and usually had better grades and job prospects.

He never understood why America would allow students from a hostile country to come to their country on a student visa, soak up all the knowledge and skills they could and then return to their homelands. It was, in his opinion, ludicrous. It had been personally and professionally gratifying, but in his opinion, ludicrous just the same.

This was not to say that America wasn't still turning out some of the brightest minds in the fields of engineering, aerospace and computer science, quite the contrary. It was because many of the top graduates of America's universities returned to their native lands, that America no longer cornered the market on bright shining stars.

CHAPTER 5

The Shooting Star

Captain Hyun-Jun Lee was doing his time in the service of the "Great One." Sadly, it was no longer unusual for someone with a job of great responsibility to have a member of their family locked up in a re-education camp to ensure their family member's "commitment" to the cause.

Captain Lee was no exception and his young wife Sing was being held at the notorious Camp 14 "reeducation" and internment center near Kuum-ni, North Korea. All Captain Lee knew was that he needed to do his assigned job according to the instructions he received.

Choosing your own career path was not in the cards for most of the population in the north. His job as a freighter captain wasn't a job he ever dreamed of as a child. As luck or providence would have it, he actually liked the sea and the responsibilities of being a freighter ship captain.

After serving in the North Korean Navy for ten years, Lee had received his license and certification to become a freighter captain. The vessels Lee was assigned to, as captain, transported goods for North Korea's various state run import/export businesses. Although the country had many such freighter captains, Lee was different. He had a rather unique knack for learning languages.

As a product of the state, Lee impressed his teachers early with his abilities to learn complex languages and dialects. Most of Lee's classmates at school were learning English or perfecting the dialects of their own country. Lee was doing far more.

During the period that Lee served in the DPRK Navy, he had learned both English and two dialects of Chinese in his free time. When the navy discovered his rather extraordinary talent, they encouraged him to focus his efforts on the languages of the Middle East. Over the past few years the government sent him to several special language schools, all located in Iran. Of the three most popular languages in Iran, Lee now spoke two fluently. At the time Lee had gone through school approximately seventy-five million people, in Iran, spoke Persian, commonly referred to as Farsi in the west. Fifty million spoke Pashto, which is descended from the oldest preserved Iranian language. As an added benefit for the young captain, Pashto was spoken in many places including both Afghanistan and Pakistan. Although thirty-two million people spoke Kurdish, it was not a language used in ports and waterways of his specific trade routes, so not a language he pursued, at least not officially.

Lee had always been a quick study, even as a child. His mastering of the Pashto language was an excellent example. He had not just learned one dialect, as most students at the school; Lee mastered several. Within a moment of the start of any given conversation he could differentiate the dialect and drop into the banter of the conversation, all without any trace of his native accent. To make it interesting, the language instructors at his last school would sit him in a circle and engage him in a conversation, all in different dialects. His role was to, without pause, participate in the conversation, easily flowing from one dialect to another. His instructors at the school had deemed his uncanny ability extraordinary.

Captain Lee's exceptional language skills led the government to assign him exclusively to Middle Eastern trade routes. His skills were especially helpful in the port of Shahid Rajaee Container Terminal located near Bandar Abbas and the Bandar Imam Khomeini grain terminal. Both of these ports receive large amounts of Iran's desperately needed imported grain in both Panamax and Handymax vessels. Lee's unique language skills were also useful in the port of Assaluyeh, which focused on the export of petrochemicals.

Lee didn't care much for these people or their cargo. He was well aware that most of his cargo was not on the "allowed" list posted by the UN Security Council. A few years back, a younger and perhaps naïve Captain Lee made mention of his misgivings only once. He paid heavily for that misstep. His government's response had been the videotaped serial rape, torture and eventual murder of his twenty-seven-year-old sister, Mi-Hi. This sealed his thoughts and lips about ever questioning his cargo, or its legitimacy, again.

Captain Lee's current assignment was captain of the freighter *Shooting Star*. She was a relatively new ship, by industry standards, at only eight years old. Historically, the shipping industry broke ships out into categories based on how much tonnage of materials they were rated to carry. The *Shooting Star* fell into the category of what the industry refers to as a Handymax carrier. These ships are routinely used for less voluminous cargos, such as containers, and their design even allows for the combining of different cargos in different holds. Larger capacity cargo of dry/wet bulk goods are shipped on larger Panamax, Capesize, or Chinamax vessels.

The *Shooting Star* was, by the shipping industry's definition, a medium size bulk carrier. She was 645 feet in length with a maximum cargo capacity of only 54,000 tons. Vessels such as the *Shooting Star* were also placed in a sub-category termed "geared carriers." Geared carriers are outfitted with onboard cranes giving them the ability to on and off load their own freight in ports with little or no infrastructure. The *Shooting Star* had five cargo holds below deck and four heavy lift cranes to load and off-load her cargo.

According to his orders, Lee's freighter the *Shooting Star* was heading into dry dock in less than six weeks' time. They had been told to arrive no earlier than 9:00 p.m., local time, at the Dalian Shipyard in Dalian, China. Lee thought it somewhat odd they would be going to a foreign dry dock when so much money and effort had so recently been put into the Rason Special Economic Zone in North Korea. The zone, earlier called the Rajin-Sonbong Economic Special Zone, had been established in the early

1990's by the North Korean government to promote desperately needed economic growth. Both Chinese and Russian companies invested heavily in the economic zone, and, as an added enticement, the use of foreign currency was permitted.

Captain Lee paced the wheel house in the *Shooting Star* hoping to make some sense of what was going on with his ship and crew. He had been running his ship and crew ragged for the past several months with the pace between ports increasing to an almost fever pitch. It was not unusual for him to do quick turns at port since this was a business where time is money and tonnage delivered was the measure of success. Now that he had received the order to proceed to dry dock, he wondered why this sudden change of tempo? The recent increase in the *Shooting Star's* work load occurred in part because container carriers like Lee's were now considered ideal for the future of services to the Iranian port of Bandar Abbas. At times, it seemed, with every passing week, the United Nations was shutting down both Iran and North Korea's access to the world markets. The port of Bandar Abbas was located at the mouth of the Strait of Hormuz on the southwest coast of Iran. It was perfectly situated, both strategically and logistically, for the safe transfer of goods, both legal and illegal, between the two ostracized nations.

Lee let what he thought was going on pass from his conscious thought and focused on the task at hand. He was on day six of his nine-day trip to Hong Kong. He picked up some machinery and several containers of some sort, in Bandar Abbas, Iran and was now working his way back east toward the dry dock at Dalian, China. Schedules and cargo in this industry were prone to change, but after a cursory review of the *Shooting Star's* manifest, he was surprised by just how little cargo he was picking up.

The final leg of this voyage would start with a two-day trip to Hong Kong. Lee liked Hong Kong. All that money from America was building the Chinese economy at an enormous rate. Even with the recent contractions in the world economy, China was doing very nicely.

After two days in Hong Kong, Lee was scheduled to deliver what worked out to be about ninety-five percent of his remaining cargo, to Shanghai.

That too, was unusual. Normally he could count on picking up an enormous load of materials at Shanghai. Perhaps, he figured, a ship without cargo was easier to work on. With calm seas, the trip from Shanghai to Dalian would take just over one day. According to the scheduled manifest he was apparently bringing several containers of equipment with him from the other ports to his dry dock appointment. It was very likely he was bringing equipment to Dalian that would be used on his own vessel.

All in all, the captain would be arriving at the Dalian dry dock in nine days. Perhaps his shipping schedule had been so aggressive, as of late, to help the government stock up on whatever they needed to make it through the threatened embargo of goods that the UN kept holding over their heads. It seemed, at this point, it was the only tool the UN would ever use. Why not stock up on necessary goods while they still could?

It was no secret that a new organization, who wore the mask of the United Nations, was developing a method to track all shipping traffic in the world's oceans. Captain Lee learned from both his government and word of mouth that this new program would go into effect in the coming weeks or months. Most ship captains have a loosely woven communication channel for issues such as these. With his often times illicit cargoes and customers, this type of informal communication between captains could mean his very survival.

In the past four months, most of the captains and crew Lee had spoken with all made reference to an increased presence of American and British flagged "research" vessels.

Those vessels had been seen supposedly placing tidal buoys for the new worldwide Tsunami warning system, or so they said when queried over the radio. They had been in international waters, so no alarm had been raised. The public spin on this technology was that it offered several benefits to the shipping industry including better logistics, fuel management, as well as the tsunami warning system to all the participating carriers. However, anyone felt about the intrusive nature of the technology, everyone did agree that it would help combat the pirate situation that seemed to be getting worse every month.

Money for this new UN program was being funneled from various participating countries to assist in the enforcement of the new UN treaty which, on face value, said it was designed to thwart international weapons sales. The more sinister side of this new program, from Lee's perspective, was that his ship's somewhat shady trading practices would be laid open for the world to see.

Of course this time, Captain Lee kept his thoughts to himself. The crew was told the ship needed upgrades to its engine and navigation systems to be more competitive in the western dominated shipping industry. It seemed to always be the fault of the "demons" in the west.

At the moment, Lee needed to get his head back to his duties. He went forward and checked on the *Shooting Star's* progress as she moved past the outer channel marker buoys and began her trek out of the Persian Gulf through the last several miles of the Strait of Hormuz. As his ship passed the port of Bandar Abbas, he happened to be scanning off his port side with binoculars when he caught a glimpse of a submarine on the surface doing some type of drill. Due to its proximity to the Iranian base, Lee assumed it was an Iranian submarine. As he watched, several men came out of the submarine's forward hatch only to go back in a few minutes later. They did this three times while he was still in visual range. After the third cycle, the submarine's conning tower slowly slipped beneath the waves of the Gulf of Oman and disappeared. In Captain Lee's mind it was seeing complex and unusual things like that, which most people would never see, that kept his job interesting.

Captain Lee had been to the Dalian shipyard before, but under very different circumstances; several years ago, when he was just getting started as a ship's captain, and again, last year, when he'd picked up a ship from the yard when it's captain had been tragically killed in a freak accident. He wondered, to this day, how a ship's captain had managed to get a ship's propeller dropped on himself from an overhead gantry crane. Apparently, the scene had been horrific. He sure hoped Dalian's shipyard safety had improved.

The Dalian shipyard has been the major focus for China's colossal investment in modern new ship building capacity for several years now. It was amazing what a few years, at 1.25 billion dollars per year, and low cost labor, can do for the expansion of a shipyard. One such investment was the shipyard's new 262-foot-wide building dock. This large dock was constructed purely to build five giant supertankers for Iran.

One of the yard's chief benefits, and competitive edge, is its in-house designing, manufacturing, installation and repair service for ships, offshore projects, marine equipment, and parts. It also undertakes steel structure fabrication work and offers a trained labor force. The yard is supported by the Marine Diesel Works group that builds slow and high-speed Sulzer pumps and engines as well as a marine propeller plant. By centralizing parts and equipment manufacturing, last minute design changes can be rapidly implemented or incorporated into an ongoing project. The shipyard has about 4,300 employees and occupies an area of more than 1,315,589 square yards. The yard possesses a steel treatment center consisting of bead blasting, shop primer, plasma cutting and other high tech industrial fabrication machinery.

The true measure of the capability of a shipyard is its ability to build ships that can carry what is referred to as "Dead Weight Tonnage" or DWT. If a ship is designated to carry 100,000 DWT, it simply means that the ship can safely carry a sum of the weights of its cargo, fuel, ballast water and provisions. The Dalian yard owns a 170,000 DWT class semi-dock building berth, a 300,000 DWT class shipbuilding dry dock and a berth for building offshore drilling platforms and other offshore structures. Essentially, the Dalian shipyard was not only *capable* of building all types of tankers, bulk carriers under 300,000 DWT class, and of course offshore structures such as drilling platforms, they were doing just that.

Time passed as it always did on a large freighter with each day wrapped in the routines of life at sea. Lee enjoyed his two days in Hong Kong and tonight he was lining up the *Shooting Star* to enter the channel outside of Dalian Harbor. On a previous visit, even though he had the skills necessary, he opted to use the expert services of the local harbor pilot. It had been a challenging experience. Navigating through a port in the daylight requires both caution and experience; entering a strange port intentionally, at night, bordered on crazy. He would be using the services of a harbor pilot to come in tonight as well. Even experienced harbor pilots are somewhat apprehensive about bringing in large ships after dark.

As they entered the port and approached their mooring site, Captain Lee gazed to starboard at the night time activity in the yard. From the work lights strung up, he estimated they were working on at least two super tankers and several large container ships. Everywhere, the flash of fifty or so arc welders cut through the night air, momentarily illuminating workers in the distance. Farther off to the right, in the distance, were two very tall structures near the water. He couldn't quite make them out at this distance but they were enormous.

The harbor pilot brought them right up to the pier and worked the controls until the ship was securely moored. He had seemed very annoyed with the whole process and very happy to be getting off Lee's ship. Lee thought about telling the harbor pilot that he had been ordered to come in at night, but thought better of it. After securing the ship, Lee overheard several comments from both his crew and shore personnel; none were favorable.

The shipyard had built a hotel of sorts to handle all of the contract personnel that came to work on the many projects going on in the yard simultaneously. For many of the workers this was a real treat. They came from farms and small poor villages all over the world. Somehow they had been fortunate enough to learn a valuable trade such as welding, electrical, or pipefitting and now had jobs that would help their parents or children get a leg up in the world. Captain Lee knew many of his crew sent money to other family members worse off than themselves.

As someone who had traveled beyond the third world, Lee rated the company's accommodations as perhaps a two star. That, he realized with some amusement, was probably generous by at least one star. For the first time in several long hours, Captain Lee grinned.

It had been made abundantly clear that everything that was to be done to the *Shooting Star* would be done on time and to utmost perfection. After its successful emergence from dry dock, the "Great One," as his lapdogs referred to him, would supposedly be at the dock to affectively re-commission her to the sea. This was all very plausible for the crew but Lee had his doubts. The vessel was only a few years old with relatively new navigational systems. Perhaps they were not at the level of other nation's ships, but they were above average for the Republic.

Although this was the first time he had brought a ship into dry dock, something seemed off. While subtle sideways glances from government officials were not in themselves unusual, averting your gaze while speaking directly to the captain of the ship was indeed. And then there were the inspections. Twice in the past two months teams of engineers had come onboard to perform special inspections below deck. It was somewhat uncustomary for him not to have been asked to join them. They had not met his gaze when they departed the ship and he had not received any post inspection report. This, in itself, was unusual. He was in this job, if you wanted to call it that, primarily because of his ability to pick-up on things that others missed. Only in this part of the world could such a talent be used to such ends. Lee kept his thoughts to himself and longed for the simple life on his small family farm outside of Chongdan. He missed his family very much. Tomorrow, it would be four years since he had last seen his little family.

The next morning, Lee decided to get an early start and headed down to the maintenance slip where the *Shooting Star* would be placed in dry dock. The term dry dock was fairly euphemistic. A "dry dock" was basically a concrete box with watertight doors on one end. After the ship was moored in the dry dock space, blocks and shims were place under the ship's keel and hull. As the water from the box was removed, the ship would gently settle onto the blocks, its weight evenly distributed. This blocking procedure normally took days to accomplish. What the workers were left with was a ship supported along its entire length and accessible for whatever maintenance it was scheduled to receive.

As Lee made his way toward the ship, he was stunned to see that it was already in dry dock with all of the water already gone, shoring braces in place and crews were already hard at work cleaning several areas of the ship's hull.

Seeing the *Shooting Star* out of the water and up in the braces of dry dock gave Lee an unusual feeling of foreboding. They had been here for less than a day. Work had apparently started the moment he and his crew departed the ship last night. Despite the clear weather, the entire forward half of his ship was entirely hidden from view, covered by large tarps.

Lee decided to make it his business to find out why his ship was now perched sixty feet above him surrounded by men, wood, and machines instead of water. He approached the guard shack at the top of the gangway and presented his credentials to the guard on duty. The guard looked at his credentials, matched the ID card photo against his face, and then presumably looked him up on the computer.

Captain Lee had no idea what information was on the computer's screen but it had changed the man's demeanor.

"You are not allowed to board," was all the guard said. Lee started to object but the man's partner slid his hand down to his holster and was resting his hand on the butt of his pistol. Lee took the not so subtle hint. If they would not allow him to go on the *Shooting Star* in his capacity as captain, he would need to find another way.

On his way to the guard shack, Lee recalled overhearing two workers speaking Pashto and it gave him an idea. His plan was risky, but his curiosity had gotten the better of him. He "borrowed" some clothes from the worker's locker room as the shifts changed and then "bumped" another man for his access pass. Fortunately, the access passes were dirty, grime covered, and rarely closely inspected. As he walked the gangway onto the ship, he thought of his wife Sing and hoped he wouldn't get caught. He paused briefly and thought of calling this potential misadventure off. The gangway behind him was full with a steady stream of workers coming on board. Leaving at this point would raise some eyebrows. As he reached the height of the deck of the *Shooting Star*, Lee looked around to see what he could in the shipyard. As he looked to starboard, he was amazed to see a ship called the *Oceans Queen*. It was identical to his ship in every way right down to the distinctive color of its cranes.

Pushed from behind by the stream of workers trying to get on board,

Lee swallowed hard, noticed his dry mouth, and went below deck. The noise below deck was incredible. Work at this decibel level wouldn't be tolerated at any other dry dock in the world. Despite all the workers wearing hearing protection, it was unsafe. This wasn't like any shipyard he'd ever seen, visited, or read about at the Mariners College.

What were they doing to his ship? He had been below decks many times and what was going on here was more than an upgrade to the propulsion system. They were fundamentally changing his ship.

Ships were designed and routinely manifested by what they carry. Grain ships have equipment on them to facilitate their carrying of grain or other dry bulk materials. Conversely tankers don't have cranes but rather have lift pumps to move the millions of barrels of oil or other liquids on and off the vessel. Even a maritime novice can look at a ship in a harbor and see the difference.

The *Shooting Star* was, or rather used to be, a container ship. Container ships were loaded both above and below deck with shipping containers. Although containers varied in size, the industry standard was eight feet wide, ten feet tall and forty feet long. Most ships configured to haul containers, moved from port to port offloading and on-loading containerized materials from different ports. The process had become almost completely automated with each container having a bar code for rapid identification for the crane operator. The cargo load on any ship had to be distributed evenly across the ship in order for the ship to remain balanced on an even keel. The exception would be ships carrying cars or other goods from a country of origin to a singular destination market.

Due to the ever increasing pressure from various countries of the west and the UN trade sanctions, the *Shooting Star* was running out of ports she could legitimately do business with. The majority of Lee's trips were to the Middle East and Iran. Captain Lee was in awe. From the outside, above the deck, his ship still appeared to be configured as a container ship. Now, below deck, he could see things were quite a different matter than they appeared.

Down below deck, beyond the passing glance of unknown foreign operatives or the prying eyes of overhead reconnaissance satellites of every nation, down below decks and out of sight, his ship was being transformed. The first thing to catch his eye was that there was no longer anything in his ship to support carrying containers. Without trying to look like a tourist, Lee noted that several mini-decks had been installed approximately sixteen yards above the keel. From his current vantage point, there appeared to be five mini-decks in total. On each of them rested some of the largest pumps he had ever seen. Perhaps this was just a refit after all.

The sanctions, despite the North's assertions to the contrary, were hurting quite a bit. Perhaps they were going to turn the ship into a clandestine tanker so that Tehran could smuggle oil to his country.

As Lee worked his way to the stern he was surprised by the diversity of the workers. They seemed to be from all over the globe. They were broken up into very efficient teams of five or six. In his brief time below decks, not a single team member had spoken to any other team. Lee mused, and bet himself, that they probably couldn't have conversed if they had wanted to. It wasn't the safest work environment but considering their work orders, not surprising. Although each man seemed focused on their specific task, most nodded as he passed as if in solidarity with their situation and surroundings.

As he approached the third mini-deck, he became aware of the massive overhead pump's plumbing. He gazed back over his shoulder, toward the bow, to see if the other pumps were configured in the same fashion. His first thought was that these idiots have their plans upside down. He was about to say something, caught himself and remembered that, at the moment, his role was not that of ship's captain, but observer.

This plumbing was clearly being installed incorrectly. Lee had been below decks on several oil tankers and knew which way these pumps were supposed to pump. All moved their precious liquid cargo from the bottom of the hold, up and out through a series of check valves and distribution manifolds just above the ship's deck.

These enormous vertical lift pumps were configured to pump whatever was in the hold up to the enormous pumps and then amazingly, to him, back down and to the stern of the ship. And, as if to make sure his eyes weren't playing tricks on him, the pipe fitters had marked the fluid flow direction with large reds arrows. The captain rubbed his eyes and looked again. All five pumps had a large screened intake a half-meter above the *Shooting Star's* steel hull. From that point, a three-foot-wide stainless steel pipe extended sixty-five feet or so up from the intake, into the pump housing. So far, he saw nothing too unusual. Then he saw something that made his blood run cold. Not only did the pipe on the other side of the pump direct the flow downward, it was half the diameter of the intake. Whatever was going to be pumped out of his ship was going to be at a tremendous pressure. Lee glanced at a specification sheet on the closest pump. This one pump could pump 210,000 gallons per minute. Lee had seen too much in his life to scare easily. Captain Lee was scared.

CHAPTER 6

Unalaska, Alaska

DUTCH HARBOR

Unalaska, Alaska is the town that supports the fishing port of Dutch Harbor. Heydar Samadi had arrived on the 12:40 p.m. PenAir flight from Anchorage. PenAir was the regional contract air carrier for Alaskan Airways and the most efficient way to get to the island. Unlike the first class ticket and all the goodies on the flight from Seattle to Anchorage, the PenAir flight was bare bones. Heydar had chosen the later flight connection so he could take advantage of the sun being at its high point for the day. For most of the flight, he stared out the window at the frigid water, snow, and ice covered land. The long flight out allowed him a glimpse into his future.

Heydar had been staying in Unalaska for just over a month now. Six weeks earlier, just days before his arrival in Canada on a tourist visa, his brother's childhood friend Rashid was killed by an American sniper team in western Afghanistan. Granted the men had been smuggling rockets out of Iran and intended to use them to kill the American GIs at their forward operating base (FOB) in Herat, but that wasn't the point. It never was. Blood had again been spilled by the infidels and he and many others were so very willing to balance the ledger.

After meeting up with his team in Vancouver, Heydar slipped over the ridiculously porous US/Canadian border into northern Washington State. He met with several Al-Qaida cell contacts in the Seattle area and worked out some critical logistic issues. In order to facilitate his mission, he was going to need some form of United States identification. They had learned from experience that new phony ID's tended to look suspicious. He needed something worn that wouldn't attract any unwanted attention. After scouting out some bars on the seedier side of town for a few evenings, Heydar found someone who looked close enough in appearance to work.

The next morning, Heydar was using the bogus name and several pieces of identification from a Seattle drifter, Mark Lamb, who would no longer have any need for identification. Heydar supposed there was always a chance that what was left of Mark's body would wash up, eventually. Was it not the coast of British Columbia where the authorities kept finding feet washed up on the shore? Seattle wasn't that far away. Maybe it had been hands? It wouldn't matter; the new Mark Lamb had no plans to return to Seattle.

Mark thought he had tolerated his stay at the Unisea Inn over on Gilman Road reasonably well so far. It was a significant departure from the accommodations he had recently enjoyed in Seattle, but they would have to do. On a positive note, the Inn was located just over three miles from the Dutch Harbor pier. It was not a large island and the route from the Inn to the pier was fairly straight forward. On clear days he would walk down to the pier to stay in shape. It was pointless to rent a car so on days where the weather was too cold to walk he took a cab or got a lift from a local heading toward the docks.

The Grand Aleutian would have normally been his first choice in places to stay, but they had security cameras and a different clientele. He did feel that both place's rates were ridiculously high for the level of accommodations. The two hotels definitely had a lock on the market. Evidently, they were both owned by the same company that owned the fish processing plant.

As it was, he went past the Grand Aleutian every day. The UniSea had not been the best place he'd ever stayed in, but certainly not the worst. It was conveniently located above the Unisea Sports Bar. As a supposed perk, they served what they called a continental breakfast. He wasn't exactly sure what continent they were thinking of...but it was none that he had ever visited.

CHAPTER 7

Dalian Dry Docks

Captain Lee left the ship at the mid shift break and didn't attempt to get onboard again that night. The weather in Dalian was dreadful in the winter. Although outfitted to dress against the weather, he was still very cold.

Lee hadn't liked what he'd seen on his ship. On the way back to his room he stopped for some noodles at a street vendor that worked at the facility. They weren't bad. They were warm and made him feel alive again. What could they possibly be doing to his ship? He finished the noodles and began his walk to the hotel. As he entered the hotel, he paused in the lounge area when he heard someone speaking loudly in Persian above the din of local Chinese.

In the left corner of the lounge, two gentlemen, one much older than the other, were having a rather heated argument. The younger of the two seemed very worried about something. Lee moved closer. Both men noticed his approach and stopped mid-sentence. The older man was neatly dressed and spoke directly to him. In perfect Persian he asked, "Do you know what the time is?" It was an old trick and without training, most people would look at their watch.

Lee mustered up his best fool's grin and said in his best clipped Korean, "I apologize sir; I don't speak your language." The man seemed satisfied that even at four feet away, Lee wouldn't understand what they were discussing. The men began anew their serious conversation.

Captain Lee was finding it difficult to keep his focus on the shipyard trade paper he grabbed in the lobby. The older man was essentially trying in vain to get the younger man to calm down and understand his place. The younger man's concerns involved the installation of some very sophisticated communication and navigation equipment aboard one of the ships in the shipyard.

Now Lee was really interested. The younger man continued, "We don't even have this type of equipment on our newest Iranian Naval vessels. It must be restricted equipment."

The older man tried to use some circular logic to dispel the younger man's concerns but wasn't being very convincing, "If it was restricted, it wouldn't be here, now, would it?"

The younger man was not convinced and put his face up close to the old man and hissed, "You can't convince me that something funny is not going on here. Why would we be installing such a sophisticated navigations and communication suite on a freighter?" Lee's head jerked straight up. In the heat of their discussion, neither man had noticed.

The older man, making no pretense now of calmness, cursed at the younger man and told him, "Let this be. Just do your job."

The younger man had had enough of this and jumping to his feet shouted at his senior, "I'm going to the *Shooting Star* and discussing my concerns with the maintenance yard supervisor!"

He never made it to the *Shooting Star*. The young man's body was found on a side street the next morning, wedged between two wooden crates. His throat was slit clear to his spine. His wallet, phone and passport were gone. On the police blotter it was reported as an unfortunate robbery that had gone horribly wrong.

CHAPTER 8

—ᨓ—

The Device

The project was on schedule for a change. Everyone in attendance today was reasonably sure failure in this particular endeavor would mean death. Saying this group of engineers and scientists were motivated and committed would be a gross understatement. For just over a year now, they had been working in such seclusion that, for all intents and purposes, they had no lives outside of this project. None of the engineers or support personnel for the project had been off the gated complex for almost fourteen months. To a visitor at today's big reveal, it would be difficult to be impressed by just looking at what sat before them.

The semicircle of eighty-two scientists, engineers, and technicians were formed up in three ranks looking at two virtually identical shipping containers. To the untrained eye these containers were rather unimpressive to look at. They appeared dented, scratched, and fairly beaten up. No one in their right mind would ship anything of value in them. And that was exactly the point. Both containers looked like they were ready for the scrap heap; that's exactly what made them perfect.

These containers, however, were not exactly what they appeared to be. First, on closer inspection, they were not dented or scratched at all. It was all an elaborate illusion to make them indistinguishable from any other container during transport to the docks or the loading onto the ship. Each had taken over two weeks and several attempts just to paint. These two particular shipping container's final cost, in American dollars, was about a quarter million dollars each. Both containers were forty feet in length, eight feet wide, and almost ten feet tall. The red one on the left weighed over five times as much as the one on the right, empty, and could easily carry its twenty-five-ton payload. This extra weight was partly due to the extra steel that had been used to construct the container so it would not twist or bend when lifted with a crane. Also contributing to the weight was the one-inch lead shielding that covered every surface on the inside of the container. The majority of the container was filled with the shining jewel of the assembled team, a massive nuclear weapon. The blue container on the right, while not as robust or exciting as its brother red container, had its own unique features. It contained all the computers and device related electronics needed to make the mission a success. It was water proof down to two hundred feet and had a self-contained environmental system that kept its contents between 50% and 60% relative humidity and at 75°F.

For the past few years, the North Korean nuclear program had been conducting one of the most clandestine operations in the 20th century right under the noses of the western powers, the United Nations and the International Atomic Energy Agency (IAEA). Rather than focus their efforts on attempting to build smaller and smaller nuclear devices, to mount on their fledgling rockets, their program had been siphoning nuclear materials off of other projects to make one of the largest fission weapons ever created. While the west and its supporters were fixated on the notion that smaller and lighter was the North Korean objective, they were quite misguided. The north had even recently gone so far as to intentionally abort or insert errors in their missile's telemetry to keep the Americans and the rest of the west off guard. They were very aware of the effectiveness of the American's Anti-Ballistic Missile program. To tell them they had successfully lied to the world, cheated on the trade embargos, mislead the United Nations, and fooled the IAEA would have been received by this group as the greatest compliment ever bestowed on them.

Their ambitious plan had been to use the design of the "Ivy King" nuclear device which was tested by the United States in 1952. Ivy King had been the largest pure fission nuclear bomb ever tested by the United States. The explosion over the Eniwetok atoll resulted in a 500 kiloton explosion. This particular series of tests involved the development of very powerful nuclear weapons in response to the nuclear weapons program of the Soviet Union.

Unlike its predecessors, Ivy King used a 92-point implosion system to bring the weapon to critical mass. Its uranium-plutonium core was replaced by 60kg of highly enriched uranium (HEU) fashioned into a thin-walled sphere equivalent to approximately four critical masses. The thin-walled sphere was a commonly used design at the time which ensured that the fissile material remained sub-critical until imploded.

Pyongyang, North Korea

The Republic of North Korea had the science of nuclear weapons worked out way back in 2005. They conducted several successful tests as late as 2013. What they had been desperately struggling with was a design that would fit their particular needs.

By today's standards, the design of the Ivy King device was relatively simple. What the North Koreans wanted to do was take that simple design and couple it with all the benefits of today's super computer modeling that made making a new generation weapon relatively easy. To increase the lethality of the older designed device, they added a new wrinkle. The engineers had decided on incorporating a design to boost and improve the older implosion design. In the world of nuclear weapons, it was referred to as a Boosted Fission Weapon. The high pressure and temperature environment at the center of an exploding fission weapon compresses and heats a mixture of tritium and deuterium gas (heavy isotopes of hydrogen). The hydrogen fuses to form helium and free neutrons. The energy release from this fusion reaction is relatively negligible, but each neutron starts a new fission chain reaction, speeding up the fission and greatly reducing the amount of fissile material that would otherwise be wasted when expansion of the fissile material stops the chain reaction.

At the first briefing where General Yŏng had initially heard about it, most of this had sounded like so much engineer chatter that had been purposely designed and presented to make generals like him feel inferior. The only part of the presentation the generals had actually cared about, focused on, and took away from the meeting a few years back was the last sentence, on the last slide, of the very long presentation, "Boosting this weapon will more than double the weapon's fission energy release." In reality, the engineers were hoping for a more realistic increase of about seventy-five percent. A successful 850kt weapon would do the job quite nicely.

Saddam Hussein capitalized on similar mistakes and leaks of supposedly outdated technology when the designs for circa 1940 calutrons were published in the late 1970's. He successfully used the outdated technology to fool the west into believing he wasn't developing a nuclear program when, in fact, he was hiding his own attempt at developing a nuclear program from the early 1980's up to their discovery in 1991. Many of the fundamental design specifications for Ivy King had been circulated for quite some time through journals, academia and other sources. By scouring open source documents and having their students attend nuclear engineering schools in the United States, North Korea had built up the capable brain trust needed for the ambitious project sitting before them today. The engineers had blended the designs of old with the technologies of the present and reverse engineered and redeveloped Ivy King's design. They made several significant improvements along the way.

The engineers had already conducted two successful small underground tests this year, using the traditional DRPK weapon design. On the third test, in order to mask the new design, they kept the yield small enough to hide the new design from the various watchdog groups and the IAEA.

Two great advantages that the project managers had, in this weapon's design, were from an engineering and manufacturing stand point. Today's advanced computerized milling machines craft components to such tight tolerances, specifications, and at such speeds; speeds that the engineers of the 1940's and 50's could have only dreamt about, that today, components could be designed, tested, and manufactured in hours not days. Perhaps the greatest advantage of all was that this weapon's design was not constrained by the usual problems that plague this type of weapon.

The design teams and engineers were not constrained by the weight of the device or its shape, size or whether or not it was aerodynamic. It wasn't going to be placed on the top of a missile or dropped out of an airplane. It didn't even need to be awesome in appearance. That was fortunate, because it wasn't. All this particular weapon needed to have was the potential to be the largest nuclear weapon detonated above ground on American soil since July, 1962. And today, as it was put through its final inspections prior to shipment, all indications were that it would be just that.

CHAPTER 9

Unalaska

Mark ordered four anti-exposure suits while in Seattle several weeks back and they had shown up in Unalaska several days ago. Survival in waters at these temperatures was counted only in minutes. Four minutes to be precise. Accurate or not, that was the widely held belief. All agreed that even if you were alive after four minutes, you'd be in pretty rough shape. Once the body's core temperature gets below eighty-five degrees, neurological impairment sets in. It can be gradual, in which case you're aware of your body's diminishing capacity such as neurological impairment and strength, or have rapid onset. In the latter case your brain essentially goes into panic mode, shutting off circulation to the extremities, function slows, your arms and legs won't move, and without flotation you simply slip beneath the waves. Maybe four minutes. Perhaps that was the record? Even with the anti-exposure suits, life expectancy was not very long once you were in the water. Not a bad way to go. But dead is dead.

At the time Mark made arrangements to lease the boat named *Dreamer* from local fisherman John O'Connell; John had told Mark that a Coast Guard approved SOLAS (Safety of Life at Sea) Life Raft came with the boat. The life raft was designed to pop out of a container kept on deck that was just over three by two feet. The raft model on John's boat would supposedly carry six men. Mark had been happy the raft would be included with the lease since new rafts booked out at four thousand dollars each. Unfortunately, upon inspection, the raft on the *Dreamer* had seen better days. For this mission Mark could ill afford to have the Coast Guard delaying his departure for something as trivial as an unsafe raft. When he'd gone back to Seattle to tie up some business dealings, he had bitten the bullet and ordered one just before he'd left. It wasn't his money. He grinned to himself. He wagered that the Coast Guard probably wouldn't ding him for too many rafts.

The *Dreamer* was a fishing boat well suited for these northern waters. It had a thick hull to protect crew and cargo from the perils of the Bering Sea ice and a relatively new diesel power plant. It had a shaft drive with a propeller configuration that let it get into shallower water than most boats its size.

One of the design features of the boat Mark liked the most was that the wheelhouse was configured in the front third of the boat. Having it forward allowed a novice captain like himself a little easier time of maneuvering without the sensation that the whole boat was ahead of him.

Mark would like to take credit for finding the *Dreamer*, but it had been his advance team from Seattle that found both the boat and its owner several weeks before his arrival in town.

The *Dreamer* was a leased vessel, of sorts. At this point in Mark's mission you could successfully argue that point. He made arrangements to lease the boat for the last few Opilio crab runs. "If it works out," he told the owner, "I'll buy your boat for cash in May." The owner, John O'Connell, readily agreed. John had experienced a run of self-made bad luck as of late and was happy to take the cash. Apparently, just like the joke that still holds true today, John had a problem with alcohol and gravity. When he drank, he fell down. A few weeks back he stumbled somewhat ungracefully out of Tony's bar, walked the one hundred feet over to the pier to relieve himself and fallen in. The fact that the fall hadn't killed him was amazing enough. When you considered the fact that it had been 2:00 a.m., pitch dark, and that someone had seen him fall in and gotten help, in time, was a miracle. John managed to only separate his shoulder and break a leg on a shallow piling, but he was definitely not getting back in the wheelhouse of the *Dreamer* this season.

On a small island where businesses were either directly or indirectly supportive of the fishing industry, a prospective employer needed to go where the prospective employees were. On Unalaska, that would be one or more of the bars on the island. It had been a chore finding the right patsies for this part of the mission. Mark needed to explore the recreational haunts of the local fisherman and dockworkers to learn what he needed. He started his search at the UniSea Sports Bar & Grill which was conveniently located below the UniSea Inn where he was staying. He also planned to visit the Cape Cheerful Lounge, the Chart Room and Amelia's restaurant which would round out Mark's search of the most popular local watering holes. It was a sin against Allah to drink alcohol, but Allah forgive him; he had to blend in. He practiced, if you could call it that, the art of drinking enough to blend in but not so much as to dull his senses. Some nights it worked. Some nights, it had not gone as well.

Several other fishing boats he had seen had crews of six or seven men. He heard that, on occasion, a woman might try it for a season, but it was rare. It was grueling, unrelenting work and not suited for most women. These fishermen went out, whenever possible, on the most dangerous body of water on the planet to catch more food that kept American's belly's full. For the most part, all had lives that included mortgages or rent, families, and lives like most of their neighbors. They just risked it all, every time they went out to sea, to have it all. Mark had recently started watching the American cable TV show "Deadliest Catch." He chuckled to himself about "the most dangerous job in the world."

Mark toured several of the local fishing boats around Dutch Harbor. They all had magnificent communications systems. All of them with up to date Global Positioning Systems tied to their computer for tracking various fishing locations. Most had two radar systems, one for weather and the other for localized targets such as other vessels. One ship, *The Grand Dame,* even installed several Sony PlayStations and Wi-Fi for the crew to pass the time while transiting the great distances out to the fishing areas. Mark smiled. He would be using equipment so advanced it wouldn't be available on the commercial market for years to come.

From beginning to end he would need to successfully navigate some of the most dangerous and unforgiving parts of the ocean known to man. His trip would cover just over 620 miles. Some tricky navigation considering that he couldn't be too early or too late. Three nights at sea, total. As the Americans were fond of saying, it would be "a piece of cake."

Mark was not looking for a full crew compliment but rather enough men to lift suspicion about his journey. He was an outsider and everyone knew it. This could potentially pose a problem in such a tight knit community as Dutch Harbor.

Unlike the other fishermen, Mark was not trying for a successful season. On the contrary, unless it happened by pure accident, no crabs would find their way into the hold of his ship. Mark set out to hire four or five men that desperately needed work and that nobody else would hire. He only needed men with enough experience to get his boat ready for the trip, stock it full of supplies, food for the crew, and even bait for the crabs. That was it.

Hiring four men once the Opilio crab season started was not as difficult as you would think. The hardest part was not letting on that you despised their type. Mark found them vulgar, womanizing, foul smelling and self-absorbed. The very thought of spending time with any of them at all, let alone on a ship, was repulsive to him. He was reluctant to hire a crew in the first place but realized it would have been suspicious to head out to sea on a boat the size of the *Dreamer* by himself.

His weeks in Dutch Harbor had taught Mark that in these Alaskan fishing ports everyone knows, or tries to know, everyone else's business. It was the same in seaports around the world. This had been an unfortunate detriment to John O'Connell, the man who had "leased" Mark the boat. John had come onboard unannounced, drunk, and had, albeit briefly, interrupted some of Mark's more covert preparations for the trip. Mark didn't know how long John had been on board or what he'd seen. It hadn't mattered. The crippled up man hadn't a chance. Mark had taken some care that John hadn't suffered. It wasn't out of any sense of compassion that Mark had been so careful. He had just needed to snap John's neck in such a manner that even a medical examiner wouldn't be able to determine that it had been caused by anything other than a fall. Mark had checked John's cell phone for texts and calls to make sure he hadn't called anyone. He hadn't. No recent pictures on the phone's SD card either. That was good. Mark mused that if John had been drunk enough on cheap bourbon whisky to fall off the pier prior to their first meeting a couple weeks ago, it wouldn't be a stretch to think he could do it again with a pocket full of cash and good whisky. Mark doubted that even if there was a medical examiner in Unalaska, they wouldn't waste too much time deeply examining the case of a habitual drunk.

Mark waited a few weeks before he started his search for a crew. He didn't want to show up as an unknown captain looking for a crew. There were far too many ways that could go sideways. He'd been patient and learned what haunts had the best potential success for what he was looking for.

The Sea Urchin bar was unlike most in town. It was not in the tourist's guide to bar hopping. It didn't serve food. It had three pool tables, an old jukebox and lots and lots of cold beer. On this particular winter evening it was too loud, too smoky, and smelled way too much like someone had either puked, peed, or both, in his booth. The first man that presented himself as a possible candidate was Terrance Moore. Terrance was relieving himself, somewhat inaccurately at the time, so Mark gave him a moment. Fortunately, Terrance was at least in the restroom. Mark asked him if he was looking for work. Eventually, Terrance finished and made eye contact. Terrance's slurred reply had been, "Who's askin?" After a no-hands-shaken, very brief introduction, and the promise of a round of drinks, he joined Mark at his table. Terrance had been recently "put ashore" for health reasons, or so he said. The snickering from nearby tables led Mark to believe that perhaps it was more related to his drinking. Mark didn't actually care. They talked for a while and exchanged numbers. Terrance left the bar around 12:45 a.m.

On his way out, he missed the already opened door and walked headlong into the door frame. He was perfect.

As Mark got up to leave, he was approached by several guys who said they wanted to have a word with him. Mark tried to remain calm for several reasons. The first reason being he didn't want to blow his cover. The second, it was becoming apparent he needed more practice drinking. Mark was hammered. Even with all his skills, these fishermen would have wiped the bar with him.

As luck would have it, it turned out the largest one in the group, Billy, only wanted to give him some friendly advice. Mark braced for it. Billy pounded him on the back and said, "Please don't take Terrance to sea." Billy shot Mark what would best be described as a painful smile. It was almost as if he had at one point been friends with Terrance. That was all Billy had said. His friends all concurred and moved off. Mark called a cab and headed back to the UniSea Inn. One down, three to go.

Mark found his second candidate two nights later. "Skip," as he preferred to be called, wasn't in as rough shape as Terrance. Mark did make note that being called "Skip" was probably as close to being called "Skipper" as this man was ever going to get. After two more beers, Mark told Skip that he still needed to do some work on the boat but plan on being ready to go on Sunday. Mark hoped a Sunday departure would give Skip enough time to get his affairs in order. He told Skip to be at the pier with his gear at 5:00 a.m. They exchanged numbers and parted ways. It was sort of sad to note that if Skip could get his act together, by the end of the week, he might actually get out on a real fishing boat again. Of course this fact made Skip overqualified for what Mark had in mind...but he'd do. Two down, two to go.

CHAPTER 10

Panama City, Panama

José Alvarez was a man without a future. He had been told that as a child, as a young man, and again last week. Before last week he thought he might be able to turn things around. That was before he thought he was smarter than the men working in the cartel.

For the past several months, José and his brother Philippe had been flirting with death by working as "tumbadores." A "tumbadore" is someone who hijacks cocaine shipments from a cartels' northbound shipment. The brothers had beginners luck on their first heist. In their case, beginners luck meant they hadn't been killed stealing the drugs. Their luck ran out when the two tried to sell the stolen cocaine to the very Mexican cartel members they had stolen it from.

Several Mexican men from the cartel tortured José's brother for a while before driving a piece of steel rebar through one side of his head and out the other. The body had been hoisted up on the town's flag pole with the message "Think" attached to the body. They apparently spared José because they had a very special job for him. If he accomplished the job, they would spare his wife and children. If he tried and failed, they died. If he succeeded and tried to run, they would die the same way his brother had.

The image of his wife and daughters strung up on the flag pole was too much to bear and he agreed to their terms.

This afternoon José said goodbye to his family. He hadn't exactly told them he wouldn't be back, but from the looks on his family members' faces, it seemed to be generally understood. Everyone in town knew he screwed up by messing with the cartel. If they needed any more proof that his future would not be all sunshine and roses, there was the matter of his brother's mangled body.

José walked the six miles to the meeting place and waited as he'd been told. The warehouse either didn't have a guard, which would be very unusual, or the guard had gone on an extended break. Sometimes breaks for cartel personnel could last up to a couple of hours. Sadly, as of late, for honest Panamanians, the breaks were often more permanent in nature.

It was dark and quiet at the warehouse and José was exhausted. He found the guard's wooden stool and just started to nod off when someone jerked the stool out from under him, crashing him to the dirt floor.

"José! You worthless piece of shit! Are you ready to pay your debt?"

José nodded. He was as ready as he was going to be. They brought him into the warehouse and sat him in front of several boxes that had been placed close together forming a rough table. One man spread a newspaper out in a vain attempt to make the whole affair more businesslike. It didn't work. They led him around the table and sat him on an overturned produce box. José cautiously glanced around at his surroundings. With the bright overhead light, it was almost impossible to see past the limited circle of light it created. It wasn't what he could or could not see that bothered him, so much as what he could smell and hear.

The past several years had been tough on the people of Panama. When the Columbian cartels put the Mexican cartels in charge of security, the violence of the drug trade exploded. With the drug trade came all the problems. In José's town the problem, as of late, was getting rid of all the dead bodies. It never took long in the sweltering heat of Panama for dead bodies to do what dead bodies do. The bodies that you could see in the streets weren't a problem. After a shooting, and with the approval of whatever cartel had done the killing, the bodies were taken away and buried.

Unfortunately, not all of the killings happened in the streets. Often bodies would be found in a house days or weeks after being killed. The smell and the sound of the flies were often so bad you would throw up when you first found the bodies and then again sometimes a day or two later when you remembered the smell. José was worried. He wasn't exactly sure what the smell was now, but he knew that sound. He could hear the flies and they were very close.

Someone smacked him in the back of the head.

"Why the long face, José, do you think you're dying tonight?"

"Yes," was all he could manage. By all the laughter, he assumed he was mistaken.

"No, José, you will live in purgatory for a few more weeks." More laughter ensued. From the way it was going so far tonight, José was starting to think that his brother might have gotten off easy.

A fat man with breath so bad, for a moment, José thought that perhaps this man's breath was attracting the flies, leaned even closer toward him. "Do you still know people up near the Pedro Miguel locks?"

José nodded with a touch of pride, "Yes, my uncle still works up there as a mechanic on the locks."

"Excellent," the man hissed and continued, "José, I hope you are learning that in this nasty business of ours, sometimes you do things *to* people and sometimes you do things *for* people that you don't necessarily want to do, yes?" José nodded.

"Your brother for instance, he was a nice boy but, like you, stole from the wrong people. We had to do something *to* him to make an example, yes?" José nodded, again.

"Tonight we are going to show you what you are going to do *for* us so we don't do anything more *to* your family. Pay close attention and remember that only success in this task will spare your family."

A skinny man with long shiny jet black hair stepped into the light with a map. "Your opportunity to help your family starts here." The man's stubby finger came down right next to the canal locks at Pedro Miguel. José wasn't sure he understood.

"For the next week or so we will train you for what you need to do here at the locks. Then you will go and live at your uncle's house, get familiar with the locks and wait for us to call you. You must not hesitate. Many things need to happen all at once for our plan to work. If you cause any part of our plan to fail..."

José finished his sentence for him, "My family dies."

The fat man with the bad breath stepped back into the shadows and disappeared from sight. José could hear them arguing but only enough to know that he was the subject of the argument. After several moments another man stepped forward and sat down at their makeshift table. Although his Spanish was passable, he wasn't from these parts.

The man placed an Apple tablet on the newspaper and after a moment an image came up. It said, "Google Earth." The man spent the next two hours explaining what he wanted José to do. He showed him pictures and engineer's drawings of the locks and all of their mechanisms.

The warm evening wore on and although the temperature had dropped some, it started to rain. The high humidity seemed to be taking a real toll on the man with the Apple tablet; sweat was running down his fingers onto the device. He swore loudly in a language José had never heard before. José was just about to ask the man where he was from when the man swore again and made the strangest comment of the evening, "If I'd known it would be this hot, I would have stayed in Seattle."

CHAPTER 11

Dalian Drydocks

Captain Lee wasn't having much success getting to sleep. The hotel was noisy with the constant foot traffic and conversations up and down the halls as various shifts came and went. As on the ship today, Lee was amazed at the number of languages he could pick out. The only language he hadn't heard all day was English. At least one of the rooms nearby was being used for "entertainment" purposes and those sounds easily came through the cheap thin walls of the hotel. Even with all that, he should have been able to sleep.

The day's events had worn Lee out both physically and mentally. He was physically exhausted but his mind would not slow down. He tried to get his head wrapped around what they were doing to his ship. As was the relationship with most captains and their ships, he felt a bond, of sorts, with the *Shooting Star*.

Lee had been the *Shooting Star's* captain for just over three years now. Even on his maiden voyage as her captain, he learned her sounds, motions, capabilities, and limits. In his brain, of course, he knew that it was not his ship. In his heart, well, that was a different story all together.

He read about some new technologies involving "pump-jet thrust" type propulsion in some trade journals a few years back. Those systems were primarily designed as maneuvering thrusters while getting into or out of tight berths at crowded ports. None of the pictures or designs he saw looked anything like what was going on below decks on the *Shooting Star*. Besides, none of the ports he visited warranted thrusters. All the articles he read noted that the ships need some type of refit for the thrusters. What would be the point? A company would invest the tremendous resources on a great new propulsion system and have no room left for cargo? It didn't make any sense. He didn't have the opportunity to get topside today but, from the bundles of wire being pulled up through the ship's wire chase ways, it was probably safe to assume that some changes were being made up there as well.

As he rolled over for what was probably the tenth time, it occurred to him that perhaps his ship was going to be used for something even more illicit than it already had been guilty of. He began to make a mental checklist of all the things he noticed on his first visit to the ship.

Lee noticed that along the entire interior length of the ship, on both sides, were what appeared to be security cameras. Perhaps they were there to monitor the refit workers? He kept his head down in case the cameras were already being monitored.

Although he hadn't noticed it on his way into the ship's hold, as he turned to leave the ship it appeared that a tremendous amount of metal work was going on toward the bow. He attempted to walk forward, but they had cut the floor away on that side of the ship. While most of the nonstructural related walls and floors had been cut away from the rest of the ship, it appeared that the front sixty feet of the ship's forward hold was being rebuilt. What added to the mystique was that the forward area of the ship seemed to have its own security detail.

Captain Lee awoke with a jump. He was certain that he heard his door latch click. He got out of bed and checked his small room...nothing. To be honest, he was actually rather relieved. Lee was only five foot five and had absolutely no training or experience in physical confrontation. His first attempt at falling asleep tonight had taken over two hours. Looking at the bedside alarm clock he could see that it was now 4:00 a.m. He'd probably gotten three hours of sleep. That was plenty. He'd had less and functioned before. Now, he was less tired and more wound up than he was before.

Going back to bed would be pointless.

After a long hot shower Lee sat down and thought about his next move. He knew he had to get back on the ship and see what else was being done. It was a given that he couldn't go on as the captain. He needed an edge but was limited by being restricted to the shipyard property. He would need to change his appearance. A haircut wouldn't raise too much suspicion. He needed to get rid of the jet black hair. He'd passed a shop on the way back from the yard the other day. Many of the workers wore what looked like a welder's cap. He could easily purchase or "borrow" one of those. Then he realized his ace in the hole. In order to change completely from the expected, he could do something most of the workers couldn't do, he could change his language! All he needed now was proper identification to go with his new persona. That might take some time and a little fancy footwork.

Lee grabbed a quick breakfast of rice and broth at the hotel restaurant. Apparently the hotel restaurant was open 24 hours a day to accommodate all the crews working on the *Shooting Star*. It was 5:00 a.m. and several of the ship's crew was either up very early or coming in very late. He asked them quite causally if they'd been past the ship. None of them had. As none of them expressed any interest in what was going on with the ship, rather than bring attention to himself, he decided not to pursue the matter. In the entire week they had been here only a few men even left the hotel. Most spent their time reading magazines or playing card games such as Godori. Several, from the smirks he received, were apparently trying to have as much fun as they could without getting into trouble. He said he'd maybe see them later and left the hotel. Only two of the crew even acknowledged he'd left.

Remarkably, the barber shop was just opening up and no one was there to see him begin his transformation. At first the barber thought he was being funny. An early morning prank perhaps?

Koreans don't shave their heads. Lee assured him it was on the level and offered him a large tip to be quick and say nothing.

In less than ten minutes Lee's head was trimmed and razor smooth. He opted to let whatever facial hair he had stay where it was. It wasn't much, but every little bit made him a little scruffier. For a couple more coins he even convinced the barber to sell him a well-used and very dirty cap out of the lost and found pile. Only one old man and the barber had witnessed the transformation. He was ready.

Five minutes later, as he walked across the yard, he caught his own reflection in one of the office windows. The transformation was startling. Without the jet black hair and with the addition of the old cap he looked very different. Later, when the stores opened up, he would buy a new warm coat and trade it for an older one with someone in the yard. He needed to look like some of the Iranian workers he'd seen yesterday.

The shipyard was vast and Lee wasn't in a hurry. The flow of workers to the various job sites was picking up and he fell into line with whatever group was heading his way. He decided to circle the yard and for no particular reason was working his way around the yard in a counter-clockwise direction. It took him just over two hours to work his way around the yard. He hadn't been challenged by any security personnel on his little adventure. He stuck to the plan and when he was spoken to by some passing laborers he had only responded in either Persian or Urdu.

One of the more impressive sites on his tour of the yard was the sight of two enormous ocean going drilling platforms. They were complete and sitting next to the water. Several small trucks were making deliveries but other than some painting on the upper decks, by all appearances, they seemed ready to head out to sea. He could just barely make out the names of the rigs "Jing qi" and "Qi wang," two names that in the Chinese culture were thought to bring good luck to a business venture.

CHAPTER 12

On The Hunt

Mark Lamb took a look at his crew so far. The two were experienced fisherman, or so they said. Both were middle-aged, semi closeted alcoholics, divorced, and thought they were having bad luck staying in port. One of them, Terrance maybe, had said he just needed the work. Neither of them had family on the island. Terrance even told Mark he could fall overboard and probably wouldn't be missed for weeks. Mark thought to himself…*how perfect was that?*

Tonight was early Wednesday night and Mark was running out of time. He was trying a different spot tonight and hoped for the best. He had a brief meeting earlier in the evening with one of the men from his advance team. For purposes of operational security, neither man was entirely clear of the other's mission. The man had been instrumental in finding the boat several weeks ago and had also taken care of the installation of the specialized navigation system. To avoid being linked to each other, it was probably best that the two of them not spend time together. The sole purpose of the meeting was basically to wish each other luck. It was unlikely they would have any more contact with each other after tomorrow afternoon.

It was poor weather for bar hopping earlier and only Mark and several of the most dedicated bar flies were here. He was looking to fill out his crew by tonight or tomorrow at the latest. Fortunately for him and sadly for his next candidate, fate intervened and presented him with Roy. Roy was a twenty-something kid covered in tattoos. Sadly, tattoo money not wisely spent. Mark thought he'd seen some needle marks on his arms and his eyes jumped a bit more than normal. Roy was dead broke and due in court in two weeks for something; he'd mumbled what it was. Mark tried to remember. He might have said "disorderly conduct." Mark didn't care at this point. It wasn't going to matter in two weeks. Roy would be missing his court date.

The *Dreamer's* forth new crew member fell from the sky, almost literally. Jonah West just arrived from Anchorage on the delayed PenAir flight #82 and stopped in for a cold beer on his way to the Aleutian Hotel. Jonah, a clean cut guy about forty, found his way to Unalaska Island in search of a new life. Mark hadn't cared at all. At this point, Mark viewed the crew as strictly a means to an end. Jonah was an experienced fisherman and was looking for work. Perfect. Apparently, the flight was boring with the exception of the extreme turbulence. When Mark mentioned he was looking to hire some men for a Sunday departure, Mr. Jonah West launched into a verbal resume. He wrongly assumed Mark cared about his experience. Perhaps it was the lighting and the alcohol, or the hour, but Mark had been unable to politely dissuade the man from talking. It was as if the man hadn't spoken to anyone in months. The man hadn't shut up. His name was Jonah but he preferred JW. He was from somewhere in Maine. He loved the sea and the cold water. He'd worked in his father's business. Blah, blah, blah, college, blah, blah, blah, some sort of special service. He apparently didn't see eye to eye with his father, on several issues. What had he said?

This is why Mark hated drinking. He had been trained not to miss things. But he had been sober then. This guy needed a job and in comparison to the others, would be the sharpest on Mark's boat.

Jonah said he'd be at the pier on Sunday morning. That was all Mark really cared about at this point.

The four men had all the markings of an ill-fated crew. And that they were.

Mark hoped the rest of his team in Seattle was having as fortunate a time in their endeavors. In Seattle, the other man on Mark's team found and duped three college girls to find out Karen Gyoh's schedule for the next several days. By using her Facebook page and Twitter, they figured out exactly where she was going to be on Sunday afternoon. Mark's teammate told the girls to call him after they grabbed her for more instructions.

Seattle
University of Washington

The two girls who were planning to grab and hold Karen were getting a little antsy about what they were planning to do. They agreed that for $250 they would hold their classmate until next Wednesday. They would get $125 to grab her and would get $125 to let her go next Wednesday night. They were told it was a simple sorority prank and that Karen was in on it and expected to be well cared for.

The reality of the situation was that Karen Gyoh was the leverage the terrorists needed to get her brother Kevin Gyoh to comply with their demands. They planned to contact Kevin's mother, explain the situation, and tell her exactly what to tell her son. They hoped that she would not die of fright before she told her son what to do to save his sister. If everything went according to plan, the girl would get grabbed next Monday afternoon and set the Cobra Dane portion of the plan in motion.

CHAPTER 13

The Iranian Submarine Yunes

On the bridge of the Iranian Kilo class submarine *Yunes*, Captain Babakan was deep in thought. Although the sub was approximately one hundred and sixty miles from his destination and his vessel, resting safely submerged under 650 feet of water in the Amchitka Canyon, Captain Babakan was, for good reason, getting a little nervous about his mission. It wasn't so much "what" he was doing on this mission, it was "where."

The *Yunes* was way beyond her normal operational range of 7500 miles and was out here without any support. He was well aware his crew was ill at ease being this far away from home. Until last year, the *Yunes* had primarily operated within sight of the shore and only recently began practicing longer submerged missions.

They had already stopped for fuel twice on the way here. Fueling at sea was normally risky business but they compounded that risk by performing the task at night. On their last refueling, off the coast of Japan, they almost lost two crewmen over the side when they slipped and fell in a brutal combination of high seas and darkness. The men were rescued but were badly shaken up by the experience.

The double edged disturbing reality of their situation was that if they were fortunate enough to survive their mission they would need to refuel twice again on the way home.

Despite his knowledge that the *Yunes* was covered with anechoic tiles, Captain Babakan was not completely comfortable in this particular part of the world's oceans. The anechoic sound absorbing tiles on his boat only helped it hide; they did not make his vessel invisible. By absorbing the sound waves of an active search sonar and distorting the resulting return signal, the range at which his sub and others like it could be detected was decreased. All things being equal, anyone hunting his submarine would have to be right on top of them to see them using sonar. Despite the technology that made his Kilo class submarine one of the more stealthy submarines in the world, he was still in the backyard of the US Navy.

Six months ago, the *Yunes* had been through drydock and received some extensive refitting. Of the more extensive modifications since its purchase and subsequent delivery was the addition of a large diver's trunk or escape hatch. This modification required the addition of two new interior bulkheads. One of the new bulkheads was just forward of the existing vertical escape hatch and one was just aft. They also redesigned the deck hatch and made it significantly larger than the one normally found on a Kilo class submarine. By using this design, the *Yunes* would only need to surface enough for the deck to be above the water for clandestine delivery of men or materials. For other missions, where they would only be delivering men, the ship would not need to surface at all. The original intention of the larger water tight room and larger hatch was to enable the delivery of Special Operations Forces, Intelligence Operatives or other special, more illicit, packages to the shores of countries of interest such as Qatar, Israel or Lebanon. The retrofit went very well and only cost them about 30,712,515,395 Rials or roughly the equivalent of 2.5 million US Dollars. Even with the American economy in apparent free-fall, the Russians wanted dollars.

Two teams of engineers and experienced workers came down from the Russian Central Design Bureau for Marine Engineering (CDB) to supervise the work. Most of the engineers that came either worked on the Kilo submarine program development or actually worked on their original construction many years ago. Although several of the men were advancing in years they brought with them both the original plans for the submarine and precious years of expertise. The only area for concern at the time, and an area that Captain Babakan had been promised would be addressed in the future, was the need for some type of counter weight or hydraulics on the new larger hatch. The men noticed that, without the benefit of hydraulics, the hatch tended to come down very quickly. Unfortunately, on several occasions, this resulted in the hatch slamming hard into place. It was not the optimum situation on a vessel designed for stealth, but the engineers claimed it would require at least six months to redesign the hatch and configure a new type of closing mechanism. It was six months they didn't have.

The *Yunes* had been running almost due north for three days and now was essentially parked just above the sea floor waiting on final orders for what Captain Babakan was told would be the most important mission of his navy career. Granted, that wouldn't be too difficult as it had been a fairly boring career up to this point. As with most ships in the Iranian Navy, it was widely accepted that they were mostly just for show. What intrigued the captain most was his special VIP passenger, Mr. Feng, on this mission. The fact that the man was not in uniform and was, what the captain surmised, to be of Chinese decent was disturbing enough. What was somewhat more disconcerting was that the man was definitely in his element and quite at ease on Captain Babakan's submarine.

After so many years of service, Captain Babakan was accustomed to receiving strange orders from his navy's leadership. What was worrying the captain of the *Yunes*, and what he found most galling, was that he had been ordered to do whatever the little Chinese man said-without question.

CHAPTER 14

Space Command

COLORADO SPRINGS, COLORADO

National Security Administration (NSA) signals analyst Mitch Kendrick had been monitoring the unusual satellite signal for about eight days now and although he was renowned for his cool demeanor and patience, he had to admit, this bugger was starting to get to him. The signal was detectable for only several moments the first few times but then, after a day of silence, was appearing at random times for indeterminate periods. The signal was coming off a French satellite that was essentially parked in an orbit above the mid Pacific. For whatever reason, it was erroneously on the books as having only one transmission frequency. He could see that one. It was this new frequency that was puzzling him. What had Mitch puzzled even more was that, even though the signal itself was scrambled, the electronic signature of the signal was somehow familiar.

Mitch was hopping on a 4:00 p.m. flight to Washington D.C. this afternoon to attend a conference on a new signals collection program. The new NSA program intercepted signals from cell phone providers by intercepting their tower to tower communications. It wasn't his program exactly but they were all in the same business of snatching signals from out of thin air, gleaning whatever they could from them.

It wasn't great timing for an out of town conference as there was a forecast for late season snow on the mountains outside of Colorado Springs. Maybe Mitch could catch the awesome spring skiing at Breckenridge Ski Resort next year.

Mitch's meetings in D.C. didn't start until Monday, but all the flights into the Washington area for the weekend were booked. Between the Spring Breakers and the folks coming into town for the Cherry Blossom Festival, the conference personnel had been lucky to even get hotel rooms. It was too bad really. Mitch smiled to himself, two extra days in the nation's capital, whatever would he do?

Mitch's briefings on Monday were to be what were euphemistically called a "Dog and Pony" show. They weren't really intended to inform or persuade anyone. Everyone was already sold on the new program. It was one of those trips that were often referred to as a "boondoggle." It was by pure coincidence that it was the same week as Washington's famous annual "Cherry Blossom Festival." Mitch laughed to himself and thought, sure it was. He'd seen the cherry blossoms before; Mitch was going to make some contacts and check out the D.C. nightlife.

Several years back, Mitch worked with the folks up at the Yucca Lake Airfield in Nevada. His job at the time was signal strength analysis for the ever expanding domestic drone program. When he left, they were already planning to break ground on a new, somewhat clandestine, facility in Bluffdale, Utah. The purpose of the new facility was to store all the data that the various programs and assets were planning to collect from around the world. Mitch had his doubts they were going to limit their collections to overseas cell phone calls and signal intercept collections, but of course, he was just speculating.

Mitch was also responsible for some of the older systems, referred to as "legacy systems" that were still flying over in combat theaters of Iraq and Afghanistan. When the drone program started ramping up in late 2003, it had been relatively simple to make sure the drones didn't electronically step on each other's signals. Back then, he might have to deconflict three drones in a day's time. As time went on, it became even busier as more types of drones and the number of flights or "sorties" increased.

Mitch was delighted when the last drone flew in Iraq. Then all he had to focus on were the drones in Afghanistan. He'd been on the short list of invited guests to watch Bin Laden's take down back in 2012. Although he hadn't gotten to go to the White House situation room, the live feed was awesome.

Mitch was good at his job and when the NSA stood up this new group in conjunction with the Department of Homeland Security (DHS), it was requested he come on board. It had been a promotion, but required a move to Colorado Springs. The move to Colorado had been a hassle in itself. Although he wasn't, by his own admission, the most social guy, like most single guys his age, Mitch had established certain routines. The Thursday afternoon that he'd heard about the job, Mitch left his office early to think about the job offer. He'd gone back to his apartment, grabbed a couple of cold beers, and dropped them into a metal cooking pot with some ice. He slid open his little sliding door that led out to his little concrete porch overlooking the little parking lot at his little apartment complex. After about an hour of introspection and four beers, he realized that he was a smart, good-looking guy with a great future ahead of him and a move to Colorado would be a good place to start fresh. Around 4:15 p.m., Mitch called his boss and accepted the position. At 6:00 p.m., he'd heard the phone ring but missed the call. When Mitch finally woke up, still sitting on his porch at 9:00 p.m., he had a nagging feeling he was forgetting something. He changed for bed and as he was crawling in, noticed his answering machine light was blinking. He had one message.

"Mitch, good decision on the new job this afternoon, I let them know that you would be there in about two weeks. I think you'll like Colorado Springs. See you tomorrow."

Mitch couldn't for the life of him think of what his boss was talking about.

After two frantic weeks of arranging for a new apartment in Colorado

Springs and fast talking his way out of his current lease, Mitch found himself unpacking his stuff into a somewhat larger apartment at the foot of Cheyenne Mountain Air Force Station just west of Colorado Springs.

His new office was located deep inside the mountain that also housed the North American Aerospace Defense Command or more commonly known by the public as NORAD. His new bosses had been relatively vague about his duties until he settled in. "Settling in" at this kind of job meant that just after a week or so of crossing T's and dotting I's, Mitch was read into his new program. Ironically, the program's name was "Neighborhood Watch." The gist of his duties was to monitor who in the world was spying on whom.

Mitch's workstations were connected to several special down link feeds from around the world and could watch what they called "chatter" in the business. What he did find disturbing was the growing number of down links and receivers here in the states. At his last count, last week, he noted three hundred and twenty-seven active links inside the United States. Big brother was not only up there, he was watching.

Mitch's job entailed a fairly simple process. It was his responsibility to track, identify, and log drone signals from satellite downlinks to ground stations. He could also track and identify signals traveling in the opposite direction. After a drone ground control station receives a feed from a satellite, he would annotate the frequency, the position of the receiver, and then compile them into a data base for either real time or future use. By using several sensors at his disposal, Mitch could usually triangulate the signal and determine both the location of the drone and the ground station.

This job would be incredibly complex and time consuming had it not been for their new software. The software had been designed with a very open architecture so it was easy to customize, customer friendly, easy to learn, and easy to use. What Mitch found most amazing was the software had been purchased from a private telecommunications firm. Since it was essentially a "commercially off the shelf" (COTS) product, the government saved a fortune in manpower and development costs in getting the new software up and running. Saving money was great, but he knew from experience that somebody, somewhere, had probably made some serious coin writing the code for this beauty.

Earlier today, Mitch called his old college buddy, Rick Wagner, at the CIA to tell him when his flight was coming in. They had talked earlier in the month about getting together at some point over the weekend to catch up. While Mitch had him on the phone, he asked if he knew who had written the *Confero* software program. Rick said he didn't know, but he'd ask around and get back to him. Mitch was just walking out to lunch when he received his answer from Rick.

"Mitch, you'll never believe me, I was walking into a meeting with my boss, Mr. Batsly, this afternoon and overheard him talking on the phone. He was saying to someone that two young ladies had written that *Confero* software. Here's the kicker, they both work here in the D.C. area."

Now, Mitch was really curious. "Where do they work, downtown?"

"They work at a new off-site facility in an office called BOATSS."

Mitch laughed, "What the heck is BOATSS?"

Rick laughed himself. "It's a mouthful, Broad Ocean Area Transit and Smuggling Surveillance."

Mitch, still chuckling, "Rick, do you guys in D.C. come up with what an office does, and then came up with the acronym to match or come up with the acronym and then figure out the job?" "Hey, I gotta run to a meeting buddy," Rick continued, "It took some doing but I've got their numbers."

"Alright," said Mitch, "text them to me."

"No freakin way dude, it's not going to be *that* easy!"

Mitch smiled, same old Rick, "What's it going to cost me this time?" The last time they had seen each other it cost him some concert tickets.

Rick didn't even have to think about it, "If they're hot, promise to double up for drinks or whatever."

"Deal," said Mitch. They were probably both frumpy looking computer nerds with no social lives.

"Cool, text ya later!" He hung up and was gone. Mitch smiled. Since Mitch had agreed, Rick emailed him the girl's names and phone numbers at the BOATSS desk. Mitch didn't care if the girls were "hot" or not.

Anyone who could make his job this much easier deserved at least one round of drinks on him. He said their names over a couple times in his head and decided he'd ask for Julie Folk. It was Friday afternoon in D.C. In his experience, Washington bureaucrats tended to go home early on Fridays. Mitch grabbed his coat off the back of his chair and headed out for a quick lunch. He would call Julie Folk as soon as he returned to the office.

Rick had ended his call with Mitch and gently replaced the phone in its cradle. It would be good to see his buddy again. The potential of going out on the town with some women this weekend was equally intriguing. Reaching over to his left he pulled the heavy brown file folder to the center of his desk. The front and back covers were clearly marked "TOP SECRET" in large bold red letters and, lower down, a stamp read TSCI (Top Secret Compartmentalized Information). Below that another stamp in black ink, "Internal Use Only." Centered on the page, written in black sharpie, were the words "Gold Sword." The folder had an *active* date of August of last year. Since that time the folder had been increasing in size every week, until now. "Gold Sword" had been taking up more and more of Rick's time and energy until last week when all updates and message traffic suddenly stopped. *Gold Sword* was the project name that had been established to track and document information that had been flowing through various channels updating them on the ongoing efforts of the North Koreans to scale back the size of their warheads and improve the accuracy and range of their fledgling ICBM (Intercontinental Ballistic Missile) forces. North Korea's tests of their missiles had concluded two weeks ago and direct observation of the tests with national assets had rolled up a week later. From where he sat, Rick had drawn several conclusions. It was not only the fact that whoever had been sending the intel had been spot on, but more importantly, when coupled with the test data, the somewhat more alarming conclusion now was that the North Koreans were getting much more successful in both their missile accuracy and performance. According to the data crunchers down the hall, it was highly probable the North Koreans now had the capability to strike the United States mainland, potentially as far south as Portland, Oregon.

Rick glanced at the large, multi-time zone display on the wall at the other side of the large office. He still had a few minutes to get to his three o'clock meeting down the hall. Standing up, he walked the file over to his four drawer safe. Rick slowly thumbed his way through the folder, one more time, before placing it in the open top drawer. Although the information had stopped, and he could get back to his normal duties, he was left with a nagging three-fold question; one, who had been supplying such accurate information, two, why had they supplied the information and, three, which Rick found the most disturbing, why had it suddenly stopped?

CHAPTER 15

BOATSS

It was finally Friday. Gina had been pestering Jewels all week about getting out and doing something fun for the weekend. She was making a fairly compelling argument when the phone rang. They watched it ring. Jewels turned to Gina and stated rather succinctly, "Last call for the day and we're out of here."

Gina grabbed the phone on the fifth ring, "BOATSS desk, Gina Hughes."

"Hi, I'm Mitch Kendrick from the NSA and I'm trying to find Julie Folk."

Gina smiled wickedly at Jewels and said, "Are you a friend of hers?" Jewels knew that look was trouble and started moving toward the phone. She wasn't fast enough.

Mitch said, "No…"

Before he could say another word Gina laughed asking, "Do you wanna be?"

Jewels was mortified. She grabbed the phone from a now hysterically laughing Gina, "BOATSS desk, Julie Folk." She was glaring at Gina which only made Gina laugh harder.

Mitch's first reaction was that they sure didn't sound like any computer geeks he'd ever met. His second reaction was a bit more personal; she sounded amazing on the phone. "Hi, I'm Mitch Kendrick, NSA, calling from Colorado Springs. I got your name from a buddy of mine who says you wrote the *Confero* software."

Jewels almost dropped the phone. To the best of her knowledge only three people knew that she had been involved with writing *Confero*. Don't panic. Just remain calm. Gina sensed her gag had gone sideways and stopped laughing.

"Yes, how can I help you?" was all Jewels could think of saying. Denying it, although tempting, seemed pointless. Mitch sensed the change in tone. What had he stepped in?

"Hey, I just wanted to say that I use the program and it's saved me a ton of work. I'm coming to D.C. tonight ahead of some meetings next week and would love to buy you a drink." There, he'd made the offer.

Jewels, despite her original apprehension, was intrigued about the opportunity to meet someone who was actually using their software. She decided to test the waters. "I don't drink," she replied, almost coolly.

Now Mitch was intrigued. "Hmmm," Mitch tried being a smart ass right back, "do you eat?"

Jewels thought her abrasive tone might have bailed her out by now. Most men were intimidated by this point and quit the pursuit.

"Sure, I eat."

Mitch smiled to himself, "That's great news! Hey, I get in too late tonight to grab dinner. Can we maybe touch base tomorrow and set up some dinner plans?"

Gina was giving her the thumbs up. "Hey," Jewels asked, "can I bring a friend to dinner?"

"Sure," replied Mitch, "can I bring a buddy of mine as well?"

Jewels paused at that point. "Can you hold for a second? I've got another call."

"Sure thing," said Mitch.

Jewels turned to find Gina standing behind her straining to hear every word. She muted the phone and looked directly at Gina, "I can't do this."

Gina gently grasped her best friend by the shoulders, looked her straight in the eyes and said, "Sure you can, I'll be right there with you the whole time."

Jewels groaned, "That's what I'm *most* afraid of." God she hated this part. "What time should I tell him?" Gina suggested seven. Jewels unmuted the phone; "Mitch, sorry about that, end of the day stuff, sure you can bring a friend, how about seven o'clock?"

"Sounds great," Mitch replied. "Can I ask you a couple questions real quick?"

Jewels' guard went back up immediately. "Sure," she replied warily, "but then I've got to go."

Mitch replied, "Super," and he asked, "most importantly, do you know of any good places to run in the downtown D.C. area, and second, I haven't had any good pizza in a while, would you mind recommending a place?"

Jewels smiled, and thought it might just turn out to be a fun weekend after all. "You're in luck, Mitch, let me get a good number for you and maybe I could show you some of my favorite running loops tomorrow morning."

Mitch gave her the number of his hotel, and asked if she knew where it was. She replied slowly and rather mysteriously, "Yes, I know exactly where that is." And she should. The DuPont Circle Hotel was on the other side of DuPont Circle from her apartment, less than a three-minute walk.

They confirmed the morning's plans and Jewels hung up.

Gina was beside herself and was trying to convince Jewels that the stars were aligning and how she should check her horoscope. Jewels smiled and for the first time in a very long time started to put some thought into what she should wear tomorrow.

Jewels awoke early and impatiently waited until 9:00 a.m. to call Mitch. It was a warm morning for March and they decided to meet in the park at the center of DuPont circle. They agreed on fifteen minutes. Mitch asked how he would find her. Jewels replied in her usual self-deprecating way, "It's a small park, I'll be the really tall girl." Mitch laughed and told her that just in case she wasn't the only tall girl he was wearing a Denver Broncos hat.

She told him that if he was going to wear that hat, she hoped he was a fast runner.

Mitch had only to walk across the street to the park. As soon as he entered the park and begun to walk up one of the concrete paths that led to the fountain he heard the first comment from a guy to his buddy, "Holy crap she has long legs!"

His buddy had responded, "She has legs?" Obviously, these two guys had different tastes in women. He had been curious just the same and followed their gazes to the steps at the base of the fountain where an absolutely stunning woman was doing some runner's stretches.

Mitch's first reaction was, "No way."

The two other guys thought he was talking to them and smiled briefly at him before looking back to the fountain. Mitch felt like he was sixteen again, awkward and goofy. He felt his face flush. What if Jewels had seen him gawking at this beautiful woman? Then much to his shock and to the significant disappoint of the two men standing near him, the woman waved in his direction, "Hey Mitch, over here."

Mitch tried to recover and attempted to walk casually over to her. He tripped twice on the perfectly smooth concrete that made up the inner ring of the circle. Smooth, Mitch, real smooth. Never one normally to be caught without something to say, Mitch was speechless. She looked amazing. Mitch's great opening line? "Wow, you are tall!" He really hoped she hadn't seen him blush. Sadly, she had.

They ran down to the Jefferson Memorial without so much as a word. They were both in great shape and the run had not been that difficult. The usual runner's hazards of dogs on long leashes and an errant Frisbee or two were all they encountered on their run to the memorial. The weather was pristine and with the leaves just coming out and the cherry blossoms in the distance it was one of those runs that required almost no effort. He caught himself glancing at Jewels several times. Only once had he been busted. She'd smiled. Maybe he could salvage this after all. The fact that they stopped for water was more of an excuse to talk than to have rest.

After they'd had a swallow of water, Jewels had led with the comment,

"So, you like my software?"

Every fiber in Mitch's body wanted him, no, begged him to say, "And everything else," but, somehow he had resisted and responded with, "Yes, very much so." It was as if he'd never been on a date before.

They talked about the usual things that two people talk about on a perfect day, the weather and where each of them had gone to school and worked since graduation. Mitch couldn't keep his eyes off of her. He had the feeling he'd been wearing the same goofy smile since they'd sat down. Jewels suggested they walk for a bit so they wouldn't cool down too much from their run.

As they passed the National Air and Space Museum, Mitch stole a glance up at the entrance, "Do you ever get the chance to go into any of these museums?"

"No," Jewels replied, "I don't really know anybody who would care to spend the afternoon walking around looking at old stuff."

Mitch wasn't sure what she meant by that. Was she saying, "Like many of my friends, I don't like old stuff and anybody who does is a dork." or "I wish I had a friend that liked old stuff."?

Before he could get his head straight on which way to go with his answer she said, "Why do you ask?"

Mitch took a deep breath and said, "I know you'll probably think it's lame but I picked up a minor in Aerospace Engineering and would love to stick my head in at the National Air and Space Museum." Mitch looked down. Her hand was suddenly on his arm.

She followed his gaze downward and appeared to be just as surprised as Mitch. She left it there and asked, "Can we do it after a shower?" Mitch was pretty sure he nodded yes. As she started to run she looked back over her shoulder and shouted, "Race you back to the circle?"

After they'd showered, they met back in the shade of the trees in DuPont circle some forty-five minutes later. Mitch agreed to eat a hotdog out of a vendor's cart for lunch if he could take her to her favorite pizza place after they toured the museum. They walked silently for a short distance when Jewels stopped him. "Mitch, I have a bit of a confession to make."

Mitch thought, Oh shit and really hoped he hadn't said it out loud.

"I haven't been on a date in a really long time," she started, "and I don't want you to misread my emotions."

Mitch was getting nervous, where was this going? "Uh huh."

"What I mean is that lots of people seem to think I'm this frigid bitch who doesn't like going out, drinking, getting crazy, and tearing up the town."

"And?" Mitch started to say when her hand was suddenly back on his arm.

"I just don't want you to think I'm not having fun, I'm just nervous."

Mitch laughed to put her at ease, "You're nervous? Half the guys we're walking by are silently praying that you're my sister."

Jewels stopped him again, and in a voice that was as sincere as he'd ever heard asked, "Why?"

He was stunned. He looked her straight in her emerald green eyes and realized suddenly that perhaps she really didn't know why. Mitch fully realized he was risking everything but said it anyway. He took a deep breath and told her the truth, "Because you're the prettiest girl on the street, Jewels."

He wasn't sure what to expect, but a punch in the shoulder followed by, "Am not!" wasn't even in the top fifty.

Mitch had the most amazing time giving her a tour of the museum. Predictably, they both lost track of the time and had forgotten to call Gina and Rick to let them know where and when to meet them for dinner. Jewels called Gina who, just like Gina, wanted her to stop and give her all the information on her day so far and to scold her for not answering her phone all day. Jewels was polite but insisted she would not need as much detail as she thought if she came to dinner on time.

Mitch called Rick while Jewels feigned being upset and crossed her arms and glared at him. Mitch covered the mouth piece asking, "Can I have some fun with my buddy?" The twinkle in his eye seemed to put her at ease. She nodded yes. "No," Mitch told Rick, "She's about what you'd expect a computer nerd to look like."

"Damn, dude sorry to hear it. Do you want to call it off?"

"No," Mitch sighed, and assured his friend that he would tough it out.

"Alright, if you're sure, I'll see you at seven then?"

Mitch smiled at Jewels and said, "I wouldn't miss it for the world." Mitch ended the call and glanced over at Jewels. She was beaming and walked a little closer as they continued the tour.

CHAPTER 16

Eareckson Air Force Station

SHEMYA ISLAND, ALASKA

Kevin Gyoh was in a jam. His mother had called and left another message on his answering machine expressing an urgent need to talk to him. Sadly, it seemed that whatever happened in his mother's life was deemed urgent. She didn't approve of him working this far away from his family. Why wasn't he married? He never called enough. While at college, Kevin often referred to his mother as "The Meddler." When he was in his senior year of college at the University of Washington, she would routinely call and check on her baby. He had been twenty-one and she was still calling to make sure he was wearing clean underwear, sleeping (alone), and eating the correct foods.

Kevin had chosen one of the newer post 9/11 programs offered at the university. His particular program focused on security policy, planning and operations dedicated to the protection of US territory. The program included infrastructure, institutional, and citizen security, as well as, instruction in national security and intelligence policy, government relations, law enforcement, security technology, communications/information technology, and homeland security. He was basically a super cop. When Kevin graduated, the big government defense contractor companies had come calling for him.

When Kevin got this gig with Boeing Aerospace on Shemya Island after Boeing's part of the Ballistic Missile Defense (BMD) contract had been renewed, he was twenty-five, single, and was happy to keep it that way. He had worked down on Joint Base Lewis-McChord for a few years but several missteps in the romance department with a local girl there in Pierce County convinced him of three things. The first, he should probably not rush into a permanent relationship for quite some time. The second, he needed to get a little farther away from his folks. The third, find a good job and build up his cash reserves. That had been three years ago and he hadn't looked back.

As the air force station's Systems Security Manager, one of Kevin's many jobs was to do physical security checks on the island's numerous facilities including each of the island's radar tracking systems. He had a weekly routine and liked to stick to it whenever possible. Kevin liked starting with the largest radar site on the island, which also happened to be the farthest distance from the central part of the base. He headed out to the monolith of technology and concrete, Cobra Dane.

Kevin had first gone to Shemya Island as an intern with the Boeing Aeronautical Systems Group in the summer of his junior year. The island was spectacular. The only way to get to the US Military controlled island was by cargo ship, cargo plane or the several times a week jet shuttle from Joint Base Elmendorf/Richardson near Anchorage. When Kevin first arrived at Shemya he was struck by both its beauty and isolation. In the waters to the west you could see the currents from the Bering Sea and the Pacific blend together. The views from the bluffs above the sea were magnificent. Ocean currents around the island could be treacherous in the wrong season or even the wrong time of day. For some periods of the year heavy fog will limit not only what you can see from the island but will create a hazardous situation for the bi-weekly supply runs. The water around the edge of the island is very shallow and in some parts you could theoretically walk out one hundred feet or so. It wasn't recommended. After WWII, and well before the concept of environmental protection, left over military ordinance of all kinds had been dumped off shore in several locations. That and, of course, the water was really, really cold.

Several weeks before Kevin's arrival a whale carcass had come ashore and become lodged in the rocks. It no longer resembled the majestically beautiful sea creature it once was. It had glided through the cold waters of the Northern Pacific for the last time. Now it more closely resembled a very foul smelling bird and wild life sanctuary. From low, scampering, skittish Blue Foxes to noisy gulls, they were whittling this carcass down to the bone ounce by ounce.

Winter on the island was vastly different. Snow and hurricane force winds were routine. The weather on the island was so severe that the contractors and military personnel who worked on the island stayed below ground when moving from building to building. Tunnels connected almost everything. Many of the island's personnel worked shift work. The commute was fairly simple. The dormitories connected to dining halls and the dining halls connected to work centers. At the end of your particular shift you simply reversed direction. There were no "great views" in the winter and no reason to be above ground. Almost no one ventured outside on purpose.

Unfortunately, Cobra Dane didn't have an access tunnel to it. To get there, Kevin bundled up, made sure he had his coded access badge, and headed out to his old beater of a truck. Kevin's boss felt that the 1998 Dodge extended cab still worked too well to be parked permanently. Kevin respectively disagreed. With the wind whistling through a cracked side window and no heat to speak of, Kevin headed out to "The Dane."

Charlie Olson worked as the maintenance supervisor and official greeter as his office was in close proximity to the door. Kevin swiped his card, keyed in his pass code and entered the relative warmth of the superstructure that housed the offices and workings of Dane. Kevin had called Charlie with an inbound courtesy call on his brick, and also quite selfishly to make darn sure that a cup of coffee was waiting for him when he arrived.

Charlie greeted Kevin with a solid fist bump and a hot cup of mocha latte cappuccino fresh from the facility's exotic coffee machine. After the usual small talk, Kevin proceeded to make his inspection of the facility. Due to the weather and other duties he needed to perform, Kevin only visited the Dane every two days. The one exception in his three years here was when he had taken some family pictures out of his wallet, passed them around to the nerds, and then left without them. He had gone back first thing the next day to retrieve them. Other than that one time, which he still got grief for, his visits were like clockwork. Everyone liked routine here on the island. It was comfortable.

On most of his inspection days, he was responsible for checking routine security items such as pass code units, secure phone code status and fire alarm panels. Rarely did he need to, or want to for that matter, go upstairs into the mission areas. These folks weren't just spooky, they were also nerds.

He didn't think many of them ever left the island for Morale Welfare Recreation (MWR) breaks. They had serious jobs, they were geeks, and they were essentially trapped on an island, and they knew it. After a few years, Kevin imagined it was difficult to blend well into the off island world.

It was Saturday morning and Sally McDaniel was celebrating her birthday with the only family she really had anymore. Kevin felt obliged to go upstairs and have some cake. Sally seemed to be a bit of a loner. Kevin had seen her around the island and she was normally alone. They had spoken several times but it had always been brief and always a little awkward.

Kevin was quite surprised by the number of candles on the cake. He thought that perhaps Sally was at least thirty. Unless someone had run out of candles, which was entirely possible out here, she was only twenty-seven. If this were true, she was certainly a frumpy twenty-seven. Her hair was always messy and obscured her face. She wore clothing that begged you *not* to look at her. Kevin figured she probably had her reasons. Perhaps it was the remoteness of the job or trouble at home in Tacoma. No one seemed to really know her story. It was widely known she had worked herself through a bitter divorce in 2008 and she lost her home in the deal.

Today, nobody really cared about someone's past or the problems of the world. Today a fellow castaway had something to celebrate and that was good enough for all concerned.

Kevin had greeted everyone and had a piece of cake but needed to move on with his day. The walk to the upper floors of the Cobra Dane array wasn't as straightforward as you think from the outside. Systems such as those housed in the superstructure were the primary concern. Convenience of the human labor force was secondary. Ascending vertically in the building was straight forward enough. It was when you needed to move through or across the building that it got interesting. Kevin needed to get from the south corner of the building over to the North. This required him to move across what can best be described as a half floor. After ascending only four steps instead of the usual nine, Kevin was on a floor unto itself. It was a full size floor just kind of pushed up and out of place. It was while moving across this half floor that Kevin thought he felt a draft. This walkway was an arm's reach away from the system's concrete face. Was that daylight? Kevin leaned in for a closer look and confirmed his suspicion. The salt air and relentless spray of the ocean was causing some of the concrete to separate along a seam in the concrete. Building maintenance was not his "hat" to wear so he made a mental note to tell Charlie on his way out.

CHAPTER 17

Washington D.C.

Gina spent the rest of her Saturday afternoon trying to figure out what to wear for this evening's adventure. Who were these guys? What were they into? Was Jewels having fun or treating this guy like an out of town charity case? God, she thought, I wish she was normal and texted me her every thought.

For her part, Jewels had gone back to her apartment, showered again, and made herself presentable. For Jewels, that meant some "Miss Me" jeans and a white designer blouse. Many years ago, her mom had given her some gold hoop earrings, but she had never worn them, maybe tonight? They sure were pretty… She thought about it and decided, no not tonight, and placed them to one side. She didn't want to look too "over-the-top" sexy on their first dinner date. Besides she might know someone at the restaurant. What would they think?

Since Jewels' restaurant of choice was only a few blocks away, they had agreed to walk. She was slipping on her shoes to head downstairs when her phone rang. She smiled knowing it was Mitch. It was the ringtone she'd assigned him right after getting home from their museum adventure. Perhaps he'd changed his mind about tonight. She wouldn't blame him. She took a deep breath and tried to be optimistic, "Hello."

"Hey, it's Mitch," he had tried to mask his excitement.

"Mitch who?" asked Jewels playfully.

"Very funny *Karen*, I'm out front, I got ready a little early and am anxious to see you." They both laughed. Jewels hung up, looked in the mirror and smiled. Well that answered that. She reached over and grabbed the shiny gold hoop earrings.

Mitch was in the lobby waiting for her when she came off the elevator. Any nervousness she had from earlier today melted away. She was radiant. "Ready?" asked Mitch.

With a smile that said she was, Jewels replied, "Very." And she was.

The walk to the restaurant was interrupted three times. First, by Gina who wanted to know, if he was standing right there and could she talk.

The second time was by Rick, who said he was on his way, two minutes out, and wanted to know if he, Mitch, had seen the other girl yet. Mitch answered, "No, not yet" and hung up.

The third time it was Gina again. They were walking up from behind her and she was still talking. Finally she must have sensed that Jewels was standing behind her. "You're mean!" she said smiling at Jewels. They gave each other a big hug then Gina turned her full attention to Mitch. She gave him the full once over and said in a sultry voice, "You're even better looking than you sounded on the phone."

Mitch blushed and mumbled, "You too."

Mitch's phone hummed again, "Have you seen her yet?" It was Rick again.

Mitch told him to hang on a moment. Mitch looked at Jewels, covered his phone and asked "Can I have some more fun?"

Jewels smiled at him and nudged Gina. Mitch lied, apologized, and said that yes, they both looked like computer nerds. He could barely keep a straight face as he hung up. He couldn't have stretched it any farther from the truth if he'd tried. Where Jewels looked like a stunner that was also an athlete, Gina was more like an athlete that was also pretty. Jewels let Gina in on the joke. Gina smirked and remarked that she couldn't wait to meet him. As they talked, Rick came hot footing it around the corner. His reaction would best be described as well, epic. Rick's jaw dropped, worked its way up and down, but no words came out. Mitch busted up, "Gina, my friend here, with his mouth moving like a carp, is Rick Wagner. Rick, this is your not-so-nerdy date, Gina Hughes." The humorous introductions pretty much set the tone for the rest of the evening. They all had a great time together and probably stayed for one round too many.

While Rick caught a train back to his apartment, Mitch walked both Gina and Jewels back to Jewel's apartment. Mitch felt he could have talked to Jewels all night long. Apparently, so did Gina. Mitch said his goodbyes, left the two of them talking and laughing while he walked back to his hotel, happy and feeling no pain.

Dutch Harbor

It was late Saturday afternoon in Dutch Harbor when the last of the supplies were finally loaded onto the *Dreamer*. Mark made sure that once again appearances were maintained and that he looked like any other fisherman leaving port. It seemed like such a waste of money. It cost him over four thousand dollars to outfit the ship for the trip including such things as ice, bait, food, etc. He gave his encrypted satellite phone a test and confirmed that his far flung team was still on schedule. Mark checked the computerized navigation system as much as he could dockside. After ensuring everyone was gone for the night, Mark went below decks and entered his cabin. On his bed lay a handwritten note. It said simply, "Don't be late for lunch." Mark smiled, appreciating the humorous reminder from his teammate that timing was critical for the operation's success. Glancing at his watch, Mark thought he'd be serving lunch right on time.

Mark locked the cabin door, unlocked, and opened his locker. It was his last chance to make sure this part was done correctly. He looked at the contents of his locker. On the top shelf were a 40 caliber Sig Sauer semiautomatic and three extra clips. Behind his hanging clothes was an AK-47 with a shoulder bag of ten magazines. On the floor of his locker was a small Tupperware container with zip ties, a remote detonator, what looked like a bottle of ear drops and boot knife. He was ready. He realized that he probably would only have one more opportunity to pray without being seen. He retrieved his prayer mat from under his blanket, lay it on the floor oriented to his best guess of where east was, and began his prayers. He knew that to make this work, he would need all the help he could get. "Mark" prayed for a very long time.

CHAPTER 18

DuPont Circle

WASHINGTON D.C.

Sunday morning came early and Mitch was awakened at 10:00 a.m. by his cell phone vibrating itself off his night stand. It was on the floor now and had finally stopped vibrating. He was just closing his eyes again when it started anew. In his only half serious dramatic voice he answered his phone. "Hello," Mitch tried to sound as if he was still asleep.

"Oh Mitch, I'm soooo sorry, did I wake you?" It was Jewels. If he hadn't been awake before, he was fully awake now.

"Good morning Jewels," trying his best now *not* to sound like a lazy slug.

"Gina and I stayed up half the night yakking and we're famished; any chance you would want to take us to brunch somewhere?"

"Definitely, yeah, sure," replied Mitch, "I trust you have a spot picked out?"

"Yes we do," Jewels said, all the while smiling at Gina. "Can you be downstairs in fifteen minutes?"

"Jewels, the jet lag is kicking my butt this morning, can I have twenty?"

"Sure thing, see you in twenty."

Mitch had started to hang up…"Jewels!"

"Yes?"

"Downstairs where?" asked Mitch.

"My place silly," Jewels said with a tease in her voice that made even Gina turn and look.

The restaurant was just around the corner from Jewels' place on P Street. Jewels loved their croissants and coffee.

After they were seated, Mitch was the first to speak. "I have to say that the primary reason I wanted to meet you two was to thank you for creating such a sweet piece of software. Somehow, in all the fun last night, I forgot to tell you both that."

Gina looked at Jewels, "He's so sweet!" and rolled her eyes.

"Yes he is" replied Jewels in his defense. Then the other half of Jewels' brain, the hidden nerd half, had to get a word in edgewise, "What do you like about it?"

Mitch laid out all the things he liked about the program, most of which the girls knew about. It was good to hear the feedback but it was getting kind of tedious to hear all about what they already knew. Just as Gina was about to say something, Mitch dropped a bombshell, "Did you guys know that you can set up the program to tell you what signals aren't there?" Now he had their undivided attention.

Mitch went on, "I was looking for a way to not only track locations that I knew about, but other areas where I shouldn't be getting hits from." Due to the sensitivity of what they worked on this was about as much detail as Mitch felt comfortable discussing at brunch. Gina was curious, "So you added more data points?"

"It would be so much easier to show you," Mitch responded.

"Mitch, what time do your meetings start tomorrow?"

"Two, but I should probably be there by one-thirty."

Jewels looked at Gina and in that silent communication that comes from being friends for as long as they had, Gina nodded. Jewels nodded back and now turned to Mitch, "How do feel about some cross-agency cooperation?"

With everyone on the same page, Mitch called his watch officer at the NSA and requested his clearance paperwork be sent over to the BOATSS office ASAP. Twenty minutes later, as they were just finishing up, he received a confirmation text. “We’re on for tomorrow,” announced Mitch, putting away his phone.

Because of the sensitive office politics that Mitch had learned about from the girls the night before, Mitch phrased the clearance request as if his boss at NSA had asked for the meeting not the girls.

Mitch wondered aloud, “What do you say we invite Rick as well?”

Gina thought that was an excellent plan and Mitch made the call, “Rick, its Mitch, what’s up?”

“You’re an asshole, that’s what’s up! You played me!” Rick hollered into the phone.

Mitch smiled and laughing said, “Like an old fiddle, my friend.”

Then, being Rick, he yelled into the phone, “Those girls are smoking hot!” Rick had yelled loud enough that the girls had heard him from across the table.

Mitch smiled at the girls. Shaking his head he said, “Yes, Rick, they are. Wait a second…Oh, they say to tell you, thanks!”

“Seriously dude, are they sitting right there with you?”

Mitch could only give his friend so much ribbing, “Not four feet away buddy. Ladies, say hi to Rick.”

Fully enjoying Rick’s embarrassing moment, they leaned forward, laughing into the phone, “Morning, Rick!”

Since Rick was being uncharacteristically quiet for the moment, Mitch asked what he had on his schedule tomorrow. Rick responded that he didn’t have anything pressing so Mitch went ahead with inviting him to their meeting.

“Hey Rick, the girls say you owe them.”

“Anything,” he replied. Rick was to the point where he almost meant it literally, “Sure, what can I do?”

Mitch smiled and asked, “Could you have your boss send the visitor request from his office and make it attention, hang on a sec…Jewels,”

Mitch interrupted the girls, "What's your asshole boss's name again?"

"Ramón Rodriquez," hissed Jewels.

"Ramón Rodriquez," repeated Mitch.

"As good as done, see you guy's tomorrow morning," replied Rick before he hung up.

"I'm not going to like this guy am I?" asked Mitch.

The girls glanced at each other briefly, smiled, and looked at Mitch. They replied as one, "Not so much."

CHAPTER 19

North of Umnak Island
ALASKA

Mark originally told the crew to be at the dock at 5:00 a.m. Sunday morning. He amended that to lunchtime to give himself some more time to prepare. As it turned out, he hadn't needed to leave that early and although he let them board, they had not departed Dutch Harbor until later in the day.

They spent the afternoon practicing several emergency drills and making some last minute runs to the store for additional supplies. Mark had spent close to $2500 for food already and these guys continued to insist they needed just one more thing. Mark had been stunned at the cost of going to sea. In addition to the food, the trip had set him back almost $18,000 for fuel and another $1,500 for drums of lubricants, oil, hydro fluid, etc. Bait, which he had little or no intention of ever using, cost him a whopping $3,200. In order to appear credible, and allay suspicion, he also spent a couple hundred dollars on gloves, raingear and assorted sundries.

Mark hadn't been surprised when Roy was the last to arrive. To compound his troubles, Roy's buddy who had given him a lift down to the boat had driven away with all of Roy's stuff still in the back of the pickup. That had taken awhile to sort out. At least Roy appeared to be sober. They left port at around seven in the evening which caused several onlookers to shake their heads in apparent disbelief.

Once they had been at sea for an hour or so, Mark had them dress out in their deck gear and do some drills with the winch and other equipment before dinner. They even tossed some buoys out and then circled back around to pick them up. They actually seemed to work well as a team. The natural leader of the group was clearly Jonah. Even though the other guys had known each other for years they still seemed to respect the new guy. Maybe they recognized that he was the only non-dysfunctional crewman on the boat. After the crew turned in, Mark had taken first watch. It gave him his first real opportunity to check out the special navigation package that had been installed this past week.

Unlike most traditional navigation and autopilot systems, the *Dreamer's* new system tied everything together. Instead of just using GPS to get a fix and plot a course, the new system allowed the boat's radar to get a fix on something and either maintain a set distance from that point, like a boat or shoreline, or close on a particular return selected by the crew. Mark picked a moving point, another ship of some sort, to their southwest by tapping the screen with his finger. He then dragged an icon shaped like a target over the point he'd selected and tapped "Radar Fix." When the system automatically displayed the distance of the target to the *Dreamer*, Mark hit "Set." After a few minutes, he manually turned the boat away from the "Target" he had programmed into the system, and let go of the wheel. The boat corrected itself back to the southwesterly course toward the ship Mark had selected as a test target. Mark thought about this. Someone had programmed in the same type of technologies used in air to air missile uses. Who would have thought you could weaponize a fishing boat?

It was important the *Dreamer* look and behave every part the crab boat she wasn't. Since almost all the other crab boats were heading north to the Pribilof Islands, Mark's trip to the southwest would have to appear as legit as possible. He was fully aware that the flight paths of most of the aircraft flying along the Aleutians flew very near to the course he had plotted. Eareckson Air Station was about eight hundred miles to the west and had routine flights to Anchorage. Closer yet, at five hundred miles to the west of his current position was Kiska Island. Kiska Island was the home of the 567th Coast Guard group. These waters were their areas of responsibility and they took their responsibility very seriously. The commercial fishermen of the area counted on them in the event one of their crew became injured, sick, or in the worst case, their boat capsized. Often times, the Coast Guard would fly at low altitude in order to check on boats in the area or just to let the fishermen know they were there. Mark really hoped that the coast guard wasn't very curious today. He was not in a location where fishermen usually are at this time of year and being asked questions he didn't have answers to would be dangerous to all parties involved.

The Coast Guard took saving lives very seriously in this part of the world and that came at a price. In order to look like a fisherman, Mark had needed to equip his boat with all the emergency trappings a Coast Guard inspector would expect to see onboard a fishing vessel. Mark found exposure suits online for just over four hundred dollars, plus shipping. He paid with his bootleg credit card. Credit card fraud would be the least of his crimes this month. The boat had come with one suit that was in decent shape, but it wasn't his size. He couldn't risk the coast guard inspectors noticing that. Boat crews drilled for the worst and needed to be able to get into their suits in sixty seconds. He imagined that it would seem like an eternity if your vessel was capsizing.

Although it was late, and dangerous to be on deck by himself, Mark conducted a short walk around inspection of the boat. He didn't expect to find anything wrong with the boat but in much the same way a general liked to get a peek at a battle field before engaging his enemy, Mark wanted to make sure, in his mind that everything was as it should be.

It was cold here...a deep, damp, penetrating chill to your bones cold. Mark thought he knew all about the cold from his previous exploits in other parts of the world. The steps of Kazakhstan were cold. Fighting the Americans in the Ghazni Province of Afghanistan had been cold. This was a different level of cold. It was as if you had gone to Satan himself and asked him to create his particular version of Hell kind of cold. His present location was just north of Umnak Island, Alaska. On his current course of 225° and speed of 10 knots he should be just north of Uliaga Island in about four hours.

According to the navigation system and the waypoint Mark had entered he would be doing a course correction to the Northwest in about three hours. The winds were gusting at over 35 knots and keeping his ship on course would have proven difficult if he had not had the navigation system. The ocean currents at this time of year averaged about 10 knots and were continually trying to push his boat to the north. There would be a time for that, it just wasn't now.

The *Dreamer's* very specialized navigation computer was doing an excellent job staying ahead of the current and the *Dreamer* was making decent time. Timing would be critical on this particular trip. He wouldn't be missing a school of fish or a basket full of the crawling, disgusting, bottom feeding crustaceans. Mark would be missing his only chance of success.

Mark could not have trained for these conditions in the seas of his homeland. Had he not truly believed that his mission was worth his life and that success would certainly place him in the bosom of Allah, he would not have come. He had studied engineering at Cairo University and graduated at the top of his class. He had trained for this mission with his laptop computer, Google Earth, and some other online resources. Reading nautical charts for a man of his education and experience was child's play. The cold he had not, and could not, have trained for. It was wearing him down and he'd only been at sea for one day.

North Korea
Special Operations Center

In the early hours of Monday morning, Capt. Qwon, Intelligence Officer, Republic of North Korea's Army, received the "confirm" message from the agent in Anchorage. He also received a message from a source he didn't recognize but the coded message was expected. "The fishing trip was very successful." This was great news. The Fort Greely part of the puzzle was in play as was the SBX. Now it was just a question of the other players. He made an inquiry from their intelligence source regarding the time of the "luncheon" on Wednesday. Apparently, lunch was running late and would be served around 2:00 p.m. local time. This quasi cryptic message basically informed him that America's SBX radar platform was due to arrive in Adak bay around 2:00 p.m. on Wednesday. It wasn't a perfect fit for the mission, but there was little they could do about the speed of the American vessel. In the bigger scheme of things, it wouldn't matter. By the time the Americans figured out what was going on, it would be much too late. Capt. Qwon had one more loose end to tie up. He sent a message to his contact in Dutch Harbor; "Menu change for Wednesday's luncheon, please be able to serve fresh crab to lunch guests at 2:00 p.m. Wednesday."

The response was almost immediate. "I'm looking forward to serving my best catch of the day to your guests." All this good news and the sun hadn't even risen above the mountains.

Seattle, Washington

Kevin's mother Cynthia was growing frantic. It was 3:00 a.m. when she had gained her composure enough to attempt calling Kevin again. She knew her son's job routinely had him away from a phone but time was running out. Where was he at this hour? She had to talk to him, now. What had her son told her about emergencies? Was it the Red Cross? It was worth a shot. Cynthia placed a call to the Office of Emergency Services on Elmendorf/Richardson. She got the out-of-the office message and was directed to the 800 number. Cynthia had forgotten to account for the four-hour time zone change. She would call back at eleven her time. She set her alarm clock and tried to get some sleep.

CHAPTER 20

BOATSS

It was 6:00 a.m. Monday morning when the girls dragged their coded access keys through the cipher lock on the door, keyed in their PIN numbers and entered the BOATSS offices. The offices were cold, again.

The girls wanted to make sure their offices looked nice when Mitch and Rick came at 8:00 a.m. Both girls took down anything they thought the guys would think looked silly. Their ulterior motive was to see the look on their boss Ramón Rodriquez's face when he opened his email at 7:30 a.m. and saw that two visitors, from two different agencies, had a meeting this morning in his section without his knowledge or approval. It should be a classic for the ages.

As predicted, they knew immediately when Ramón opened his email because Gina's phone rang. "Yes sir?" Gina loved to patronize the man.

As expected, he wanted to see both of them in his office immediately. He didn't even wait for them to get all the way in before he let loose, "What the hell are you two up to?" The girls tried to be coy but he was having none of that. "Tell me now!" he bellowed, in his best wavering and yet pathetically insecure voice. It was sad really. Apparently Ramón was more concerned about the fact that visitors were coming than he was about exactly who was coming.

Gina offered, “Sir, these gentlemen have some concerns and questions about the *Confero* software we are using and asked for our help.” That didn’t work.

He now focused his rage at Jewels. “Why wasn’t I notified about the visit? I didn’t give permission for them to visit.”

Jewels knew she should probably keep quiet but she’d had enough of this little piss ant already this morning, “Sir, they called Friday afternoon around 3:00 p.m. I believe you had already left for the day...”

He was burning mad. He hadn’t signed out or told anyone he was leaving and they knew it. He recovered enough and announced loud enough to be heard outside his office, “I’ll brief them on our operations and funding requirements and limitations. If they have any specific questions I may call you two in. Stay in the office and be available if I need you.”

Wow, she really disliked this man. She went back to her desk and the message light on her phone was blinking. She hoped it was Mitch. Nope. “Hi Jewels, its Rick, I wanted to tell you this in person, sorry I missed you. Be sure your asshole boss reads the addendum to the visitor’s request. We’re even. See you at eight.” Jewels wondered what that was all about.

Jewels called her boss and asked him if he had read page two of the visitor request letters. He hadn’t. He burst out of his office demanding to know what the hell an “eyes-only” meeting was. One of the new folks on the floor thought that he would be helpful: “Sir, an eyes-only meeting is one where only a certain restricted group of people are allowed to attend the meeting.”

Jewels’ phone rang. She quickly answered it, saving her for the moment from the awkwardness of the situation.

“Miss Folk,” It was Ken, one of the security guys from the front desk. She occasionally brought him coffee in the morning. He was always pleasant to her and today was no different. “Two gentlemen are here to see you. They’re badged up and ready, do you want me to show them back?” “Sure thing, Ken,” Jewels replied in her very best smooth-as-butter voice.

The guys came around the corner in their very best suits, both making every effort to appear dead-pan serious, "Miss Folk?" They feigned introductions all around. Jewels couldn't resist. She stuck her head into Rodriquez's office "Mr. Rodriquez? Sir, the men I told you about are here."

Rick curtly introduced himself and Mitch to Ramón and asked if there was a secure area where he and his colleague could speak to Miss Folk and Miss Hughes. Caught off guard, Ramón gestured them into the secure conference room. As he attempted to follow, Rick placed up his hand. "I'm sorry Mr. Rodriquez; you're not cleared for this meeting."

"But I'm their boss!"

Rick raised his hand in a gesture that indicated that he needed Ramón to stop, "Sir, you're not on the list."

They had barely made it into the conference room when Gina started to giggle, "Oh my God, that was awesome!"

"Alright, let's get down to business, "Jewels directed her attention to Mitch, "Why don't you log onto the system and show us what you were talking about last night."

"Sure thing Jewels." As he logged in, he started to explain, "What I noticed was that I could set the parameters of the system to subtract certain elements of collected data. For example, I normally track drone signals all over the United States, right? So what I did was open up my signal search to areas that were local, national, or world signal events where you wouldn't expect to find or detect a specific event. Last week I started detecting and tracking a signal emanating from essentially the middle of the Pacific Ocean. From what I could tell from the very short bursts of signal, it matched almost identically a signal that I had previously seen in the States. I'm still trying to figure out what it is and why I'm picking it up for such short periods of time."

"You said it's similar to another signal you're familiar with? What do you think it is?" asked Rick.

"Well, now this might sound crazy, but it's almost identical in amplitude and wavelength to a US drone link that I've only monitored both into and out of Nevada and Iraq. Anyway, I was thinking on the way over here about your specific collections. Everything you get in here is raw data correct?"

Gina piped up, "Yeah, it comes in over a secure link with very little signal degradation."

Leaning forward now, Mitch asked, "So you could, in theory anyway, strip away parts of the signal if you wanted to?"

Both Gina and Jewels responded together, "Sure, but why would you?"

Mitch smiled, "I spend a lot of time thinking about better ways to skin a cat; sometimes they seem crazy but sometimes..." He shrugged and smiled at the girls. "Here's my thought, what if you could not only isolate what ships make what sounds but what parts of those ships make those sounds?" He continued, "Say Vessel "A" has a hatch that makes a certain sound when slammed shut. If this happens at sea you don't usually hear it because the sound is interspersed with everything else, right?"

Everyone nodded, although Rick's eyes appeared to be starting to glaze over a bit from the technical aspect of the conversation. Mitch wondered aloud, "What if you could break a signal apart and identify not only the sound of the ship's motor but specific sounds emanating from specific ships?"

"So what?" asked Rick rather academically, "What's the value added to the program?"

"The value, my unimaginative friend, is that if you were to hear a particular hatch door slam without the accompanying motor sound you would potentially still know where a particular ship was."

Jewels was drumming her finger tips together. She leaned back in her chair and stared at the ceiling for a moment, closed her eyes, "So if we recorded and logged the sounds of a particular vessel's activities at one port we could potentially, just by processing the signal collected at its destination port, determine what activities were being conducted on board that ship at a particular point in time."

"Exactly!" shouted Mitch.

Gina turned to the system and with fingers flying over the keys created a "test mode" for the program. It would take a bunch of time for the system to collect all of the information from all the ships but the logic appeared sound. "Somebody give me a normally quiet area in the ocean."

"Northern Pacific?" suggested Rick trying to be helpful.

Gina smiled at him in acknowledgment. He smiled back. He'd guessed. Rick felt he was on a roll and continued after a moment, "Could the system be tweaked to pick up sounds that shouldn't be where you hear them?"

Everyone was staring at him. He wasn't sure if he was being humored or if they really wanted him to go on. Mitch broke the awkward silence, "Go on, Rick."

Rick so desperately did not want to sound like an idiot in front of Gina this morning. Cautiously he placed his idea before them, "What if your acoustic system heard a sound that shouldn't be in the middle of the ocean, like a car door slamming? Could you set the system up to notify you of the anomalous sound?"

No one said a word.

Rick hesitatingly asked, "Did I embarrass myself again?"

Mitch looked at Gina who in turn looked at Jewels. Jewels turned to Rick and with a smile told Rick, "Not yet." It was cold blooded but everyone laughed, even Rick.

"How long Gina?" asked Jewels. Gina tipped back in her chair looked Rick straight in the eye and said, "The idea was the hard part; I can have the code done in about five hours."

Jewels smiled and piped in, "I'll help you."

Gina leaned over and loudly whispered in Mitch's ear, just loud enough for Jewels to hear, "Make that six hours."

Fortunately, Jewels knew how to take it as well as dish it out. She laughed at the joke and suggested they get to it. "Alright, everybody back to work. Remember not to smile when you walk out."

They wrapped up their "eyes-only" meeting. As Mitch walked out the door he brushed his hand ever so slightly against hers, "Dinner?"

Jewels looked at her watch, and then at a nodding Gina, "It'll be a late one, but sounds great. Let's say 7:30ish? I'll call you when I get home."

Mitch dropped his smile as they walked out the conference room door. They had been in the room just over two hours. Some of the staff raised their eyebrows, but no one said a word. Gina moved quickly to her desk, put her headphones on, and dug in. She had learned to write code as if it were her first language. She rapidly filled screen after screen. Jewels, although not as proficient at writing code as Gina read over her shoulder for a while occasionally making an observation or comment. After twenty minutes or so, Jewels went back to her computers. She opened her email account on her unclassified government computer system and already had an email from Mitch. It read simply, Can I pick the restaurant tonight? ~ Mitch. Jewels smiled and responded quickly. All she sent was a smiley face emoticon.

The girls worked best in tandem, sort of like human dual core processors. As Gina wrote the code, she would push it through the system to Jewels. Jewels would integrate it into the front of the system. Jewels wrote the operator interface. Creating things such as menu tabs, search parameters, and building links to numerous classified networks and resources was her specialty. They had been writing together in one manner shape or form for several years. It would have been foolish to approach the project any other way.

Jewels and Gina had worked straight through lunch and were about to grab a cup of coffee when Ramón walked up. Often times he wouldn't make an attempt to interrupt you, he would just tend to stand there glaring until you stopped what you were doing and granted him an audience. They both finished the lines of code they were working on and said, "Yes sir," within seconds of each other. It was obvious from his facial expression this was not a social call. They were right.

Ramón started with, "What I would like to know is how you two pulled off a meeting with two different guys from two different agencies with no pre-planning and to my knowledge, no approval from anyone?" After a few minutes of ranting, he ended with, "I'm your boss and I demand your respect." It was classic Ramón. This time something was different and they had both noticed it, he seemed a little more edgy than normal.

The girls waited a few minutes and then popped out for some vendor coffee. Jewels got a double shot of espresso just to take the edge off. Sitting down in the foyer of the lobby in their building they drank their medicine. "So?" Gina started. Jewels stared out the lobby window. "Jewels, is everything okay, sweetie?"

"I like him," Jewels said into her still steaming cup.

"Really," Gina tried to sound surprised. "I hadn't noticed."

"Seriously Gina, I'm scared because I…" her voice trailed off for a moment.

"You what?" asked Gina.

Jewels replied in a voice that Gina had heard perhaps only once in all the years they had known each other, "I don't want to screw this up."

Gina, the girl who normally talks nonstop, said only two words to her best friend, "So don't." Jewels looked up after a few moments and Gina was gone. She needed a minute and Gina knew it. What the hell? Tears? Really? Jewels dabbed the corners of her eyes with a tissue. Her nose was stuffed up, her eyes were watering and she was feeling a bit flush. Jewels realized what Gina had already known. This spring was the first spring in a long, long time, that moisture in her eyes and rolling down her cheeks was not from the spring flowers and pollen. She was falling for Mitch. Now what?

Seattle, Washington
Gyoh Residence

It had been a long night and Mrs. Gyoh had not slept very much. She'd been up since 6:00 a.m. watching the news. It was depressing. Tensions were high everywhere in the world it seemed. The President and his cabinet seemed very apathetic or apologetic about almost any event in the world that might cast his administration in a poor light. As she dialed the number for the emergency services office at Richardson/Elmendorf, the timer on the stove went off with a loud buzz. She jumped, spilled her coffee and almost dropped the phone. It was ringing and the automated system hadn't picked up. Mrs. Gyoh took that as a good sign.

Debby Waters, the Red Cross representative at Joint Base Richardson/Elmendorf took the call at 8:02 a.m. having just sat down at her desk. Mrs. Gyoh explained she had an urgent message for her son who was stationed out on Eareckson Air Station. He didn't work by a phone and it was imperative that she get a message to him to call home. Ms. Waters asked all the questions you would expect. What was his name, his unit, did she know what shift he worked? They were easy questions for the most part. Fortunately, they were right off the sheet that Kevin had made for her before he'd left. Then she asked the $64,000 question. "Mrs. Gyoh, what is the nature of the emergency?"

"It's my daughter, Kevin's sister, she's seriously ill."

After what seemed like minutes, she could hear some sounds in the background. Did she know she was lying? What was the delay? "Mrs. Gyoh? Sorry about that. We get so many calls from relatives up here worrying about their loved ones. I had to make sure Kevin had a sister. You understand, I'm sure?"

She did. She didn't like it, but she did. After another long moment of silence, suddenly Debby was back, "Mrs. Gyoh? I'm so sorry this has taken so long. My computer is working great this morning. Its operator, on the other hand, isn't doing nearly so well without her coffee." Mrs. Gyoh feigned a laugh.

"What would be the best time for him to call you?" asked Debby.

"Anytime," replied Mrs. Gyoh, "he has all my numbers. Could you express to him that's it's critical that I speak to him as soon as possible?"

"Yes, Mrs. Gyoh, I'll tell him. Wish your daughter well for all of us up here at the base."

Kevin's mom had already hung up. Now all she had to do was wait for Kevin's call and give him the number to call. Where had she put the number? On her nightstand was the pink sticky note with the odd number. She didn't ever remember seeing that prefix before. She knew 011 was the international prefix but where was 886?

CHAPTER 21

The Yunes

Mr. Feng, which Captain Babakan, in a moment of curiosity, had looked up and found to mean "sharp blade," had impressed on the captain that precise navigation and stealth were going to be an essential key to the success of the operation. The plan as it stood was to drift with the current from Amatignak Island to a point just north of Kasatochi Island. By drifting with the current, the *Yunes* would not need to use very much power and would be virtually silent. This time of the year the prevailing currents north of the Aleutians were toward the east. Upon reaching their position off Kasatochi Island, surface, off load his cargo, submerge, and continue drifting with the current east to a point just west of Seguam Island. Just to the west of Seguam, the current made an abrupt turn to the south for about twenty-five nautical miles, dropped down the South Aleutian Slope and headed west.

Captain Babakan planned to use every bit of natural forward momentum he could to avoid using his batteries up. Once over the edge of the South Aleutian Slope, he could then dive his boat deep and drift silently west at 273° back to the south of Attu. At this point he felt he would be able to safely engage his engines, still at their minimum power, dive to the *Yunes'* maximum depth, and proceed west. The captain wasn't entirely sure what he was dropping off, or for whom, but he did know that he was expected to do it with as much stealth as he and his old Kilo sub and crew could muster.

The explosives and accompanying electronics had been carefully packaged in large waterproof briefcases and then sealed a second time at the sub's home port in Bandar Abbas. The six-man team practiced for hours putting the briefcases into modified crab traps and closing the submarine's hatch. In the drills, it had taken just over eight minutes. The goal had been five. However, after several runs, on dry land, without wind, on a stable floor, in warm conditions, everyone agreed that five minutes was, to put it simply, overly optimistic. The process was practiced for three days. The first step was placing the men and materials in the diving trunk. The trunk is a self-contained room with a hatch to the inside of the submarine as well as a hatch to the sea. By using the outside hatch, divers can exit or enter the submarine while it was still underwater.

It has an inner hatch that could sustain the pressures of several hundred feet and an outer hatch that was flush with the deck. When exiting the submarine, the crewmen enter the trunk, close the inside hatch, and then activate a pump allowing the dive trunk to fill with water. Once the trunk is full of water and the pressure equalized, the outer hatch can be opened and the divers or crew can swim to the surface or, using scuba gear, perform other types of missions.

The design of the trunk's hatch and this mission were well suited for each other. Since the submarine was only going to surface to wave height, the hatch to the actual interior of the sub would protect the ship from a rogue wave over washing the deck and flooding the ship.

The mission called for a six-man team. Five men brought the equipment up onto the deck and the sixth manned the hatch, watched for rouge waves, and coordinated the operation. As the captain watched, his handpicked team set about readying themselves for the harsh conditions outside. The men had not been given exposure suits. In the event they were to fall overboard they wouldn't be found. They understood the risks. For security reasons, only the six men he had chosen were briefed on the mission or even seen the cargo. The six men had no idea what they were delivering. The very fact that they were delivering anything called for a higher than normal level of operational security.

The boat was sitting at a depth of thirty-two feet with only its periscope and radio mast above the surface. The helmsman was awaiting his orders to continue the *Yunes*' ascent. Captain Babakan supposed that to someone with a sense of humor, they must have looked like very desperate crab fisherman to say the least. The plan itself, at this point, was relatively simple; it was the implementation that would be the tricky part. His team was already in place in the forward dive trunk. Even in the event of an emergency, a rogue wave etc., only the escape chamber open to the sea would flood. The amount of water that would enter the chamber would have no bearing on the operation of the boat. The captain knew that he wouldn't be allowed to pump it out due to noise concerns but he would save the boat. He also knew he would most certainly lose his team.

At 8:00 p.m. local, the burst transmission came confirming the mission was green. The *Yunes* was ready to surface. "Captain Babakan, a moment sir?" The captain was startled by the voice. Mr. Feng spoke flawless Persian. Mr. Feng smiled and seemed to enjoy the surprise. He continued in Persian, "You do understand that, as per your orders received at the start of this mission, from this moment forward I essentially have control of the operation of your vessel?"

The captain felt his jaw move but wasn't sure that he had actually said anything. He tried again.

"Yes," was all he could muster. Although he had known, somehow when it was spoken out loud it sounded almost profane.

Then it got awkward and a little more embarrassing. "Captain Babakan, please immediately inform your crew of the temporary command structure change." What was this all about? This wasn't in his orders. As if he had anticipated this very action, Mr. Feng produced a sealed set of orders with the Iranian Navy seal and handed them to the captain.

Captain Karim Babakan and senior officers of the Yunes;
Mr. Feng is assuming command of your vessel, mission, and personnel, until you are otherwise directed by this office.

All Captain Babakan could do was nod his understanding of the orders and make the announcement to his crew. Mr. Feng gave them a moment for the change of command to sink in. As if in a dream, Captain Babakan felt himself take a step backwards, salute crisply, and hand Mr. Feng the microphone. With a smile that changed slowly to a look of complete concentration, Mr. Feng ordered, "All stop! Surface the boat! Zero feet."

"Zero feet sir?"

Captain Babakan placed his hand on the young man's shoulder, "What Mr. Feng means is he wants the deck of the boat to be just above the level of the sea." The young man controlling the ascent looked to Captain Babakan for some type of encouraging sign, but all he received was a smile and a nod.

In the forward wet compartment, the team of six men checked the seal on the door between their compartment and the rest of the boat. The green light indicated a positive seal. The hatch could no longer be opened from the outside.

The compartment's hatches had been configured like most modern submarines in that only one hatch may be open at a time. The team did a communications check. The team lead was on a channel that connected him to the inside of the boat as well as his men. They opened the outside hatch leading to the deck. Immediately they could feel the tremendous cold air pouring down into the compartment from the frigid arctic sea.

As they prepared to haul their cargo to the deck of the submarine, Mr. Feng came over their headsets, "Due to the present sea conditions, each man must secure himself to each of the packages in order that they not wash overboard."

Each of the team clicked their throat microphones twice to indicate they understood. Each "package" consisted of a half scale crab trap, two "shots" or four hundred feet of line with a yellow crab float, and of course, the large black briefcases. Captain Babakan started his clock. The men brought the cages, up on deck, one at a time. Each man, as they had practiced, left the door of the trap open. One at a time, as ordered, they secured themselves to the trap with a ten-foot cord and a carabineer.

Two minutes fifteen seconds. The team leader then handed them each a four-hundred-foot coil of lightweight rope. At one end of the coil was a yellow crab float at the other was a fixed eye hook for securing the line to the trap. Four minutes, thirty seconds.

Captain Babakan stole a glance at Mr. Feng. He was smiling. They were significantly behind schedule and he was smiling? The men placed the coil of line over their left arm and secured the end with the hook to the trap. The last things brought up on deck were the specially wrapped briefcases. Each waterproof briefcase was placed in its respective trap and the door secured with another small carabineer. Each man then walked twenty feet forward of the hatch and placed his coil of rope squarely on top of the trap. Six minutes and ten seconds.

The team leader had barely reported, "Ready to deploy." when Mr. Feng ordered, "Close dive trunk hatch! Open all forward torpedo tube doors! Vent bow tanks only! Dive the boat." The crew hesitated for less than a second then quickly complied with Feng's orders.

The team leader protested and was heard yelling, "What about my men?" Yet even he complied with the orders and quickly closed the hatch with a loud bang. The hatch closed indicator light turned from "red" to "green" indicating a positive seal. The moment the forward torpedo doors had flooded, the bow of the submarine lurched forward just enough to throw the men on deck off their feet. Through the periscope, Captain Babakan watched helplessly as the bow pitched downward into the cold sea. The men had heard the team leader's comment and out of the corners of their eyes seen the hatch close. One by one, the cages with their heavy packages slid off the boat and sank like stones. The men who, only moments before, had been screaming for the hatch to be reopened and then frantically trying to get back to the hatch, quickly followed the cages over the side. The mission leader, still isolated in the dive trunk, was demanding that the interior hatch be opened and was demanding that he speak to the captain. "Flood the trunk," was all Mr. Feng said in response to his tirade. The mission leader lived for a while as the chamber flooded and was getting very creative in the use of profanity until the combination of extremely cold water and lack of air silenced him...forever.

Mr. Feng looked coolly into Captain Babakan's face, "We were never here. This mission never happened. If information of the mission ever leaks out, your entire crew and their families will be killed. Do you understand?"

Captain Babakan hissed, "yes."

Mr. Feng smiled again, and with the authority and cockiness of an experienced submarine commander, whispered the most shocking thing the captain had ever heard, "Captain Babakan, relax, we do this kind of stuff all the time. It would serve you well to remember, I don't like loose ends."

Mr. Feng turned away from the captain grabbed the microphone and ordered, "Helm, make your depth three hundred twenty-eight feet. Navigation, place us on a heading of 054°. "Remain at silent running, zero turn on the screws." Not another word was spoken.

Seattle
Gyoh Residence

The phone was ringing. Mrs. Gyoh got it before the second ring. "Kevin?" She was almost nauseous.

"Hi Mom, how's sis?"

"Kevin you must listen to me very carefully."

Kevin started, "What's this all about Mom?"

"Kevin, hush! Do you have something to write on?"

Kevin sighed, "Hang on...okay shoot."

Kevin's Mom read him the number very slowly, number by number. It was unfortunate but there was an echo on the line which made the whole process seem to take much longer. She read it twice to him and he read it back to her twice.

"Kevin you listen to me very carefully, do you remember the books you used to read when you were a teen?" Kevin started to answer, but she cut him off. "Just listen, this is just like that!"

Kevin sensed something was seriously wrong with his Mom. He read all the espionage and spy thrillers he could get his hands on when he was younger. His mom wasn't making any sense.

"Alright Mom, I'm listening"

"Your sister is in real trouble and only you can fix it. Some men called and said they have your sister. I don't know what these men want, they wouldn't say. They did say they would hurt her if you don't do exactly what they say. Kevin, let that sink in for a moment."

"Mom, what could they want from me? I don't have any money."

"They wouldn't tell me, they just gave me that number and said you needed to call them as soon as you could."

He had managed to say, "I will Mom, I love..." when he heard the click.

"Mom?" but she was gone and the line was dead.

Kevin looked at the number he'd written down. Where the heck was country code 886? He got himself organized and dialed the number. He used his Skype account to make the call. As it rang he looked up the number. His answer came up in Bing search just as the other end answered the phone. Taiwan?

A man answered in a heavy accent that almost sounded British. He hadn't expected that. "Is this Kevin Gyoh?" he demanded.

"Yes," Kevin answered cautiously and still a little off guard with the accent business.

"We have your sister; we will kill her unless you destroy the Cobra Dane radar by Wednesday afternoon."

Kevin was floored. "I can't do that," he stammered. "I wouldn't."

"Shut up fool! We don't care how you do it, or when you do it, as long as it's done by this Wednesday afternoon. It's off line in two days or she dies." The connection went dead.

Holy shit Sis, what are you mixed up in? It was just coming up on 9:00 a.m. and Kevin needed to think. Who were these people? Kevin thought for a minute. Wait a minute, it was March. March is pledge month. Maybe it was some of her sorority sisters pulling a pledge prank. He remembered all the stuff his sister had to do when she was pledging Tri Psi's. He used to call them "Try Psychos." As an upperclassman this year, she would be the target of all the spring pledges and their required pranks. Kidnapping upperclassman for a day or two was standard fare as long as all parties had agreed in advance and appropriate safety precautions were taken. Spoofing the country code of Taiwan and altering that dude's voice was awesome. I guess the kids had an app for that as well. Kevin hoped that the students were putting as much energy into their studies as their pledging rituals. The business about burning down the Dane was a little over the top, he would have to talk to his sister about that.

The phone calls had forced Kevin to start his day a little late but nobody seemed to notice. He made his loop past the various communication uplink sites, checked in with a couple of other site managers around the island. After a while the shock of the call wore off and Kevin got busy with the rest of his day. He went to chow early then racked out in his room. It had taken a while longer than normal to fall asleep but he was dead to the world by 10:00 p.m.

CHAPTER 22

Anchorage, Alaska

Terry Grabowski had been delivering fuel to the bases in Alaska's interior since 1976. He loved the job and, although his trips normally took him about six and a half hours, he enjoyed the long drives. At sixty-six years old, the job was beginning to wear on him physically. Thankfully, it was nothing out of the ordinary, just the usual aches and pains from working outside all his life.

The summer months were terrific and with the almost twenty-four hours of daylight, the trips were an easy day of travel. It was the cold Alaskan winters that were starting to take their toll on him. Often, temperatures at some of Alaska's interior bases plummet to forty below zero. It was getting tough on Terry's aging hands and legs to be that cold. The doctors said he had arthritis in his hands and back and should probably consider another line of work. Yeah, sure. At sixty-six, in Alaska, he would just find a different line of work. Where do these doctors get their smarts? His doctor would have appeared somewhat more intelligent if he had shaken his hand, looked him in the eye and said, "It totally sucks to be you." Terry would have respected that. So now, he sort of walked, sort of limped through his days. At night, a long hot shower was a real blessing.

Glenda, Terry's wife of thirty-nine years, had passed away just over five years ago. Three years ago, Terry's son, Dwayne and his little family moved north from Ohio to keep an eye on him. Terry made a big deal out of that at the coffee shop he frequented every morning in Anchorage. Terry felt he needed to at least "publically" assert that he hadn't wanted them to come. For several years now, his fellow customers at the coffee shop by the fuel depot had been his family. Secretly though, Terry had been delighted the kids moved up. He supposed the bad economy had an upside after all. Your kids don't mind moving home when you ask them to, if they don't have jobs.

It had been a "transition" from being alone to having the kids and a grandchild at the house. God knows he had the room. It wasn't that. It was more that he had developed his own various routines and they worked. After Glenda passed away, he'd had to gently tweak some of his routines. When the kids moved up, there wasn't much left of his routines as he knew them. It was mostly silly stuff, like walking around in his briefs; that was taboo now. Farting and belching were also frowned upon.

He had slowly parted with a bunch of "old stuff" he and Glenda had accumulated over the years and then rapidly filled in the empty space the "new stuff" of his kids and granddaughter. The effect on his actual house was minimal. The effect on Terry's empty heart was immeasurable. His granddaughter was the new center of his universe. He lived for that smiling little bundle of sunshine.

Shama Wazeri liked Terry's routines as well. Shama's orders had been very clear. He was to get onto Fort Greely by any means necessary and do as much damage as possible. Shama's name would be placed among the many who had martyred themselves for the great cause.

Shama had legally entered Alaska with a Canadian tourist visa last fall and had been cooling his heels at The Hotel Captain Cook in downtown Anchorage ever since. It was a pricey place to stay for as long as he had, but then again, it wasn't his money.

The Hotel Captain Cook was an amazing property: four restaurants, fifteen retail stores, and a giant flat panel TV in each room for watching movies. The hotel also offered free access to the athletic club, massage service, and an indoor pool. Shama only knew the generalities of his upcoming mission but did not have an execution date. That was fine with him. He would be ready. In the meantime, Shama would patiently wait for his orders and enjoy as much of this life as he had left. When the orders did come, he wouldn't need to pack, he wouldn't be returning to the hotel.

Shama had been watching for a person just like Terry Grabowski for several months. Terry was perfect. In Shama's eyes, Terry was a very weak man. First, he was old and weak of body. Second, he had developed numerous relationships and routines that Shama could exploit. One such routine was his daily stop at Lou's Truck Stop for a cup of coffee. It should have been a quick stop, but Terry would be there for almost twenty minutes. Terry loved to talk to everyone in the shop, about anything and everything.

Everyone here in Alaska seemed to know everyone else's business and seemed to trust each other. It was annoying. They liked to say how much they relied on each other, like that was a point of pride or something. Shama had feigned relationships with several of the other patrons at the coffee shop in order to gain their trust. What information Shama couldn't get from Terry, he had easily gathered from Terry's friends at the truck stop.

Terry lived in an isolated part of the county and had no neighbors within a mile or two. Sadly, in this hellish prison of ice and barbaric cold, that was not unusual. Terry's fuel route would take Shama exactly where he needed to go. Terry had almost boasted to Shama last week how he knew almost everyone at the fort. "Private Donnelly's wife had given birth to a baby daughter last week. This other fellow at the post had wrecked his truck." If Shama could have felt pity, it would have been pitiful. To "ice the cake" as he heard so many times, everyone at the shop also knew that the shining star in Terry's life was his granddaughter. Not even his son, his granddaughter. It was pathetic. As was the nature of today's technology based communication, Shama received his message to "execute" the mission in a cleverly worded email from his associate in Toronto. The email simply stated, "Tomorrow through Thursday would be an excellent time to view the Aurora Borealis." Due to Terry's route schedule, Shama had explained to the planners of this operation, that he would need a "window" as opposed to a specific date.

Terry's next run to the Fort would be Wednesday morning. Shama suspected that he wasn't the only player in the game so he sent the following reply, "Wednesday night works best for me. What do you need me to bring?" Whatever plan had been cooked up was bigger than his small piece of the puzzle. For this timeline to work he would need to get his special equipment ready. He had two days left. Maybe one more full body massage before he left?

Several time zones away, deep in his own underground bunker, copies of the message traffic were also received by General ShahAb Tehrani. The general was, of course, quite pleased with the good news. As the general readied himself for morning prayers, he was thinking about the next phase of the operation and how pleased Allah would be with him when he received a message on his secure computer network. "Thank you for all your help with this project." It was cryptically signed, L.Q. General Tehrani paused, smiling to himself considering the irony of the situation and thought, Oh no Lieutenant Qwon; it is I that should be thanking you.

Shemya Island

Tuesday arrived cold and dreary on Shemya with nothing out of the ordinary on the schedule. Kevin spent some time down by the water on the western side of the island gazing across the half mile or so to Hammerhead Island. He loved this particular spot. On many days, providing the sun was out, the water would sparkle one moment then suddenly turn to an explosion of foam as it crashed against the rocky outcroppings along the shore. Kevin often thought this spot represented his life up to this point. It was truly an amazing place. He thought about his mom and sister and about the folks that were for the most part his "Island Family" here.

It was Tuesday and that meant a trip over to Cobra Dane. Charlie met him at the door with his usual cup of coffee. Today they toured the underbelly of Cobra Dane. They looked at the facility's security system, ran some diagnostic tests, and even conducted an in-place fire alarm test.

The fire control system was the rather old fashioned overhead heat activated sprayers. The system would work in the event of a fire but everything electric below the sprayers, for several floors, would be destroyed or seriously damaged. Kevin hadn't thought of the crazy phone call all day but as he reviewed the emergency procedures for the folks at the Cobra Dane facility his mind wandered back to the man's strange demand to destroy Cobra Dane. As a purely academic exercise and out of shear boredom he began to wonder if it could be done.

CHAPTER 23

Wednesday Morning

RICHARDSON HIGHWAY

As was the norm, Terry's run up to Eielson Air Force Base, or today's run up to Fort Greely, required him to leave the house at around 7:15 a.m. Today's run of fuel was a mixed load. The truck had three compartments that could carry up to three different types of fuel. Today's load was comprised of one compartment diesel fuel, for the three dozen or so base vehicles, and two compartments of 85 octane gasoline called MOGAS, which is used at the base motor pool by both the base personnel and contractors. He made the run twice a week to Fort Greely and three times per week to Eielson. Terry didn't splurge on much in life but before his Glenda passed away he had promised her he would upgrade his ride to something more comfortable.

He had kept his word, and then some. Terry's truck was a new Kenworth W900L with an 86" studio sleeper cab. It was a real head turner. He had only used the sleeper cab itself on a few occasions when he had been running late and wanted to catch a few winks. It was loaded with all the bells and whistles.

After three years Terry still wasn't sure how to use half of the gadgets on the truck. The salesman had even talked him into a door that exited from the sleeper. What Terry would ever use that for he hadn't a clue. Maybe some younger driver could pretend that it was an apartment if he didn't have to climb in past the steering wheel. Maybe his son Dwayne would use it someday?

The route to the bases was committed to memory and he had his routine stops for food or to use the bathroom. In this business, routine was helpful because if something went wrong, and you were overdue, someone might come looking for you. In the winter season though, far fewer places were open. Here he was in the middle of March and the temperature for most of his trip today was never going to go above five degrees. Shit.

Terry stopped by Lou's for his usual large black coffee and the latest gossip. It always amazed him how much could happen in one day. He had been here just yesterday and thought he was all caught up! Mostly everyone would be talking about their favorite TV shows. Summer was all about fishing and hunting, winter was TV season. He really didn't have time for TV with the kids back home. He'd listen intently to who was winning on "American Idol" or "Survivor" or whatever show was being discussed. He had no idea what they would be talking about but participated by interjecting an occasional "Wow" or "You're kidding me." He always left with a full cup of coffee and a smile.

The Fort is located one hundred miles southeast of Fairbanks, Alaska, in an open field close to the Richardson Highway. Fort Greeley was one of the smallest bases Terry had ever delivered to.

With some installations, the actual footprint of the base was relatively small in comparison to the actual geographic size of the base. He had watched Fort Greely grow, contract and grow again over the past twenty years. The Base Realignment and Closure (BRAC) folks had taken a swipe at it back in 1995. They consolidated and realigned the fort but not closed it. It was the home of the Cold Regions Test Center (CRTC). The facility had been designed to test the operational effectiveness of military gear in the harsh northern environment. It was also the home to the 49th Missile

Defense Battalion. The 49th supposedly tested and successfully launched Anti-Ballistic Missiles. He'd heard about it on the news. Usually, it was the multimillion dollar failures that made headlines. That was tough on the people who referred to themselves as "Team Greely - Home of the Rugged Professionals."

To call Fort Greely a "wide spot in the road" wasn't too much of an exaggeration. It was basically a flat section of real-estate cut out by retreating glaciers tens of thousands of years ago. He guessed that maybe five hundred or so people were assigned there?

The base was, in fact, a perfect match for its two primary missions. The weather was perfect for the CRTC and the fact that it was out in the middle of nowhere, meant if something went wrong with a missile test, very few people would be affected. That was the plan anyway.

Over the years, Terry had gotten to know many of the folks at the post. He had been delivering fuel when they'd arrived on the post and had watched them grow, heard about their families, and then eventually, seen most of them leave the post years later. He felt a connection to these folks. Not just the folks at Greely, but all the bases he hauled fuel to. He thought of what his idiot doctor had said and looked out the window of his cab at the frozen ground that stretched before him. Quit? And leave all this? Terry laughed. He pulled his old grease covered coat a little tighter, flipped up the fleece collar, took a couple gulps of water to swallow the aspirin for his aching hands and laughed again.

Terry merged onto I-A1 E toward the town of Palmer. He had nothing to do for another one hundred and forty-six miles except enjoy watching the darkness transform into the half-light of a new spring day.

CHAPTER 24

The Dreamer

NORTH OF ATKA ISLAND, ALASKA

Mark plotted his course to bring him to an exact heading of 274°. Exact was important. Timing was important. The success of his part of the mission was paramount to the larger mission. At this heading and speed, he would be at his destination shortly. It would be dark and extremely dangerous.

So what, he thought? You could say that about most of his whole life up to this point. Why should tonight be any different?

Everything on the trip had been fairly normal up to this point. The crew was curious as to where they were going since he had been traveling west instead of north. He would need their help getting the crab pots on board with their very special cargo. From that point forward, the crew was expendable.

According to the coordinates Mark had put into the navigation system, they should be at their destination in about twenty minutes. Although he didn't think it would be necessary, he removed his Sig from its hiding spot and slipped it into his waistband in the small of his back.

Arriving at the coordinates, the crew spotted the yellow floats within one hundred feet of where they were supposed to be. Mark made his run on the port side of the floats so the winch could grab them and bring them onboard. He was very glad he had the experienced help on board because it looked very much like one third art, one third skill, and one third sheer luck.

He was receiving some puzzled looks from the deck crew about the proximity of the floats to one another but he just shrugged his shoulders. The first line was hooked and the winch strained under the load. As he watched, he saw the deck crew recoil in horror from the side of the boat as the trap cleared the water. Terrance lost his lunch all over the deck. What was wrong? Moments later, in the glaring starboard spotlight, he saw a man's body hanging by the waist from the trap.

What the hell was this? This wasn't part of the plan? The crew struggled with the winch to get the man's body onboard but despite their efforts the ship caught a wave and the man's body slammed into the side of the boat. He couldn't hear them but he could see their body language. The men had been so preoccupied with the man's body that they hadn't yet noticed the trap contained a large black case instead of crabs. Then the flailing and finger pointing started. They'd seen the case.

The men appeared both scared and pissed at the same time. Mark reached back and felt the heft of the large Sig in his waistband. Maybe he would need it after all. Skip grabbed the waterproof case out of the trap and with Roy's help ran it up to the wheelhouse. Out of breath, they were difficult to understand but Mark did notice a recurring theme of, "What the Hell?" Mark needed to think quickly as the dead body business had him scratching his head as well.

The crew proceeded to pick up the other four floats, small traps, and similarly attached bodies.

"I don't know what my friend was into but we better get these cases to the folks at Adak as soon as possible." It was off the cuff...but it worked. Actually, the more Mark thought about it, it had worked out perfectly.

Mark called the harbor master at Adak who said he should put the bodies on ice, if possible, and make his best time to Kulak Bay at Adak. Mark acted very concerned but relented and said they would be at Adak tomorrow afternoon. Probably around two, he'd said.

The harbor master signed off with, "I'll be waiting at the dock. Adak out." Mark smiled quickly to himself as he thought of the view the harbor master would get tomorrow from the dock as the *Dreamer* entered the harbor.

Needless to say, the discussion at dinner was all about what everyone thought had happened: the size of the traps, what idiot would tie themselves to a crab trap, and, of course, what in the world was in those waterproof cases? The suggestions ran the gamut from drugs to cash. Then everyone seated at the table had gradually gotten quiet. Mark looked at his hapless, unconscious crew and smiled a knowing smile.

Anchorage
Terry's House

This morning, after Terry left his house at 7:15 a.m., Shama slipped into Terry's house with the key Shama had made from an impression of Terry's house key. Shama felt ashamed for Terry that his son Dwayne was such a disappointment. Shama killed the sleeping man quickly.

The quick kill wasn't as much fun for him as he was used to. Normally, Shama enjoyed making his victims suffer and beg for their lives. It was all such great theatre. Shama wiped his still bloody knife on Dwayne's sleeping wife. When she had awoken to the sounds of the very brief struggle, he had quickly beaten her into submission. Shama had been tempted to rape her, but had not wanted to soil himself on what he determined to be an "infidel whore."

Shama had tied the terrified mother and daughter into chairs and placed them together in the front living room by the fireplace.

Using his laptop and a camera he'd purchased from the Anchorage Radio Shack, he established a live web link that could be accessed from his tablet or phone. It took a few minutes to find Dwayne's truck keys. Dwayne had been too lazy to hang them up. The man's wallet and keys were still in his pants pockets, lying on the floor of the bedroom. Shama mused to himself that unemployment must be so exhausting.

As Shama passed the bloody bed, he paused briefly to admire his handy work. He liked using his knife...that wasn't exactly true, he *loved* using his knife. He'd had lots of practice. He found the experience most exhilarating. He felt an indescribable rush each and every time he used it. Maybe he would get to use it one more time before he died.

Shama was running a little behind schedule now and would need to step on it to get ahead of Terry for the plan to work. As he pulled past the Shoreside Petroleum fuel depot he could see Terry's truck in line to pick up his load of fuel. Terry's truck was easy to spot. When Terry had upgraded to the deluxe sleeper cab a few years back, he changed the factory paint scheme to a crystal blue sky with a picture of bright sun shining down. It was obnoxious. It was probably to pay homage to his granddaughter. If anything, Shama was glad that after today he wouldn't have to hear about the little miss perfect granddaughter again. For the second time today, Shama actually smiled.

Shemya Island
Kevin's Room

Kevin was up and dressed by 6:00 a.m., had eaten morning chow and was back in his room by 7:00 a.m. He glanced at his watch and figured he'd call his mom and see how his sister had done with her "kidnappers." All phone circuits were tied up. It wasn't that unusual for the lines to be busy first thing in the morning. Anybody who needed to get anything done back in the States, either on a personal or professional note, had to take into account the time change. Kevin tried several more times before heading out the door for work.

Wednesdays were usually catch up days and today was no exception. Kevin went past the motor pool to inquire about some overdue parts for his truck.

Tom, the parts guy, chuckled at his inquiry. "Cheer up Kevin, in two more weeks you won't even need a heater for that truck anymore." He was right about that. It was really starting to warm up. Most days they were getting temperatures up into the mid-fifties. Kevin smiled, "And the rearview mirror?"

Tom put on his best fake serious look and said, "Always look ahead Kevin, always ahead." Tom then smiled, waved and got back to inventorying all the parts that had come in for those folks lucky enough to have received them.

It was almost noon when Kevin swung past his room to drop off his coat and grab a bite to eat. He opened his email and found he had several emails from his friends and some reminder emails about coming social events on the base. The one that caught his eye had the subject line: Your sister.

Kevin didn't recognize the sender but did notice it had a video attachment. He opened the message. The text in the body of the message was very brief: It's noon where you are and Cobra Dane is not on fire. See attachment. Kevin double clicked on the attachment. To his horror it was a twenty-three second clip of his sister tied to a chair in pure terror. She looked horrible. She didn't appear to have a mark on her but that didn't mean they weren't there but out of sight or that they wouldn't do something to harm her in the future.

Kevin felt sick to his stomach. It had been real and he hadn't done anything in almost three days. His phone rang. "Kevin!" his mother was screaming at him, "Do something!" Most everything else she said was unintelligible. Kevin tried in vain to get a word in but his mother was inconsolable. He hung up the phone.

Kevin wasn't scared of something physical or tangible, that he felt he could deal with. It was the head game that had him nervous. Kevin was scared he was going to make the wrong decision. He slowly walked to his desk and wrote a note on some stationary. After several moments of writing he folded the paper in half, placed it in an envelope and placed it on his pillow. Better safe than sorry.

CHAPTER 25

Wednesday Morning
THE DREAMER

The men were tied up together in one cabin below deck. Mark couldn't kill them yet. It was too bad really. It was actually tough work keeping them alive. He had rather unimaginatively drugged them at dinner the night before. He had prepared and served them Goulash from his Grandmother's old country recipe. Of course he had added his own "special" secret ingredient.

In his lifetime, Mark had poisoned and drugged many people. Until now, all the people he had drugged, he had killed while they were still under the effects of the particular drug. He needed to be careful this time on the dosing and ensure it wasn't lethal. Mark still might need one or two of them alive for leverage.

Mark had purchased this drug from a contact in Seattle. It was very fast acting and left no trace in the body after twenty-four hours. He derived a somewhat perverse academic pleasure in watching the drugs take effect. The two alcoholics just nodded off like it was another cheap Friday night drunk. The boy had a much different reaction. Mark thought that perhaps he had been correct about the young man's drug use. The boy seemed to have had an allergic reaction of sorts. He wheezed, gagged, and eventually vomited his dinner on the galley floor. He was comfortably unconscious now, lying on the floor with the others. The surprise in the group was Jonah. He had had a different look in his eyes as the drug took effect. It wasn't fear. More like... resolve or perhaps determination?

It really didn't matter anymore. He would wake up tethered with zip ties just like the others.

Mark needed to get his head in the game and start focusing on his target. Mark's target was SBX1, the navy's first Sea-Based X band radar platform. SBX-1 is part of the Ground-Based Midcourse Defense (GMD) system deployed by the Missile Defense Agency (MDA). Because the radar was sea-based allowed it to be moved to areas where it was needed for enhanced missile detection and defense. Recently it had been positioned farther to the west watching several attempts by the North Koreans to launch something, anything, successfully.

Fixed radars provide coverage for a very limited area due to the curvature of the Earth. The chief benefit of the SBX was that it could pull up stakes and move past that curve and spy on whatever it wanted. The primary task SBX was carrying out was the discrimination (identification) of real warheads from decoys, followed by precision tracking of the identified warheads.

Mark had studied the pictures available online and seen that the vessel had many small radomes for various communications tasks and a central, large dome that enclosed and protected the 1,800 ton X band radar antenna. By looking at the pictures of the system online, Mark was able to easily identify the SBX system's Achilles Heel as its exposed and unprotected twin steel hulls.

Power is supplied to the SBX platform by six 3.6-megawatt diesel generators. The generators are housed in two separate hull compartments, three generators to a side, one group in the port hull, and one starboard. They were designed with the intent that half of the generators could be lost and the platform would remain functional. The engineer's concept of "lost" was "broken." Marks plan would hopefully breach both hulls with seawater and cause the electrical systems to go off line, permanently.

Mark learned everything else he needed to know from the various prime and subcontractor's websites. Along each step of the SBX project, the various vendors and contractors involved had discussed and described in great detail the system's various construction techniques. The internet had been a virtual treasure trove of information for someone like himself, someone searching for the system's vulnerabilities.

Below deck now, Mark carefully unwrapped the waterproof packages containing the large black pelican type briefcases they had plucked from the crab traps. Each briefcase contained 35 pounds of the plastic explosive Symtex and remote detonator assemblies. He worked on getting the explosive charges all synced with both the Bluetooth in his cell phone and the wireless connection to the *Dreamer's* specialized navigation system.

He positioned the explosives in the forward hold at shoulder height, against the forward most part of the bow. He then placed everything he could: excess equipment, floor boards, and even the bodies of the Iranian sailors, against the explosive charges to direct the explosion upward and outward toward his target, the SBX's hull.

Before leaving port, Mark had filled the *Dreamer's* tanks with enough fuel to stay at sea for three weeks. He wouldn't use a fraction of it. Each massive fuel tank had an explosive charge wired to its side and each of the explosive charge's detonation control lights was bright green.

Back in the wheelhouse, Mark chuckled to himself how the final charge, under the captain's chair, was the "paradise" charge. This charge was a bit different than the others. It was smaller and its intentions quite a bit different. This charge was designed to remove him from the equation, forever. It had been specifically designed to remove all evidence that he had ever even taken this trip. The light on this charge was also bright green.

All of the explosives throughout the boat were showing they were successfully synched to the *Dreamer's* navigation system and with his phone. Mark found it amusing that all of the various connections to the explosives and their operational status were now visible on his computer screen in the wheelhouse. It was as if they were now integral parts of the boat's systems. Mark smiled. He supposed they were.

With the rest of the crew still unconscious, and all of the connections green, Mark returned below deck and took his time welding the hatch to the forward hold closed. When he was finished, he threw the cutting torch assembly overboard. The weather report was calling for calm seas around Adak Island tomorrow afternoon. He would need them. Allahu Akbar.

BOATSS

Jewels was reviewing the sensor deployment updates for the past week. Remarkably, for a government project, they were not falling behind schedule. This had a great deal to do with the designed pace of the schedule being managed by the abilities of the installers not the needs of the program. Even still, they had successfully placed the new hydro acoustic sensors from Japan almost all the way up to the eastern Aleutian Islands. The Arabian Sea, Bay of Bengal, and the South China Sea locations had all been just recently completed. The South China Sea proved the most time consuming. This was due in part to politics, where the sensors were being placed, and the somewhat more clandestine nature of their installation.

The Dreamer
Below Decks

Mark was correct. Jonah had woken up, but not just like the others. Jonah was not disoriented or surprised. He was angry. No, retired Navy Seal Lt Col Jonah West was really pissed off. He had let his guard down twice in the past twenty-three years. The first time he'd had his heart broken by a woman he had trusted for seventeen years. The scars were still fresh. But when asked, he would always say he was healing. Now he found himself on the floor of a fishing vessel, out at sea, zip tied to two drunks and a kid, who'd obviously, at some point during the night, shit his britches. This was not starting out to be a very good day.

The last thing Jonah remembered was eating dinner. He thought back to last night. Dinner had actually been delicious. What had he missed? Everyone sat down for dinner. No, the captain hadn't sat down. He tried to focus. The captain was standing on the other side of the galley making coffee while they ate. Had he been smiling at them? Watching them eat perhaps? He was sure now. The bastard had drugged them. But with what? He wondered? It didn't matter really. Jonah just wanted to know who he was dealing with.

Jonah summed up the situation and knew a couple things right off. First, he needed a plan and real soon. Second, Jonah knew that even after only knowing these guys on the floor next to him for a short time, he'd assessed they would be of little to no value to whatever plan he managed to come up with.

Then, strangely enough, amidst all that was going on around him, Jonah did something only a Navy Seal would do under these circumstances, Jonah West smiled. He thought of what his young teenage nephew back home in Maine was so fond of saying when things seemed out of hand; "Well ain't that just absolutely freakin great!" Then Jonah smiled again. This time it was a different kind of smile. This time his smile more closely resembled that of a very large, very hungry; shark.

Shemya Island

Kevin called his boss and said he needed to go over to the administrative building to check on some new requirements that had come in. He hated lying, but really couldn't think of a way to expedite this process by involving more and more people. He headed up to the base commander's office; but his secretary said he was at a base function and wouldn't be back until three.

"Can you be sure that you tell him I was here to see him, and that it's really important?" The commander's secretary wasn't hired just for her looks, and knew something was up.

"Mr. Gyoh, the vice commander should be back in about forty-five minutes. Would you care to wait for him?"

"No Ma'am, thank you." And he was gone.

Kevin went back down to his truck to think. The way Kevin saw it, he had two choices. The first plan was to get the Security Police or the Office of Special Investigations (OSI) involved. The problem with both of those organizations was that neither organization would have the chops to evacuate Cobra Dane. They would, however, probably detain him for questioning and not let him out until it was way too late to do anything. It was 12:40 and Kevin sensed he was running out of time.

Plan two had better work; his life and the lives of many others would probably depend on it.

Richardson Highway

Shama's plan had been in motion for several months and he was well prepared for today's events. About thirty miles from Fort Greely, literally right alongside the Richardson Highway, was the Black Rapids Airport. The airport, if you wanted to call it that, was no more than a wide spot in the road that in the summer doubled as a little airstrip. No one manned it, and it didn't have any instrumentation or lights. Before flying into Black Rapids Airport, most pilots would go on the internet and get a series of time lapse photographs of the day's recent weather from a camera mounted several miles away across the valley but pointed in the general direction of the airport. It wasn't ideal but seemed to work well for the local bush pilots. The runway wasn't even paved and the website described its surface as "unimproved soil with ruts and small brush up to six feet."

Shama had stashed what, at this point, was about two hundred pounds of dynamite behind one of the out buildings in a large waterproof, and, more importantly in Alaska, bear-proof box. It had taken three months and several trips to the borders of both Western Canada and Washington State to accumulate the amount he felt he needed. Ordinarily this would have been a significant task. Fortunately for Shama, he wasn't working alone and his support team had started early. Even in a post 9/11 atmosphere, his team had almost no difficulties accumulating the needed materials. His team brought the materials to the hotel and they had assembled the devices in his suite.

Shama carefully placed the dynamite into four equal packages with their associated electronics. He wirelessly synced them to his Garmin navigation device and placed them all in waterproof Pelican briefcases. Each briefcase weighed just over fifty pounds and would fit easily through the maintenance ports on the top of Terry's fuel tanker. Years of testing and his experience with IEDs in Iraq and Afghanistan had proven that an explosion that started in the interior of the fuel compartments would be significantly more powerful than one attached to the side of the tank.

The plan with the truck hadn't been the original plan. Originally the planners of this operation had wanted him to pilot and subsequently crash one of the local bush planes loaded with explosives onto the base. Shama hadn't personally cared which plan they'd picked. Although the effect on his life would be the same, he had convinced the planning committee that a fuel truck would be much more likely to cause the affect they were looking for.

Just over two weeks ago, Shama had stolen a car from the hotel's parking garage and used it to drive the devices up to his hiding spot at the Black Rapids Airport. This morning he had left it behind the garage at Terry's house. Shama was really enjoying today's ride to the airport in Dwayne's pickup truck. He was gaining a better understanding why these Americans had such a love affair with their trucks. This one was very comfortable indeed. It had heated seats, tinted windows, and a Kenwood sound system. After about thirty minutes, Shama was finally getting used to the smells of Dwayne's truck. Old food wrappers were everywhere he looked and the smell of old stale cigarettes sitting in the ash tray had been almost nauseating.

Shama had planned ahead and knew to bring his own music for the trip. He popped out the CD Dwayne had in the player and replaced it with his own. Shama had a good five hours drive ahead and he couldn't afford to be late. He scanned the music list, picked his favorite song, turned the volume up until it almost hurt and stepped on the gas. He would be in paradise by sunset. "Allah Akbar!"

The Dreamer

Jonah could tell the others were beginning to wake up. The smell from Roy's "accident" was overpowering in the confined space of the galley. One by one, the men had begun to wake up. As they realized their predicament, they tried to come to grips with their current situation. They were all zip-tied, hands behind their backs in the same chairs they sat down in for dinner the night before.

Jonah had a plan but would need everyone's cooperation to make it work. Skip was the first to speak with a profound, "What the hell?" These initial comments were promptly followed by increasingly harsh metaphors regarding abnormal acts of a savage nature.

Jonah was in a tight spot. In order to save the rest of the men, they would have to trust him, a man they had only known for three days, with their lives.

"Gentlemen," Jonah began, "As you know, my name is Jonah West. I'm a recently retired Navy Seal." He had decided to go with humor on the off chance that some of them might have attended an AA meeting once or twice.

Since both Skip and Terrance had laughed, and sarcastically said, "Hi Jonah," he knew he was probably on the right track. Jonah continued his attempt to keep it light hearted despite their current grave situation.

"We are all really screwed unless we work together as a team, make no mistakes and do exactly what I say." Jonah listened for a response; there was silence at first and then a long exhale from one of the men.

"Oh good," sighed Skip, "I thought for a minute we were in real trouble."

His strategy of keeping at least some of the guy's calm was working. Jonah realized he hadn't heard anything from Roy. "Roy, are you okay?" He still had no response from the young man. Jonah realized that the young man was probably absolutely mortified regarding his current situation and tried a somewhat softer tone, "Hey Roy, I need an answer buddy."

Finally, he heard Roy's weak voice say, "If we live through this, will you guys keep quiet about me shitting my pants?" That did it, they all busted up laughing and then quickly, like four little boys playing hide and seek, started shushing each other so "Mark," or whatever his real name was, wouldn't hear them.

Jonah explained to them that in his experience they were still alive for a reason. He explained he had heard Mark speaking an Arab language earlier on either a radio or cell phone. Jonah knew it wasn't Arabic per say, but for these guys, the nuances of Middle Eastern languages would certainly be lost. He decided to cut to the chase and lay out what he thought the plan was. In his opinion, the boat was going to be used for some type of terrorist attack on something. The good news was that if they could get off the boat just prior to whatever Mark had planned they might be rescued with the rest of the incident's survivors.

"And what's the bad news?" asked Terrance.

"The bad news," replied Jonah, "is that we don't know where or when or how he's going to do it."

Jonah began with a whisper and laid out his plan of action. When he was done, Skip said, "So let me get this straight, both your "successful plan" and your "failed plan," end with us in the water?"

He made a good point and Jonah thought of several things to say and arguments to support his plan but ended up saying only one word, "Yup."

Skip laughed at that and said, "Well then, what could possibly go wrong?"

"All right," Jonah started, "Let's put this thing in motion.

Remember guys, the longer Mark thinks we're still secured down here the better. Skip, you're facing the door, keep an eye out while I cut us loose."

And with that, retired Seal Jonah West, in what appeared to be almost one fluid motion, reached down and back behind his chair, produced a six-inch blade out of his boot and was cutting his zip-tie free. The guys were in awe and started to think they might actually pull this off. Jonah had just moved to untie Skip when he thought he heard a plane.

Flying over the *Dreamer* at 1500 feet was PenAir flight 5310. Flight 5310 was supposed to be flying back to Anchorage this morning, but had been stolen and was currently flying almost due west at just over 320 knots. The only person on board was heading west to fulfill his part of the mission. He needed to be at his destination no earlier than 2:00 p.m. and no later than 2:30 p.m. and he was running behind.

CHAPTER 26

Black Rapids Airport

Terry was near the end of the run and had made his usual stops. He often had to weigh pulling over and taking a wiz in a pee-can he kept for such emergencies or getting out and stretching his back.

It was just past 1:45 p.m. as he approached the Black Rapids Airport. He was startled by what appeared to be his son's Dodge truck parked just off the road. As he gently applied the brakes and pulled off the road he was certain that it was Dwayne's truck. Way out here? Terry had driven past Dwayne's truck in his front yard on his way out this morning. Terry got out and approached the truck. The plates matched and it had the same crap in the back seat that he'd been nagging Dwayne about since last fall. It was definitely Dwayne's truck. The foot prints in the new snow, however, definitely weren't Dwayne's. Something wasn't right.

Terry looked up and saw that the door to the office was open even though the office was closed for the season. Terry touched the hood of the truck as he passed by on his way to the office. The hood was still quite warm; it hadn't been here long. Terry had just stepped through the open door into the half light of the office when he saw what he thought was one of those new phone computer tablet things. Technology wasn't his thing but even Terry quickly grasped what he was seeing.

The screen clearly showed that his daughter-in-law and granddaughter were tied to chairs in Terry's living room. At their feet was a device of some sort and it had a blinking green light. What the hell was going on here? As he approached the tablet he heard the unmistakable double click as the hammer of a large revolver was being pulled back. By the sound of the cocking mechanism, it was a very large caliber revolver. Whoever was behind him now had his complete and undivided attention.

"Put your hands behind your back and they might live to see the sunset today," said a familiar voice. Terry felt as if he was in a nightmare. Only the cold air pouring in through the open door convinced him it was not a dream. Terry slowly complied.

Terry heard the sound of a zip tie and then the sharp tug as it pulled snug against his wrists. Whoever this was now turned him around. Terry sucked in his next breath so hard he began to cough. Standing in front of him was "Sam" the guy from the truck stop. What was going on? "Sam, what's this all about? Where's my son. What have you done?"

Terry's questions were met with a sharp wrap of the revolver's barrel against the side of his head.

As he secured Terry to a support post in the office he whispered coarsely in Terry's ear, "By the way, Terry, as you've no doubt guessed by now, my name's not 'Sam,' it's Shama." Shama laughed.

Terry wasn't amused in the least but thought it best to comply with his captor for the time being.

Shama made two trips back to his cache of explosives behind the outbuilding at the rear of the structure. He placed the briefcases and some other equipment into the sleeper cab section of the truck and returned to the office.

"Why are you doing this?" inquired Terry once again.

"We've been here long enough," was all he could get out of his former truck stop friend "Sam."

Shama cut the zip ties binding Terry to the post but kept his wrists secured together. He pointed the large gun at Terry's midsection and ordered

Terry into the semi-truck's cab. Shama ordered him to place his wrists up by the shoulder belt mechanism. Terry complied and, within seconds, had his wrists zip tied to the mount of the seat belt. Terry knew from what he'd seen so far, that this wasn't this guy's first rodeo, he was very experienced.

About a mile down the road, Shama turned right, he drove about fifty yards down the road and stopped. Shama took the keys and made sure that Terry remained secure. "Sit tight old man." Shama figured he still needed about five minutes to arm his bomb and place the pelican briefcases into the three tanks.

Shama climbed up the access ladder on top of the tanker and dropped his large canvas bag of equipment. Amongst the tools was a pair of metal shears and three ten-pound dumbbells. Each dumbbell had a three-foot length of wire securing them at one end to the dumbbell and the other end was secured to a red carabineer.

He was working swiftly now because, although he was off the main road, he didn't want any surprises coming down this side road. Shama quickly snipped the old tamper tags on all three compartments. He then attached a red carabineer to each pelican case. After ensuring he wasn't being watched, he slowly lowered the heavy cases into each tank. The cases themselves were buoyant and needed the weight of the dumbbells to hold them at a fixed position at the center point of each compartment. Another lesson he had learned in both the countries of Iraq and Afghanistan. The closer the explosion was to the center of the fuel; the more explosive force was generated in all directions.

Shama said a silent prayer and lowered the lids of the fuel compartments. Out of his bag he removed three new seals for the lids. Starting at the back of the tank, he moved forward applying new tamper tags to the lids. At a quick glance it would appear that the original tamper wires had never been disturbed.

Terry could hear him up on the truck doing something. All he heard during the whole process was the sound of what might have been heavy objects being dropped on or maybe in the tank. He strained to see with the side mirrors but could only see the ground. Shama had adjusted all the mirrors downward as he exited the cab.

No more than five minutes had passed when suddenly Shama was back in the cab with what appeared to be a switchbox of some sort. The switchbox had a cord like his daughter's iPod, what had she called it? A UBS or USB? Whatever it was called, this man plugged it into his truck's Garmin navigation system. Shama set the GPS destination for 63°57'7.27"N 145°43'39.89"W and smiled a wicked smile.

Shama turned slowly to Terry and said, "Listen to me very carefully old man, I have done you one favor today already by killing your miserable excuse for a son." Terry felt the blood drain from his face. "I need to get onto the base, and I presume you don't want your precious granddaughter to be blown into the Alaskan wilderness for the animals to feed on. Am I correct?" Terry nodded.

"Alright, here's what we are going to do." As Shama cut the zip ties binding Terry to the seatbelt, he outlined the plan. Terry would get them onto the base using all his supposed friends. The man actually sneered when he said friends. After they had made it past the initial front gate checkpoint, Shama would switch positions with Terry and Shama would drive the truck to its destination.

Terry felt the plan had "failure" written all over it, but moved to the driver's seat as instructed. He stared out the front windshield of the truck, his grip on the steering wheel turning his knuckles white. Terry thought about his son Dwayne and said nothing.

Terry must have appeared to not be paying attention because Shama gave him another sharp rap to the side of his head, "Do you understand the plan? Do you want to see your granddaughter live?"

Terry turned to Shama, "Yes, I understand your plan."

Twenty-eight miles up the road, they passed the Delta Industrial Services Company on their left. Someone had waved an Alaska greeting. Terry did not wave back. A short distance later they approached the turn off for Fort Greely. Shama asked him again if he understood the plan and showed him his cell phone. On the screen were his daughter-in-law and precious granddaughter. They looked absolutely terrified.

Shama spoke in a flat almost surreal tone, "All I need to do is push the pound key and they both will be food for the animals. Are we clear?"

Terry nodded yes and turned a slow right turn into the Fort's entrance as Shama climbed into the back of the sleeper cab and sprayed some type of aerosol. It smelled absolutely horrible.

Private Steve Donnelly and his partner Private John Makleroy saw Terry's truck approaching and smiled. They both agreed that Terry reminded them of their grandfathers back home. They waved as Terry slowed the truck to a stop. Terry had to somehow communicate with the guards about the bomb; but how?

"Hi, Mr. Grabowski." Terry only nodded a greeting. John waved and walked around the back of the truck. "Bill of Lading, sir?" Terry silently handed him the manifest and then casually asked about his son.

"My daughter's doing fine, sir" replied Donnelly.

Terry mumbled, "Mine too."

Donnelly laughed and said to his buddy, "Only odd plates for inspection today, right?"

"Alright, sir," said Private Makleroy, "Pull on up ahead."

"Have a great day, Mr. Grabowski."

Terry drove away without a word. Private Donnelly turned to and asked his partner, "What's eating Mr. Grabowski today? And what the hell was that smell coming out of his cab?"

Four hundred feet up the road they made the switch as planned. Shama reapplied zip ties to Terry's wrists and shoved him into the back of his sleeper cab. Shama un-muted the Garmin and drove away with one hand on the wheel and one hand holding his phone, finger poised above the pound sign.

Shama listened to the Garmin and smiled. He obediently followed her somewhat stilted voice directions and took the first right at the traffic circle and shifted up.

"Turn right in one hundred fifty feet at Patricia Pike." Terry couldn't see out of the cab but already knew they were not going anywhere on the base that he had ever been.

Private Donnelly had watched Terry pull away and stop several hundred feet away for a minute or two before moving again. What was that all about? Mr. Grabowski knew the way to the fuel depot by heart. And what was with the "Mine too" comment about the daughter? Mr. Grabowski had a son.

Private Donnelly's partner John then yelled over to him "Hey, dude, I remember where I've smelled that smell before. The only thing that smells that bad is the stuff the drug dealers spray on their loads to screw up the K-9s."

And in that one brief second on that cold afternoon, just after 2:30 p.m., Private First Class Steven J. Donnelly knew he had screwed up, badly. He hit the alarm button in the guard shack as hard as he could and for what seemed like an eternity, but was in reality only seconds later, the base alarm klaxon began to sound.

The klaxon system was base wide and primarily used to notify Fort Greely's population of an accident. It had never been used for a real emergency and many people walked outside to see what was going on. The klaxons stanchions were along each of the key driving routes of the base. As Shama made his left onto East Post road, the klaxon at that intersection went off. The sound was so loud and so unexpected; Shama had dropped the cell phone. Terry didn't hear the phone fall but as Shama accelerated and turned onto Big Delta road the truck had swerved just enough for Terry to see that he no longer held it.

Terry wasn't sure what the end plan was but he was sure it probably ended with him dead. It was time to go. Shama continued to accelerate the truck. As Terry sat in the back of the sleeper, staring at the wall of the sleeper cab he realized that today he should probably use one of those fancy options in his truck.

Shama could see his target. The truck was approaching fifty miles an hour and accelerating. He had been told that the first building on his left after the turn was the control building for the Antiballistic Missile battery, field one. Shama felt a thump, and then a cold blast of air; he glanced over his shoulder to see the sleeper cab door open. It no longer mattered.

Suddenly and quite unexpectedly loud, he heard a woman's voice say very calmly: "Arriving, Fort Greely, missile field one, on right." It was the last thing he heard before his world turned to fire.

CHAPTER 27

The Dreamer

LAST RUN

While the rest of the men kept a look out, Skip had slipped down the hall to the lockers and retrieved each man's anti-exposure suit. Jonah was relieved they had done the survival suit drill before this. He had lots of experience with these suits, but it had been a while. It was one of those tasks where muscle memory was key to donning the suit quickly and correctly.

Once on, everyone except Roy agreed that the best part of the suits so far was that they couldn't smell Roy's shit anymore. Roy had gone down the hall and gotten rid of his briefs but that had only helped a little.

Whatever Mark was doing was certainly preoccupying his time. Timing was going to be everything for Jonah's plan to work. With everyone suited up, Jonah used a mirror to take a peek out from the galley and see where Mark was. Jonah tried to see where they were but could only see through a small dirty section of a portside window. He saw land.

As Jonah brought the mirror around the door frame, he could see Mark sitting in the bridge, staring forward. Jonah was just about to pull the mirror back when something caught his eye. On the bottom of the captain's chair was a little green blinking light.

Jonah had seen that type of light many times before. It was a bomb. The bad news, at this point, was of course that it was a bomb. The good news, and at this point it was a stretch, was that he'd been right. They needed to get off this boat as soon as possible. Without trying to scare the men too much, he implied that he had seen something alarming on the bridge. He was just starting to explain when the radio in the bridge came to life and the man on the other end was sounding very angry. Then Jonah heard the best thing he'd heard in quite a while..."Captain of the vessel *Dreamer*, this is the United States Navy."

Mark had made the initial call to the harbor master relaying his position as just east of Great Siskin Island. On the horizon, like a building out of place, was the SBX platform. The SBX was just north of Cape Adagdak turning to starboard and making its approach to the harbor. Mark knew it had to come almost to the middle of the sound or it would run aground.

Suddenly the *Dreamer* was being hailed by the SBX.

"Captain of the *Dreamer*, this is the US Navy, you are entering a restricted area, bring your vessel to a new heading of 175°." Although taken aback by the radio call, it played perfectly into Shama's plan.

"Turn your vessel to port, immediately!" came the new instructions from the SBX. It was time for Mark to stall.

"The harbor master is expecting me," he said in the best broken English possible. The security team on the SBX hesitated. Then they repeated their demand that he turn to port. Mark's answer was to select "RADAR" on the autopilot. On the next touch screen he selected the looming mass of the SBX. Mark selected the icon "MAX" as his closing rate. He locked the autopilot, and continued trying to stall. Below his feet he could feel the powerful engines spinning their way up to maximum power. The bow of the *Dreamer* began to slowly rise as she picked up speed.

At 1500 feet it was time for a little more showmanship. Mark got on the radio and started his final performance. His rudder was out, he said, his English was not so good, his crew were "stupid morons." Whatever he could think of to do to stall, Mark was trying. The autopilot was recalculating his approach rate and increasing his speed to intercept the giant radar platform before it entered Kulak Bay. Mark figured he needed fifteen more seconds.

The *Dreamer* was closing on the SBX quickly now and it appeared to Mark for a moment that the SBX might actually be slowing. He couldn't actually see it slowing down but his computer indicated that the closure rate of the two vessels was slowing. It wouldn't matter. The SBX platform took almost a mile to stop. Mark could sense a change of tone in the man's voice. He was no longer demanding the *Dreamer* turn to port. He was ordering him to stop. At this point the boat was going where the computer wanted the boat to go. The autopilot had taken complete control. The engines of the *Dreamer* were running into the red zone and he had one over temp light already flashing.

Mark was no longer making any navigational decisions. All he could hope to do in the wheelhouse now was to make a grand show for all the people now watching him through the binoculars from the watch tower of the SBX.

Jonah felt the boat speed up and took a quick peek over the gunwale. He saw how close the harbor was and could also see the massive looming shape of the SBX. He estimated they were less than a thousand feet from the platform and closing rapidly. If what he thought was about to happen, was going to happen, it would be very soon. It was time to leave. He reminded the others of the bodies they had pulled up with the crab traps. The others were nervous but ready. He reminded them to run straight off the back of the boat, take a deep breath and not to let it out until they were back on the surface. One last thumbs up and, with Jonah bringing up the rear, they all made a break for the back of the boat.

From the forward security watch tower of the SBX, Ensign Moody had seen enough and was going to give the order to open fire when he saw four men in survival suits run off the back of the crab boat and land in the water. Ensign Moody switched the radio to internal communications, squeezed the button on the hand mike, and screamed, "STOP THAT BOAT NOW!"

Mark had seen the crewmen running out of the corner of his eye and for a moment, panicked. The *Dreamer* was traveling at just over 11 knots when he thought he heard a "pop" and saw a hole appear in the window of the wheelhouse. He didn't have much time to reflect on it when a second hole appeared that matched the one in his chest.

The *Dreamer* was being riddled with automatic weapons fire now, but it was far too late to change the outcome of what was to come. At just past 2:40 p.m., the fishing boat *Dreamer* impacted the inside front starboard leg of the SBX platform. Simultaneously, over two hundred pounds of Symtex high explosive blew a fifty-foot hole in the starboard steel hull of the SBX as well as ripping open a seam on the port hull. The secondary charges detonated less than three microseconds later and turned what remained above the surface of the water into lethal shrapnel and a secondary pressure wave. The SBX immediately began to list to port, take on water and sink. The thrusters which propel the vessel were electric and immediately went offline when the seawater penetrated the SBX's twin hulls.

All personnel on the forward part of the platform that were not immediately killed by the tremendous overpressure of the explosions and shrapnel wounds, died when they had fallen to their deaths from the high platform.

CHAPTER 28

Shooting Star

Captain Lee had not attempted to get back on the boat for several days but had been carefully observing what he could from a safe distance. From the first morning here he had been surprised to see the *Shooting Star's* sister ship, the South Korean flagged vessel *Oceans Queen* in the next drydock over. He thought it must be more than mere coincidence. Over the past few days, he had proven his original thought correct. On more than a few occasions, he watched small delivery vehicles shuttling parts and yard workers from his ship, the *Shooting Star*, over to the *Oceans Queen*. Several hours later, the delivery vehicles would reverse the process, and return personnel and tarp covered items back to his ship.

Lee received word that the progress on his ship was proceeding ahead of schedule and that the refit supervisors anticipated him leaving as early as tomorrow night, after dark. Lee wasn't a stupid man. The shipyard personnel's original storyline tried to convince him that scheduling and availability at the shipyard were what required his ship to come in after dark when it arrived several days ago. That story was plausible to a point. Often projects run late and extensive work is normally required to get a drydock ready for a ship to come in. Now they were telling him that he would also be leaving under the cloak of darkness; that was far beyond plausible. It was quite obviously a lie.

Fort Greely
Alaska

Terry had left the truck as gracefully as he could for a man in his sixties. Out of pure luck he managed to miss several steel fence posts and was rather ungraciously caught by a section of a contractor's plastic debris fence. He was still on the ground when the blast and heat from the explosion tore over his position removing both the debris fence and the posts.

He wasn't feeling well enough to get up right away so he just lay there for help. Later, watching the base surveillance video, he was certain his guardian angel must have been watching over him. Both the debris fence that had broken his fall and the berm behind it were supposed to have been removed and the area graded flat last Monday morning. A last minute delay had changed the removal date to tomorrow, probably saving his life.

The Yunes
Sonar Station

Sitting safely deep in the Aleutian trench and drifting silently westward, the captain of the *Yunes* and his "advisor" had anticipated the explosion at around 2:15 p.m. local but it was actually a bit late. The simultaneous explosion of the almost three hundred pounds of Symtex explosive was quickly followed by the unmistakable screeching of metal and the distinct splash of debris as it came raining back down to the sea. The only two men on the *Yunes,* on the sonar station's headsets at the time to hear the explosion, were Mr. Feng and the captain. Of those two men, only Mr. Feng knew what they had put into motion.

In his official capacity in the Chinese Navy, *Admiral* Feng, had been the architect, mastermind, and commander of the submarine that successfully conducted the ballistic missile test off the California coast on November 10, 2010, wasn't sure at this point how the rest of this plan was going to work, but at this point, they had performed their part of the mission flawlessly. He thought back to his meeting in Taiwan and hoped the other parts of the plan were going as smoothly as his. As Feng continued to monitor the sonar station, the captain gestured that he would stay on this heading for ten more minutes. Feng smiled, nodded, and thought to himself, one more to go...

Fort Greely
Alaska

It took every bit of the twenty seconds of time from the klaxons going off to having almost everyone tucked into the control facility. It had been for naught. The explosion erased the building, all of its personnel and contents. All that remained was the concrete pad and a smoldering heap of burning rubble. Despite the magnitude of the explosion, the missile field and the missiles beneath it were undamaged.

The smoke hadn't even cleared Fort Greely when a flash message had gone to the Pentagon notifying them that missile field one had been the target of a terrorist attack. Because of the four-hour time difference, the night shift at the Pentagon was just finishing up their shift change briefings. It took the personnel at the Pentagon ten minutes to come up with a plan of action and send out a warning to all military facilities worldwide.

Six minutes after the Pentagon's notification of the Fort Greely attack came word that the SBX platform had been hit as well. Causality reports began to flow in as well as the news reports from Adak Island and the communities around Fort Greely.

Reports from the Navy Commander on the SBX indicated that the SBX platform had sunk and was resting partially submerged on the bottom of Kuluk Bay. Due to its immense size and design it literally sank straight down to a depth of fifty-four feet and stopped. The radar's super structure was still above the water as were many of the crew areas. The causality count was twelve confirmed dead and three missing, presumed dead. The engine rooms were inoperable due to flooding and consequently the system generators were off-line.

The SBX system was not available for tasking and was on the mission status board as "Red" with no posted readiness date. The news out of Fort Greely was higher in lost personnel but less impact on the site's mission status. Between the folks in the building and those caught outside when the truck hit, the fort had lost twenty-seven people. The site's mission status was on the board as "Yellow."

At 2:27 p.m. PenAir flight 5310 suddenly popped up on the Eareckson Air station's approach radar. It was just east of Shemya Island and began its mayday calls to the air controllers at Eareckson. According to the pilot they were low on fuel, had thirteen passengers on board and needed emergency clearance to land. In the confusion and time compression of the moment, and the calls coming in over the other emergency channels, the controller immediately vectored him in on runway 28. Assam grinned. They never learned.

At 319 miles per hour and accelerating, the SAAB 340 flew straight over the runway banked right, and crashed into the sheet metal southeast side of the Cobra Dane radar building.

On impact, the plane and Assam's share of the dynamite he'd received from Shama in Anchorage, approximately two hundred pounds worth, detonated fifteen feet inside of the Cobra Dane building. Every floor above ground level was destroyed by either the initial explosion or the resulting fire.

The Yunes
Sonar Station

The only man on the *Yunes* still on headset to hear the explosion from Cobra Dane was Mr. Feng. Feng knew the significance of the explosion and smiled. They had accomplished three out of four of their assigned tasks. It dawned on him that his grade for the mission when looked at from that perspective only gave him a low "C." After all, the young man on Shemya had been a wild card at best. When he considered that three out of three targets had been successfully engaged he felt better. Three for three gave him an "A" for the missions. An "A" had a much better ring to it so that was how he was going to spin it in his report. He gave the thumbs up to Captain Babakan. They adjusted the boat's course to a more southwesterly track.

Shemya Island

It had been a long shot but it had paid off in a big way. At 1:30 p.m., Kevin had called his friend Charlie Olson at Cobra Dane and said he was coming by for a visit. Charlie met him at the door but didn't have his usual cup of coffee waiting for him. Charlie had sensed something was wrong. Kevin had just been there yesterday. This was apparently not going to be a routine visit.

Kevin walked into Charlie's office and sat down. "Charlie, you've known me for a while right?" Charlie just nodded.

"Well, I've got a very crazy story to tell you that you have about fifteen minutes to believe."

Kevin filled him in on the particulars about how he had been instructed to burn down or otherwise destroy Cobra Dane. Then he showed Charlie the video of his sister. Charlie looked at Kevin and reached for the phone at the same time.

"Kevin, I think you're a great guy and you do a hell of a job here on this rock but you can't think I'm going to let you damage the Dane?"

"No, Charlie, I don't, but if you could hear me out for a minute longer I think that we could have everyone be alive at the end of the day."

Charlie removed his hand from the phone. "You've got five minutes."

"Alright, fair enough, the problem with terrorists is that they usually have a backup plan. You would, wouldn't you?"

Charlie nodded, but looked rather uncomfortable with the whole discussion.

"The most important thing we need to do is get everyone out of here as soon as possible. Could you spray for rats or something?"

Charlie shook his head, "I did that last week, remember?"

"Charlie, what about a fake electrical fire?"

Now Charlie was smiling, "What's your idea?"

Kevin leaned a little closer, "Could we kill the power so everyone in the facility would think a transformer had blown? Then maybe we could burn some motor oil in the barbeque or something to make smoke."

Charlie shook his head, "That would cause the alarms to go off, and the building would be full of firemen in ten minutes."

Kevin smiled. "I'll worry about the alarms."

The plan worked flawlessly. Kevin put the smoke alarms in bypass/test mode. When the smoke was noticed by the guys in the airfield's tower they called the fire department who naturally had nothing showing up on their alarm panel. They in turn called Charlie who explained it away as another Cobra Dane cookout gone amuck.

Everything was going according to plan when by shear chance a couple of Cobra Dane guys at the Base Exchange bumped into some Fire department guys they bowled with. One of them happened to be the Eareckson Air Station fire battalion chief. He was rather curious to know why two guys from Texas weren't at the Cobra Dane barbeque. The two guys had looked at the chief dumbfounded. "What barbeque?"

In less than five minutes, every fire truck on Shemya Island was racing toward the Cobra Dane Radar site. At 2:29 p.m. when the aircraft hit and destroyed the facility almost eighty personnel from fire, police and EMS were less than three hundred yards away and closing fast. Not a single person had been hurt.

Pentagon
Washington D.C.

It was quite clear to all parties in the room that the United States Missile Defense system was under attack. A few naysayers thought it might be random until they received the call from Eareckson Air Station. Apparently an aircraft had feigned an emergency landing on the Eareckson runway and instead slammed into the back of the Cobra Dane radar system. According to the report, the catastrophic explosion that followed seemed to indicate it had not been an accident. That news seemed to clinch the deal with the former naysayers. The illuminated status board for the Ballistic Missile Defense System went from "Green" to "Yellow."

The Pentagon would need to hold a press conference for the morning news cycle and get out in front of this story. They would have to try and somehow convince the American people that everything was fine and that the nation was still safe. In the meantime, the Army immediately dispatched additional teams of maintenance personnel to Fort Greely. The navy immediately rerouted two AEGIS cruisers that were scheduled to deploy to the Sea of Japan, north, to take up the slack left by the disabled SBX and the now destroyed Cobra Dane System.

CHAPTER 29

BOATSS

Like most Defense Department employees, the girls were stunned by the terrible news coming out of Alaska. The death toll kept climbing and the talking heads on the news were extolling their various spins.

The left was blaming America for having bases that were seen by other countries as provocative. Some pundits were even suggesting that these events were probably the actions of several lone wolf or homegrown terrorists.

Of course, as they flipped through the channels, guests on other networks were convinced it was a combination of the usual suspects. In less than two years' time, the nation had been attacked several times. Things had been relatively quiet until the Benghazi fiasco. The administration had really taken it in the shorts for those perceived mistakes. Several local events had occurred in New York and Los Angeles, but nothing major. The nation was tearing itself apart on issues such as border protection, gun control, and the economy.

A story was just breaking on the news about a plane crash on Eareckson Air Force Station. The news was way off the mark but they were getting their information from someone. With access to a Department of Defense top secret computer, what had really happened on Shemya was already widely known to those with access. The PenAir SAAB 350 had been stolen from its hanger earlier in the day and been used as a cruise missile to take out the Cobra Dane radar site at the end of the EAS runway.

It was pretty apparent with the attack on Fort Richardson's missile field, the SBX platform, and the Cobra Dane radar, that someone was trying to break the back of the United State's Ballistic Missile Defense system. From the looks of things, they were doing a pretty damn good job.

The intelligence community was coming unglued at the seams. It had already been calculated that the explosion on the SBX platform had been caused by the impact of a large fishing vessel with what had been already calculated to be several hundred pounds of plastique explosive.

Four men, all Americans, had been pulled from the water after the explosion. Witnesses that survived the initial explosion on the SBX reported they had seen the men jump off the back of the boat just before it impacted the SBX. All four men had been stabilized for their various wounds and placed on a medivac back to Elmendorf for more advanced care and treatment for exposure. Three of the men were currently being questioned by various government officials. A fourth man had apparently suffered a more serious bullet wound, allegedly fired from the SBX, and was still in guarded condition.

The big question in the intelligence community was how someone could get that much high explosive out to a fishing vessel in Dutch Harbor in the first place. It couldn't have gone by air and the Coast Guard keeps a fairly good eye on the comings and goings of vessels in the ports closer to Anchorage.

Jewels called Rick on the STU IV secure line. "Rick? What are the chances that someone could drop off a package on one of those remote coastlines in the Aleutians for someone else to pick-up?"

Rick hesitated, "It would be tough for a couple of reasons. First, you still haven't solved the question on where it came from. This wasn't dynamite. My sources are telling me that this was high grade military grade stuff like Semtex or PETN. Then there's the amount. If the agency is correct in their assessment at a couple hundred pounds? This was professionally done."

Jewels stewed on that for a moment. "What if I could figure out how it got to the fishing boat? Can you guys get me any overhead stuff?"

Rick glanced up at the row of clocks on the far wall thinking of whose satellites would have been over the Aleutian Islands during the time period Jewels was suggesting.

"Jewels, I'll see what I can do. It's crazy over here, let me run for now." He hung up before she could say thank you.

That's all she needed to know. Jewels entered the coordinates for the island of Unalaska and hit "Search." Using the new search protocols, the computer was subtracting out all normal sounds it heard in the last twenty-four hours. Jewels moved her search west, closer to Adak. Again, nothing. She was apparently missing something. What about five days? She rolled her cursor over to the "Time" cell. It wanted it in hours. Her brain wasn't in gear today. She entered 120 and hit "Enter." This search was different. There were almost no sound files for the period except for one large boat. Jewels "grabbed" the file from the list and placed it in the "Search" box that would then compare it to all files of known sounds and hit "Enter." It came back immediately as the same boat that had left Dutch Harbor Sunday evening. Alright, she'd figured that part out.

Despite running searches in the immediate area and radiating out in each direction the system didn't have another wave file matching any known ship.

It was getting late and she was exhausted. Her head was pounding. She put her head down on her desk and wished that Mitch wasn't going home in two days. He had been spending as much time with her as he could but with the unfolding situation before them it had mostly been splinters of time as they grabbed a bite of food somewhere.

She heard something and wasn't sure it was what she thought it was. It sounded an awful lot like a beer can being crushed. Sounded like fun, just not in the right place. Her head flew off the desk.

"That's it!" she said out loud to nobody in particular. After five minutes the system had automatically logged her out for no activity. She logged herself back in. She wasn't tired anymore and rapidly moved her cursor over to "Previous searches" and hit "Edit parameters." In homage to Rick she had created a parameter using his off the wall suggestion "Anomalous sounds." She selected 120 hours and hit "Enter." She had anticipated the system would detect many sounds it didn't recognize. It chimed after only 48 seconds.

The system found only one file. She double checked her search parameters and found the default setting was "Known sounds." She selected "All" and hit "Enter." This time hundreds of files came back. She selected "Store files" and put her head back down. Way too many. Alright, you win, she thought. What's the one sound? She went back into the system and extracted the file from the previous search. She played it on her head phones. "Baanng!" She played it several times before she put it on her larger speakers attached to her desktop. She called out to several coworkers and asked them to listen. "Baanng!!!"

"Does anybody have any ideas what that sound is?" She asked to the gathering group.

She played it two more times before someone said, "It sounds like a heavy metal door or a hatch." That was it. She was just too tired to place it. She put the file in the "Compare" folder and ran a search against all known data bases. The search was designed to get you an exact match or three similar matches. This search took just over two minutes.

1. Ship cargo door
2. Empty cargo container
3. Miscellaneous ship bulkhead hatch

Nothing had matched it exactly but she had a good working theory. Some type of vessel had been in the area that only made the one sound. No engine sounds on the way to the location or before the sound and no engine sounds after the sound.

Jewels walked to Ramón's door and knocked.

"What is it?" he demanded as he put on his coat.

"I have a working theory on how the explosives were delivered to the fishing boat." Jewels said in a rush of excitement. He never even stopped putting his coat on.

"Ball game tonight, theories can wait until tomorrow." And out the door he went.

Jewels was dumbfounded. She knew he was an arrogant ass but people were dead and still dying and he was worried about a televised college basketball game. It brought to mind and illuminated the expression, "March Madness."

Jewels turned off the computer system, said goodnight to the cleaning crew, and walked out the door. The cool air felt wonderful and helped clear her head. As she rode the train the three-minute trip up to her apartment she hoped Mitch would make her feel better. Just saying his name seemed to help.

Yunes
100 miles Southwest of Shemya

It was Thursday morning. After ten hours of drifting silently westward in the current and using the batteries, the *Yunes* had only been traveling at a combined speed of 11 knots. With the crew getting impatient with running silently, Mr. Feng relinquished command of the *Yunes* back to Captain Babakan.

With command of his vessel once again, Captain Babakan ordered the ship up to periscope depth. They had not been making the best time but they had been traveling as silently as possible and putting as much distance between the Aleutians and their present position as possible.

Captain Babakan had several reasons for bringing his boat so close, perilously close, to the surface. First and foremost, he desperately needed to charge the *Yune's* batteries. In order to do so, he needed a relatively safe place to bring the *Yunes* up close enough to get the air intake to the diesel engines above the surface. This was called "snorkeling" and it was perhaps one of the most dangerous things he could do. At snorkeling depth and running the diesel engines several more sub hunting capabilities could be brought to bear against them. It could be a potentially lethal combination. The captain was out of options. The engine room had called him twice in the past hour letting him know the batteries were rapidly approaching the end of their useful limit.

Secondly, by bringing the boat up to periscope depth he would not only be able to bring the diesel engines back on line, he could charge his batteries, increase the boat's speed to 12 knots, and get some fresh air in the boat. While on the surface they could use their diesel engines for both propulsion and to recharge the batteries. After two hours of charging the batteries he would have enough power to dive the boat if a situation arose that made surface travel dangerous.

Although not mission critical, the other reason the captain was glad to be on the surface was to stroke his own ego. Captain Babakan desperately wanted to find out what was going on in the world.

Needless to say, the news coming out of the States was exhilarating. Reports were still coming in over the news about the sinking of the American SBX radar platform and the attack on Fort Greeley, Alaska. He hadn't been aware of that part of the plan.

To the best of his knowledge, no one was actively looking for him. Sonar hadn't reported any threatening contacts so they had remained at snorkel depth for almost five hours.

The crew of the *Yunes* had been listening to the news broadcasts for almost the entire time. The captain was about to turn it off when the news broke about the apparent accident of a PenAir flight out of Dutch Harbor. Apparently it declared an in-flight emergency and attempted to land on Shemya. Although the aircraft had been cleared to land, it had attempted to go around for a second approach and struck a large building on the end of the island. More details were promised as they became available.

Captain Babakan smiled. He'd heard all the details he needed yesterday when Mr. Feng had told him about the attack on Cobra Dane. It had taken almost seventeen hours for the military to release the information to the press. The captain ordered the diving officer to dive the boat, level at three hundred and fifty feet, new course 275°, and increase speed to 18 knots.

"Yes sir, dive the boat, level at three hundred fifty feet, new course now 275°. Increasing speed to 18 knots."

The captain had been thinking about his dead crewman still in the dive trunk. It certainly wouldn't help crew morale for his body to be found by other crew members or worse several days from now all the way back in port. He decided that he'd better talk to Mr. Feng about it discreetly in his cabin. Not now though. He'd been enjoying his day so far and didn't want to spoil his mood.

Elmendorf/Richardson Base Hospital—Security Wing

For the second time in less than a week, Jonah West awoke disoriented and somewhat confused. He recognized his surroundings and therefore knew he wasn't dead. He surveyed the room. He was definitely in a large hospital room that had most of the bells and whistles. Some of which he noticed were attached to him. Jonah couldn't move his head very far, so he instead rolled his eyes enough to see most of the room. The first thing that stood out to Jonah were the two Marine guards standing at his doorway with MP5s. One was facing out and the other one looking straight at him. The one looking at him had a look that Jonah recognized oh too well. He wanted Jonah dead.

After hitting the water, the three men had floated in the cold water for almost ten minutes before being hauled out by unseen hands. Everyone it seemed had fared better than Jonah.

Although the gunner on the SBX had not intentionally targeted the men as they leapt from the back of the *Dreamer*, his eyes and arms had worked together in perfect harmony and he had followed them off the back of the boat with a burst of bullets. Under normal circumstances this would have been ideal. Unfortunately for the men, and especially Jonah, the young gunner's index finger had not relaxed from the trigger and the bullets had raked over the men before he realized what had happened. Sadly, the young marine's heroic efforts to save his vessel placed him directly above the *Dreamer* when it impacted the SBX and exploded. The young man was still missing at this point and presumed dead.

The bullets from the burst had caught each man in order as they left the boat. Kevin was hit in the calf, Roy was caught in his left buttock, and Skip had been caught in his right shoulder. All of their wounds were more grazing than penetrating because of the steep angles involved.

Unfortunately, Jonah had been the last man off the back of the boat and had caught one round high in his left shoulder and one through the right side of his neck.

The doctors were stunned that he could have been so lucky. Although he had significant tissue damage to his neck, no nerves or major vascular areas had been affected. It hadn't taken long for the guards to notify the medical staff that he was conscious and the room was filling rapidly with two distinct groups of people, medical personnel and what he assumed were law enforcement of some kind. The former group seemed very concerned about his condition; the latter had the same look as the Marines.

"Can you move your head?" someone on his left was asking.

Jonah tried to speak but quickly realized he was intubated. If they wanted him to do more than nod at them, they were going to have to pull the damn tube out of his throat.

He nodded. That hurt significantly more than he had anticipated. His pain must have been evident because the next thing they asked him was if he was in any pain.

He heard someone say something about needing to talk to him. The voice seemed very muffled and he couldn't make out who had said it. Jonah wasn't even considering trying to move his head again to nod "yes" to the question so he'd blinked twice. The nurse smiled at him and moved toward one of the many IV's hanging off the stand to his left. The stand was heavily laden with a bag of blood, a bag of dextrose solution, and a bag of antibiotics. In a moment a warm feeling not unlike being in a warm bath seemed to flood over his entire body. He drifted for a moment then was out cold.

The FBI agent who had been in such a rush to talk to him sighed heavily and got everyone's attention in the room.

"For those of you who don't know, I'm special agent in charge, Max Robertson, from the FBI." He now had everyone's undivided attention.

"I want all of you to know that the man you're taking care of had no part in the attack on the SBX ship. He is a highly decorated, recently retired, Navy SEAL. From all reports and interviews conducted so far, he was perhaps even a hero in this whole fiasco out at Adak. We do know for a fact that his efforts saved at least three other men who were on the vessel with him. Please take good care of him."

At Jonah's hospital room doorway, the two Marines, who only moments before wanted Jonah dead, quietly whispered to each other. With the precision of an honor guard the men changed their respective positions at his doorway. Where before, they had been standing in Jonah's room, securing a prisoner, they now moved and were stationed just outside, one on either side of his door. Their facial expressions had changed significantly since hearing the news of who the patient was. Each Marine's face now reflected the pride, honor, and unwavering dedication of protecting one of their own.

CHAPTER 30

DuPont Circle

It had been a long day physically, mentally, emotionally and Jewels felt spent. Even the three-minute train ride seemed to take forever. She called Mitch, as promised, when she got back to her apartment.

"Hey Jewels. How's my favorite computer geek?"

"Tired," was all Jewels could think to say.

"Are you too tired to dance but not too tired to eat?" teased Mitch, trying his very best wit to lighten her mood. Jewels appreciated his efforts but wasn't sure she wanted any company.

Jewels really wanted to see him but wasn't going to be up for anything more than some quiet company. "What did you have in mind?"

"I found a restaurant not far from here called Urbana. Ever heard of it?"

Having an apartment less than two blocks from DuPont circle had its perks. One of them was a restaurant named Urbana. It was the place she would always try and end up on special occasions such as her birthday or when friends were visiting.

Just surviving the stress of today would seem to qualify as an occasion. In reality, they'd written some new code, potentially solved a National

Intelligence riddle, and Mitch was, in fact, from out of town. Those were enough reasons right there.

"Sure, I've heard of it. How did you hear about it?"

"I heard it was the place to take someone special after a very long, difficult day." "Really?" asked Jewels.

"No, actually I made that part up," laughed Mitch. "There was a trifold brochure about the place at the front desk of my hotel."

Jewels smiled for the first time in hours. "Are you coming to get me?" Jewels inquired in as alluring a voice as she could muster.

Wow! Mitch thought, she sure sounded great on the phone.

"You're just walking in the door, right? Why don't you call me when you're ready?" "I need ten minutes," replied Jewels. "Did you make a reservation?

Mitch's rather sarcastic reply was that he was from Colorado, not the "sticks" was much too easy for Jewels to let pass without comment.

She smirked and said, "So that's a yes?"

Mitch had not wasted any time and was waiting for her when she got to the lobby. He mused to himself that he could get used to this.

It was less than a five-minute walk from Jewel's apartment to Urbana. They certainly weren't in a hurry and Mitch's reservation wasn't for another forty minutes. They walked slowly, with Jewels holding Mitch's hand. It felt comfortable.

Their timing was actually perfect. They got there right after the majority of the happy hour crowd had left for the evening. Happy hour at Urbana was always a very lively and noisy event. Their specialty was hand-crafted cocktails and a superior wine list. On most of the evenings she had been there, it had always hosted a very lively local crowd. For several years it had earned the title of one of D.C.'s "Hottest Restaurant Bar Scenes." On any other night, that would have been a welcome break. Tonight just wasn't the night. Many people, both inside and outside the beltway, were wondering just what yesterday's events in Alaska signaled.

The twenty-something hostess bounced her way up to Mitch and asked if he wished to be seated early. Apparently several large parties had cancelled and they had a booth available for them almost immediately. The booth was in a quieter section of the restaurant and Jewels opted to sit next to Mitch instead of across from him. From the look on Mitch's face she knew she had made the right decision.

The waiter brought Mitch their menu's and the wine list. Mitch perused the menu briefly. "This menu is sure different than the restaurants in the Springs."

"I'll bet," Jewels responded.

Mitch had actually been referring to the prices, Jewels the selection of dishes.

The food was always excellent here and Jewels had probably, at one time or another, personally tried or heard about most of the dishes. She offered her opinions on several and Mitch decided to opt for the roasted duck, Jewels the lamb.

Mitch selected a wine he thought would work best with both entrees and they leaned back into the seat and into each other. He closed his eyes and enjoyed the moment. After a few minutes of silence, Jewels spoke. "Are you seriously headed back to Colorado Springs tomorrow night?"

Mitch looked solemnly at Jewels, "There's something I need to tell you."

Jewel's heart sank. Here it comes. Jewels thought the worst. He had a girlfriend back in Colorado Springs.

Mitch saw her face change. "What's wrong?" he asked.

"I just know you're going to tell me something horrible," Jewels sighed, slumping slightly in the booth.

"I'm sorry you feel that way," replied Mitch. "Should I call for the check?" "No, let's get it over with." Jewels appeared sullen.

"Alright, here goes. My boss said I can stay another week. He said since we are working on basically the same things here that I'd be working on back at my office, I might as well stay and learn something. There, was that so bad?" Mitch was smiling.

Jewels, on the other hand, was crying. She threw her arms around his neck as if in fear of falling from a great height. "Oh, Mitch, that's great news!" She broke her embrace and quickly wiped her tears away with her napkin.

"A toast," Jewels declared.

"To what, pray tell?" Mitch was smiling.

It was Jewel's turn to smile now. With her glass raised high, she turned, looked at him and said, "To whatever brought you to my doorstep, Mitch Kendrick." With that, she shifted ever so slightly and gave him just the lightest peck on the cheek.

Shemya Island, Alaska

Kevin Gyoh had completed all of his post incident reports. It was odd to see his name in the reports. It seemed that every base agency from the Base Commander down had wanted to speak to him about the incident. All Kevin really wanted to know was if his sister had been released and what her condition was. The Red Cross was able to get that part of the equation solved for him relatively quickly. Kevin had been able to talk to both his mom and sister for a while, with each of them taking turns crying. Even after his sister's whole ordeal, his mom seemed to be the worse for wear.

Kevin had needed to be debriefed by all of the major agencies on base and they told him to expect several more debriefings in the coming days. It was the rehashing of the obvious that made Kevin even more certain he had handled it the only way possible. They let him drive past the still smoldering ruin of Cobra Dane facility. It was a total loss. The impact of losing such an important system would certainly be felt for years.

Although two days had passed, Kevin still felt physically and emotionally whipped. Today he at least had his appetite back and felt he couldn't take another step without eating. He'd just made it through the line when he spotted Charlie Olson at his usual table and went over to join him. Charlie looked up, saw his friend, and with as much feigned frustration as he could muster said, "FINALLY!"

Kevin was so tired he hadn't even noticed that all of the personnel from the Cobra Dane, both shifts, were seated all around Charlie. First, all the people from Dane stood up and started clapping and hooting. That was embarrassing enough. Then the surrounding tables also stood up. Just as it started to die down someone started chanting, "Kevin, Kevin, Kevin!" The whole place erupted. Kevin sat down and put his head in his hands. These people no longer had jobs and they were in enough of a good mood to chant and clap?

Somebody was clinking a water glass with a spoon to get everyone to settle down. Kevin looked up. It was Bill Davis, the Cobra Dane project leader, who was essentially the supervisor of all the Cobra Dane personnel on the island.

"Kevin, I'd like to thank you for your quick thinking and more important quick actions. More clapping and whistling ensued. "You may notice that there would seem to be a lot of people here at these tables you might not recognize."

Kevin glanced around and now that he mentioned it, there did seem to be more people sitting at the tables than usual. Bill continued, "I imagine in all the hubbub of the past two days you may have forgotten what was significant about Wednesday afternoon at Cobra Dane." Kevin nodded.

"Kevin, last Wednesday afternoon, in addition to having both shifts at the facility for a meeting, we were hosting twelve visitors from the Missile Defense Agency (MDA) at the site when you kicked off your little "Hail Mary" plan. If you had not been able to convince Charlie, and the two of you hadn't done what you did, we would have lost a whole lot more than that system. We would have lost thirty-one of our best people."

The applause and back slapping started again and Kevin realized that maybe, just maybe, things would be okay. As things began to quiet down and the sounds in the chow hall were returning to normal, Kevin noticed that several people from the Dane site kept glancing at whoever was sitting to his right. As casually as possible, Kevin looked to his right. At first he didn't recognize the person and assumed it was someone from the MDA. The woman was somehow familiar but he just couldn't place her. He'd smiled and gone back to eating his dinner. A voice he did recognize said, "Thank you, Kevin."

He turned to his right again. Now he knew who it was. It was Sally McDaniel from the Cobra Dane crew. She looked incredible. Her transformation from last week at her birthday party to now was startling. Sally had pulled her hair away from her face and she wasn't wearing her ill-fitting, shape hiding clothes anymore. She had cleaned up beautifully. Kevin smiled. Always the ladies' man, Kevin managed to say, "Hello."

CHAPTER 31

Shooting Star

On the evening of the fifth day at sea, Captain Lee was now three days from the closest land he would encounter for the next several days. His ship, the *Shooting Star,* continued to radiate the bogus identification code of the *Oceans Queen* that had been secretly changed while in the Dalian drydock. To even the most experienced maritime personnel seeking to locate the *Shooting Star,* she now appeared to be under repair in the Dalian drydocks.

Two days ago, the *Shooting Star* passed through the Tsugaru Straight between the islands of Hokkaido and Honshu. Captain Lee watched in wonder as the late afternoon sun glistened off the many snow covered peaks on Hokkaido. The weather had been good for this time of year with the swells at only three feet or so. The ship was making excellent time and maintaining a speed of 22 knots. Lee allowed his mind to drift for a moment to a different time, perhaps someday soon, when he could see things like this with his family.

After a late supper, Lee did his usual late night walk around his ship. For three days now, he had successfully avoided thinking about the "why" the changes had been made to his ship. He had instead busied himself with the "what" he was supposed to do in Los Angeles. Ocean voyages are steeped in routine. Maritime tradition dictates that each day be divided into six four-hour periods. Three groups of watch keepers from the engine and deck departments work four hours on then have eight hours off watch keeping duty.

A mariner's off duty time is largely a solitary affair, pursuing hobbies, reading, writing letters, and sleeping. As Lee walked the ship he greeted his crew if their doors were open and respected their privacy if they were not. Most ocean going vessels now operate an unmanned engine room system allowing engineers to work days only. Although the engine room is computer controlled by night, the duty engineer will often make inspections during periods of unmanned operation. Engineers work in a hot, humid, noisy atmosphere. As Lee entered the engine room he was greeted by his chief engineer. Mostly through the use of hand signals and some lip-reading, he determined that everything was operating well.

As Lee continued his evening walk; he visually reviewed all the changes that had been made to his ship and wondered why, in fact, they had been done. Of course the big changes were obvious like the removal of entire sections of the ship and the installation of what he determined to be some type of water jet propulsion system.

What he found most disturbing were the little things. A so-called new "anti-pirating" system had been installed on the ship. It was true that pirating had picked up, as of late, off the coast of Africa and that pirates were getting bolder as the months went by. But why the rush if he was heading across the Pacific? Part of the system, he noticed, was what appeared to be motion sensitive cameras. Lee had noticed them when the ship was in drydock and assumed they were temporary in nature to keep an eye on the workers.

When Lee had finally been allowed to board his ship on the day of sailing, he noticed the cameras had not been removed. As he walked through the lower levels of the ship this evening, he couldn't help but notice the lights along the catwalks turned from red to green as he passed by. He could only assume the cameras' recorded images were being sent to a hard drive system somewhere in the ship for security records. Although he hadn't made a specific effort to find the room where the images were being sent, he expected someone on the crew to have mentioned it.

Lee stopped up near the bow when something caught his eye. He was on the lowest deck of the ship in the number two container hold. Due to the reconfiguration of the holds, there was no longer any capability to have containers below deck. Although the deck of the ship was covered with containers, they were only one level high. He watched them being loaded and knew they weren't empty, but generally speaking, the ship had been loaded with very few containers for a trip all the way across the Pacific.

While most other areas of the ship below deck had been cut away and removed to accommodate the new pump system, this forward part of the ship had obviously been added to. The length of the number two hold had been decreased by at least sixty feet. The lightweight bulkhead normally separating the number two hold from the forward most part of the ship had been replaced by a new and very robust bulkhead. In the middle of this new bulkhead was a very secure looking cargo door that was easily fifteen feet high and thirty feet wide. The unusually large door was secured with at least three locking systems he could see. It appeared as though they had constructed some type of secure storage facility right here on his ship. Lee examined the bulkhead's construction. Someone expended a great deal of effort to create this new bulkhead and had even gone so far as to make the welds appear older than they were.

Lee glanced at his watch and realized he still needed to check the galley and swing through the bridge before turning in for the night. As he turned to go he noticed the newly reinforced metal floor directly in front of the new door. The reinforced floor extended aft at least thirty-five feet to a point just past the forward deck loading hatch. Conscious of the fact that he was probably being watched, he feigned dropping something out of his pocket. As he bent down to pick it up, he gave the floor a quick cursory inspection and realized it had also been made to appear as though it had always been there. The exception was where two long drag marks extended to and, Lee surmised, past the new wall and door structure. He couldn't help having a sense of unease as he made his way topside.

The Yunes

After several hours, Captain Babakan had gathered the courage needed to knock on Mr. Feng's cabin door.

"Enter."

"A moment, sir?" inquired Captain Babakan.

"Ah, captain, good news about the missions, yes?"

"Yes, sir," replied the captain as enthusiastically as he could muster. "I wanted to talk to you about the crewman's body that's still in the dive trunk."

"What about it?" Feng remarked without as much as an upward glance from his papers. Captain Babakan swallowed hard.

"I feel we should dispose of the body over the side or somehow explain what happened to the crew as an accident and bring his body inside. He was a dedicated soldier of Allah and his body should be treated with some measure of respect."

Feng looked up. "I don't want his body on the boat. It will create too many questions that cannot be answered. What's your other plan?"

The captain detailed his other plan which involved removing the crewman's body and putting it off the ship with some weights attached to ensure it would sink. Feng thought that was reasonable and told the captain to proceed.

The problems facing the captain for this task were numerous. First and foremost, he didn't trust Feng. He really couldn't let anyone help him because Feng had made it clear there could be no witnesses. While hoping those instructions did not include himself, Babakan formulated his plan. He would have to remove everyone out of the forward part of the boat. The crew would be very suspicious of the captain getting into the dive trunk by himself. Feng could order the men to the rear of the ship and keep them occupied watching something for twenty minutes while he carried out his task. He would then pump out the dive trunk, enter and bring the crewman to the deck of the submarine. Babakan had already found some chain to secure around his crewman's waist to aid in his sinking quickly. What he liked best about his plan was that he would not have to actually leave the submarine.

Feng approved the plan and had suggested they take a long look through the periscope before surfacing the boat. Feng, it was clear, didn't want any surprises. They planned it for the top of the next hour.

Captain Babakan ordered the crew to a special meeting at the rear of the boat which was to be conducted by Mr. Feng. After venting the dive trunk and getting a green light on the seal, the captain opened the bulkhead hatch. His crewman's body was just inside the hatch. None of the normal issues associated with a dead body were yet present due to a combination of the low water temperature and tremendous depth and subsequent pressure of the water.

Using the communications system Babakan keyed the "mic" two times. He received one "click" in response. That was Mr. Feng's signal that the deck of the boat was above sea level.

Now it was just a trust issue. With the hatch to the sub closed and secured behind him it was theoretically possible to open the hatch to the deck even if the boat was still slightly submerged. It wouldn't be enough water to sink the boat but looking down at his dead crewman he was reminded that his drowning out here was a distinct possibility. He really didn't have a choice at this point and opened the hatch.

Cool moist air, a beam of sunlight, and a small splash of cold seawater greeted him as he pushed the large heavy hatch upward. Please, he silently prayed to Allah; don't let the hatch come down with me outside.

He hoisted the dead crewman onto his shoulder and carried him up the five rungs of the ladder to the deck. As he lay just over the lip of the hatch, the captain wrapped the six feet of chain around his crewman's waist, securing it with a carabineer. Babakan pushed the body out another foot or so, said another quick prayer to Allah, and began to lower the hatch. Just as the hatch had cleared its neutral position, a small wave hit the port side of the submarine. The unexpected motion caused the captain to lose his footing momentarily and in a sudden panic he'd reached down to steady himself. In the brief second it took to reach down, he momentarily released his hold on the hatch. Immediately realizing his mistake, and with only a second to spare, he pushed back off the ladder and dropped to the bottom of the dive trunk. The massive deck hatch came down very hard, with a loud bang.

On the bridge of the *Yunes*, only Mr. Feng had noticed the sound. He quietly looked over and saw the deck hatch light was green. He smiled. He resisted the temptation to flood the compartment with the captain still outside. He knew Babakan didn't trust him. If the roles had been reversed, he wouldn't have trusted him either. Frankly he had been surprised the captain suggested the plan.

Moments later the captain appeared and, pretending to be annoyed, ordered everyone back to their stations and the dive officer to dive the boat. He watched through the periscope as the crewman's body sloshed back and forth several times before sliding off the starboard side of the boat.

Pyongyang, North Korea

In a small room, off to one side of the enormous operations center, two people were intently watching a bank of security monitors. On the screens, from every angle imaginable, they were watching Captain Lee inspect his ship. Although it was not unusual for him to do so, tonight he seemed to give it more than just his usual cursory inspection. Tonight it appeared he was looking for something. On several occasions he could be seen staring directly into the various cameras. This in itself wasn't any cause for alarm. The moment the captain examined the floor of the cargo hold, everything changed. With only four days left in the operation, they would have to report this up the chain of command.

The two admirals and three generals in their own offices just off the command center's main floor were grateful for the information. It was agreed, by all, that they would have preferred this particular scenario taken another day or two to play out. Everything in the mission had been rehearsed and scripted down to the hour. Some flexibility existed in the plan but everything needed to be coordinated when the script changed.

After several secure and very cryptic messages to other high level key players in the game as well as assurances that all was in order, the generals ordered the go ahead for phase thirteen of the operation.

CHAPTER 32

BOATSS

Jewels and Gina were both in early Friday morning to get any kinks out of the new program. The thermostat on the wall read 62°. Jewels swore if they ever got fully funded she would get them out of this ice box forever. Funding of any kind was quite the dream in Washington these days and the thought made them both laugh.

Jewels showed Gina what she had found late yesterday afternoon with the sound profile she'd discovered. Over their first cup of coffee for the day they discussed what they could do with the file.

Gina's fingers were once again flying over the keyboard and without looking up, she asked Jewels, "What is the maximum time value you can put in the search window?"

"365 days," Jewels replied. "It allows for faster searching. Most of the information older than that resides in offsite servers. I thought that for testing purposes a shorter time span would be prudent."

Gina ended her typing with a flourish. "Here's my idea." She took three long slow gulps of coffee. "We know where and when you heard the wave file you found yesterday. Instead of asking the system to identify what it thinks your file is, let's ask it instead to find any file that matches it. We really don't care what it is right now, do we? What we need to do is find out where the sound went, or came from."

Gina may have had her issues and demons, but when it came time to solve problems, she was the one you wanted on your team. Jewels agreed and after some initial massaging of the new search program they uploaded the mystery hatch file Jewels had found and instructed the computer to find a match. What the system had to do now was search all wave files it had in its data banks back one year in time.

The girls were wise enough to know this was going to take several hours. Since no one else was in yet, Gina asked Jewels how her evening had gone. "So when I left here yesterday you were pretty down in the dumps. Did you go home and crawl into bed?"

Jewels looked her best friend in the eye and with the most wicked smile she could muster said, "Almost."

"OMG, you didn't," gushed Gina. Her eyes were as big as Jewels had ever seen them. "I want details right now!"

Jewels busied herself with some things on her desk that suddenly needed arranging and gave Gina a curt, "Nope."

"Pleeease," Gina's begging was getting pathetic. It was very funny, but pathetic just the same.

Although Jewels hated receiving Gina's postdate wrap-up reports, she relented.

"Alright, just this once," She turned quickly in her chair and told Gina all the good news.

At 8:10 a.m., Mr. Rodriquez made his entrance. After talking to all the men in the office, who had been there on time at 7:45 a.m., about his new bracket position, team scores, and everything else he could think of other than work, he went into his office and closed the door.

Everyone who was still in the office late yesterday afternoon knew Jewels was on to something. They looked in the direction of Rodriquez's office and then at Jewels and Gina. Despite how they might have felt about Jewels personally, they knew she was the best chance they had of finding the answer of where the explosives had come from. Most of them gave her a nod that said to her "we know." She hadn't thought peer recognition would ever mean much. Of course Jewels hadn't thought she'd ever meet a guy like Mitch either.

Pentagon

Across town at the Pentagon, Mitch had just finished up his last presentation of the conference and retrieved his cell phone from the security locker when he got a text from Rick. "Contact me ASAP." It took another twenty minutes of small talk, handshakes, and more small talk before Mitch could get out to the metro stop below the Pentagon. As he dialed Rick, he put some more credit on his metro card. The phone picked up, "Rick Wagner."

"Hey, Rick, what's up?"

"Mitch, we've got something you need to look at as soon as you can. How long would it take for you to get over to my office?"

Mitch laughed, "Rick, I don't even know for sure where your office is."

"Mitch," he laughed, "I'll send you the directions. By the way, your clearance paperwork is already here."

Mitch started to ask how he'd pulled that off and remembered who his friend worked for. He then placed a quick call to Jewels. Their planned lunch date appeared to be in jeopardy.

BOATSS

Jewels would have been crushed if Mitch was both cancelling and leaving tonight. They were just starting to talk about dinner plans when the program she had searching for the odd sound chimed. It had found a perfect match. Julie Folk was a multitasker by nature. It was how she was wired and probably what made her so good at her job. When she saw the location of where the sound had been detected she told Mitch that she needed to go. She hung up even as he was still saying goodbye. She needed to talk to Rick on a secure line. "Gina, look at this." Jewels was pointing at the illuminated search box in the center of her monitor.

"Can that be right?" Gina looked at the location on the screen and had the same reaction many others would later in the day. Her jaw dropped.

The sound of the mystery hatch was as clear as a bell and had been made one mile off the coast of Iran less than three weeks ago. She dialed Rick and hit the "Secure" key when he answered the phone. "Rick Wagner, I've got you secure."

"Rick, Julie Folk here."

"Jewels!" Before she could even speak, he started to apologize about stealing her lunch date.

She cut him off. "Rick, you read my email about the mystery sound I found yesterday off Adak Island?"

"Yes, I..." he started to say.

"I found it again, this time just outside the harbor at Bandar Abbas. According to our cross check of signatures the only vessel in that area at the time was the Iranian submarine *Yunes*. It's an old Kilo class diesel electric but certainly quiet enough to ride the currents undetected along the Aleutians."

Rick looked at his watch and told her that they were coming her way. Rick hung up the phone on Jewels and went to find his boss. This whole thing was quickly getting way past his pay grade.

CHAPTER 33

The Shooting Star

Captain Lee awoke and thought briefly about his current situation. Even if he could buy into the whole changing of the ship's registry to a South Korean vessel, which he didn't, he still had no idea what his leadership thought a trip to L.A. would accomplish. What could they possibly be delivering to Los Angeles that was worth such an enormous financial investment and tremendous risk? What was so important and required such secrecy? They had added systems to increase his speed, changed his capability to carry containers, gave the ship what looked to him like a sonar package, built what amounted to a vault in his ship's bow, changed his GPS signal and signature to make him appear to be a different ship and run the South Korean flag up his flag pole. To what end?

Lee readied himself for the day. After a quick shower he headed for the galley. The galley on the *Shooting Star* was on deck five and required he walk through the crew's quarters. The ship seemed unusually quiet this morning. Normally at this time he would have heard the sounds of the crew moving around the ship. Perhaps a dropped hammer, a slammed hatch door, something. This morning he heard nothing except the sound of the ship's engines.

The stress of the previous weeks was clearly taking its toll on him. He needed some coffee. As Lee entered the galley it became clear something was indeed amiss on his ship. He poured himself some old cold coffee, placed it in the microwave and set the timer for one minute. As he waited he looked at the galley. The galley was in exactly the same condition as he had seen it at 11 p.m. last night. Clean. No smells of cooking, no crew waiting for him to encourage them to finish up and get the day started. Nothing.

Lee jumped and let out a shout when the timer on the microwave beeped. It was almost a law of the sea that hot fresh coffee always be available for the crew. Lee was starting to sense that old stale coffee might be the least of his problems today. He finished his coffee in three big swallows and headed for the bridge. Again, he passed no one. Something was clearly wrong. The hairs on the back of his neck tingled and his stomach began to turn ever so slightly. Why had no one come to get him?

Captain Lee began to run. He turned the lever on the hatch to the bridge only to find his first officer lying prone on the floor. Lee rushed to his side but it was rather obvious the man was dead. When he tried to move him he was stiff. Rigor had set in. Sadly, in his life, he had moved many dead bodies and he knew his first officer had been dead for several hours.

Lee attempted to assess the ship's situation. The ship's autopilot was engaged. This was not unusual when ships were transiting the wide expanses of the open ocean. Whatever had happened to his first officer had happened very quickly. First Officer Jae Dahn was nothing if not predictable. Every night at 10:45 he went to the galley just before it closed for the night and made himself a large black coffee. Jae Dahn had often said that one of the perks of being at sea was good coffee and all the sugar you could put in it. Sugar was one of the many commodities that were deemed luxuries in North Korea. Jae Dahn would return to the bridge, place the ship in autopilot, and work a crossword puzzle or some other type of mental stimulation while his time on watch passed. How the man wasn't twenty pounds' overweight and toothless was always a point of amusement.

Lee looked at the floor and estimated that most of his first officer's coffee was now on the floor of the bridge. Lee wasn't laughing now.

Sounding general quarters on a ship was always taken very seriously. Either your ship was in great peril or it was a drill. In either case, it was meant to get you to your station immediately. The captain pushed the button to sound the general quarters alarm and then, using the ship's public address system, verbally ordered the crew to report to the bridge. After one minute with no response, Lee's stomach turned over ever so slightly. After three minutes without communication with any of the crew, he reached over and turned the alarm off. Nobody was coming. He was alone on a 54,000-ton merchant vessel traveling at 22 knots in the middle of the Pacific. Alone. With a gut wrenching heave, Lee's coffee joined his first officer's on the floor of the bridge.

Captain Lee checked the newly installed navigation system and saw they were on a course of 091° degrees taking them thirteen hundred miles north of the Hawaiian Islands. That was right where he should be. Lee moved to the radio suite and noticed something very odd. The signal strength indicator for the ship's transmitter was in the red. It wasn't really in the red. It was at zero strength. His radio's receiver was in the green. Although this was new equipment and he honestly hadn't spent the time he should have getting to know the system, green was still good and red was still very, very bad.

Like most ships, the *Shooting Star* had redundant systems and spare parts on board. Those spare parts were normally there for his engineer to troubleshoot and replace. Lee was fairly certain he was not going to be able to count on his engineer's services.

So many changes had been done to the ship in drydock it was almost difficult to fathom not only how it had all been accomplished, but why? As Lee turned to leave the bridge he noticed something odd about the hatch leading out off the bridge. Up in the corner of the hatch was a new device of some sort. Standing on his toes to get a better look, the device appeared to be some sort of locking mechanism. It had a slightly recessed hole in which a deadbolt seemed to reside. On the top were what appeared to be three LED lights? One was bright green, one was a faint yellow and the third was a faint red. He grabbed the stool that was kept in the bride for just such reasons. Ships were built for men of average height or taller. He was neither. As he reached up to further examine the device, the light that had been bright green only a moment before, changed to amber. The effect on Lee was electric. He recoiled from the device as if he'd been shocked. A tamper-switch on a lock? After a moment the light turned back to green. This was very odd. Lee approached the device again. As before, the light turned to amber as he reached for it. Lee was stunned. With everything that had happened in the past few weeks and all the changes that had been done to his ship in drydock, he shouldn't have been. He needed to find out what happened to his crew.

Freighters normally carry a compliment of six officers and twelve crewmen. This normally broke out to be the captain, chief, second officer, boatswain, and several able seamen.

The crew's berthing areas, or state rooms, were four decks below the bridge. Like most ships, his officers enjoyed somewhat better accommodations than the rest of the ship's company. With many of the more routine duties accomplished during the day shift, most of his crew would have been in their berths at 11:00 p.m. No sense in delaying the process.

Captain Lee headed down to the crew deck. He opened the first door he came to. Lan Van, the ship's engine room maintenance officer was right where he should have been just in worse shape than he should have been. He was very dead and whatever had killed him was the same as First Officer Jae Dahn.

Lee proceeded down the passageway, opening doors and finding most of his crew dead in their bunks. The ship's cook was in the head, pitched forward off the commode and into the sink. The only one of his crew that appeared to know something was amiss had been Cargo Officer Hyun Su Rang. Lee found him collapsed over a clipboard that contained the ships manifest and load data. Perhaps in his capacity as chief mate he had read a Material Safety Data Sheet (MSDS) along the way that described the symptoms. An MSDS listed a material, and all its particular hazards including flammability, toxicity, and any other pertinent information. Listed below the hazards were all the ways to handle each specific issue mentioned.

Hyun's duties had included the responsibility for the ship's stability and special care for cargoes that are dangerous, hazardous or harmful. In the case of the *Shooting Star's* cargo, it was often deemed illegal by the United Nations and several other countries. Lee smiled briefly because he knew that quite often it had been.

Lee approached the ship's officer suites. Lee's Chief Engineer Wan Hoe, hadn't faired any better. He and the chief had spent many hours together talking about everything from life on their ship to the future of ship design. His engineer had held the same rank as he did but with a separate list of responsibilities. His responsibilities were great in both scope and importance.

While the captain took responsibility for navigation and deck operations, the chief engineer took responsibility for engine room and maintenance. The chief had not been happy since they had arrived in the Dalian shipyard. He was very distressed over the changes to his ship. But, like the captain, had learned the hard way not to ask questions. They had decided to talk about other things. Up to the point they arrived in the shipyard, the only subjects the two never discussed were politics or life at home. The subjects were far too depressing and with the new regime in power, far too dangerous. Then they had faced the very strange changes in their vessel. They agreed to add that to the list of taboo subjects. Much the two had learned, could be communicated, with far greater safety, with just a glance. He would be missed.

Captain Lee had looked in each cabin and the results had been the same. His crew had all died very quickly and without struggle or sound. It was apparent to him that they had been poisoned, but with what? His medical officer would have known immediately. Although he had suffered the same fate as the others, he could still help. His stateroom was filled with all manner of medical books.

Surely in all these books Lee could find the answer.

CHAPTER 34

BOATSS

Mitch had almost literally bumped into Rick as they met at the security desk at Langley. Rick smiled and said, "Not today," while placing a guiding hand on Mitch's shoulder he walked him right back out the front door. "We're having lunch over at the BOATSS office if that's okay with you." They really couldn't talk about the why they had changed their plans until they were back in a secure location so they talked about what they could do this weekend.

Gina had ordered Thai food for everyone and they ate in the conference room. Rick asked where Ramón was and Jewels told him, "Out to lunch." Mitch almost coughed up a lung laughing. No truer words had ever been spoken.

Mitch grinned but with a somewhat serious tone told Jewels, "You guys know that at some point you're going to have to let him in on what's going on." "Way to spoil lunch, Mitch," groaned Gina.

Jewels looked at Mitch and shrugged, "I tried to tell him last night, but he didn't want to hear anything about it, maybe after basketball season."

Rick nodded his understanding. "Alright Jewels, show us your stuff." Nobody said a word...then Gina laughed, Jewels blushed, and Mitch buried his fist into his friend's shoulder.

"What are you guys, eight years old?" Rick asked.

The verbal gaff had broken the tension of the moment and they got down to business. Gina showed Rick how they had found the original sound and then its subsequent match three weeks earlier. Rick called his boss. "Boss, it's complicated to explain but it's a 97% match. Yes, I'll tell them." He hung up.

"He says he knew you two would work it out and good job."

It was just past 1:00 p.m. when the girls decided it was time to head downstairs for a coffee run. The guys stayed behind to work on Mitch's almost forgotten mystery satellite signal.

"Mitch," Rick started, "the reason I was having you come up our way for lunch was that besides showing off my cubicle of an office I wanted to show you some information you might find interesting. We had an overhead asset grab some happy snaps of the Dalian shipyard yesterday and compared them to a few weeks ago. Here's what our analyst found."

This wasn't Mitch's area of expertise and his facial expression let Rick know he had no idea what he was looking at.

"Look here," said Rick as he pointed to the image of two large cargo vessels berthed right next to each other in drydock. "We know this one on the right is the *Oceans Queen*. She got here just over four weeks ago. To the best of our knowledge she's had nothing obvious done to her. The ship on the left, the *Shooting Star*, showed up here about a week later. It appeared that several areas of the *Shooting Star* were covered with tarps. We thought perhaps it was due to the weather, but it's been relatively nice over there for this time of year."

"That's it?"

"Well, no, a couple things are strange about this ship. We looked back at the previous week or so of pictures and it was in none of the afternoon shots. The overhead assets are programmed to take pictures at first light and late in the afternoon. The angles are better and normally all ships are in port by 6:00 p.m. local at the latest. The *Shooting Star* isn't there on the afternoon pass but is there first thing the next morning. That would mean it came in after dark." He stared at the images on the screen. "Not only that, notice it's 6:30 a.m. local and the ship's already covered with tarps and the water has been pumped out of the drydock. I'd say, looking at this, they began work on this ship the minute she pulled in and tied up her lines."

Jewels and Gina walked in with fresh coffee from the cart downstairs. "Anyone need a pick-me up?"

"Our heroines have arrived!" bellowed Rick.

Jewels took a few swallows of her coffee and glanced at the screen the guys were staring at.

"What are you guys working on? What ships are those?"

"That's the *Shooting Star* on the left. It's flagged as North Korean. We took this picture of it in the Dalian drydock a little less than three weeks ago."

As Jewels walked away, slowly sipping her coffee, she paused, turned back and, to no one in particular said, "Oh, the ship that came in after dark a couple weeks back."

Rick nodded and continued, "For about a week our overhead assets hadn't seen anything due to a combination of crappy weather and bad luck. Then four days ago the weather broke and we could see that the *Shooting Star*, or the ship we thought was the *Shooting Star* was no longer in the left drydock."

"Where was it?" asked Jewels

Rick scratched his head and in exasperation said, "We're not sure how, but now it's in the right drydock and the ship that was previously there, is gone."

"That's rather implausible don't you think? How can you tell which ship is which?" asked Gina.

"Oh, that's easy enough," replied Rick. "Each ship has its own unique transponder signal."

CHAPTER 35

The Shooting Star

From everything Captain Lee had found so far, it would appear his crew had been gassed with a cyanide based gas. It was fast acting and dissipated relatively quickly. Lee had gone back to his room and thought about why or how he had been spared. Whoever was doing this obviously had access to the onboard computer system. He noticed when the ship was in Dalian hundreds of feet of blue communication wiring had been strung throughout the ship. Perhaps they had tied all of the ship's systems to the computer?

If the ship's environmental systems had been tied to the computer system whoever was at the controls could have, in theory, controlled not only the temperature of the air into the crew's quarters, but also the dampers in the system that controlled the amount of air that flows into the quarters. All the operator would need to have done was to shut the inflow of air into his cabin for a short time. By isolating his cabin from the rest of the ship, he would have been spared the fate of the rest of his crew.

With everyone else dead, Lee felt no reason to limit his investigation of the newly installed systems on the ship. He had seen the massive pumps being installed while they were in drydock but had never explored the system in its entirety. While in the engine room he also noticed two new pipes that came through the rear bulkhead of the engine room. The only thing to the rear of the engine room, at that height, was container hold seven and eight. One pipe had red arrows indicating it supplied water to the common manifold in the engine room; the other had red arrows that indicated it supplied water to perhaps a pump in container hold seven or eight. The supply end of that pipe went through the engine room bulkhead and sat level with the floor about twenty feet forward of the hatch.

Lee climbed up the two decks, to a level at which he could then walk aft to the holds. As he had almost expected at this point, container holds seven and eight had been gutted and a sixth pump, although somewhat smaller than the others, had been installed in container hold eight. Shaking his head in a mixture of awe and disbelief, he went back down to the engine room.

From each of the massive pumps rearward, the discharge lines from each pump extended through the forward bulkhead of the engine room and connected to a central manifold which had a total of eight lines. Each line had a specific code. Along with a large red arrow indicating direction of flow, each pipe had a number that correlated to what pump it came from and what position left to right it was attached to the manifold. At the bottom of the common manifold were two smaller lines that split off, one to starboard and one to port that exited through two new holes on the engine room floor. Lee looked at the quality of work on the system and nodded in appreciation. The guys who had done the welding and fitting work had done a top notch job. Even the welds that connected the sections of pipe had been ground down smooth before they were painted.

Lee had seen the exterior of his ship just briefly on that second visit to his vessel while she was still in drydock and had seen the large nozzles on either side of the ship's stern. The nozzles protruded to the rear of the ship just in front of the maneuvering propellers. He could also see that on at least one side of the ship, near the keel, was a newly attached synthetic blister shaped device.

He had drawn a blank until, just as he was walking away, had heard the word sonar.

As he walked back from the rear of the engine room, he noticed the door of the engine room now had some type of electrical actuator on the engine room side of the hatch. Apparently the door could now be closed and locked remotely. How had he missed that? He looked around at all three container holds and marveled at the transformation. All of the walls that used to separate the holds had been removed. The only thing remaining were support columns and some lateral bracing. It looked like the inside of an oil tanker. With the exception of the addition of the five large pumps and their associated plumbing, the forward holds were completely empty. The ship was eerily quiet as he made his way to the upward decks of the ship.

Lee was just getting back to the wheelhouse when most of his questions about whether someone was monitoring the cameras were seemingly answered. At exactly 9:00 p.m. he felt a vibration and heard a hum on the ship he had never experienced. He checked his gauges and could see that his ship was not only slowing it seemed to be settling lower in the water. For a moment he panicked. He was sinking!

He began running down five decks to the stairs above container hold five. With each deck he descended he could hear the sound of the pumps increasing. He opened the hatch to the hold and saw one of the most frightening scenes a ship captain can see. His ship was quickly filling with water. He was beginning to get quite concerned when suddenly all of the pumps stopped. For a moment the ship was quiet. It was 9:10 p.m. The normal sounds of the engine were somewhat muted by the water that now filled the ship and absorbed much of the vibration normally transmitted through the hull. For the briefest moment he reflected on how nice it was to have a ship that made very little sound.

At exactly 9:15 p.m. the pumps abruptly started again. In addition to jumping because the noise had startled him, he was immediately thrown to his right as the ship suddenly lurched forward. Grabbing a handrail, Lee glanced over the port side and estimated the ship had easily gone from its previous 10 knot speed when he'd left the bridge to what was clearly currently closer to 15 knots and still accelerating. He leaned into the motion of the ship and began jogging back up the five decks to the bridge.

Several minutes later, and rather out of breath from both the climb and the whole experience unfolding before him, he reached the bridge. Lee couldn't believe his eyes. According to the gauges he was traveling at close to 32 knots. That was almost 37 miles per hour! He was traveling faster than most naval ships. He tried to steer but the helm wasn't taking inputs from the wheel in the bridge. It was probably best at this point. He had no experience handling a ship of this size at that speed. Someone somewhere had their hands on the controls of his ship. He hoped they knew what they were doing.

The cycle of pumping the hold full of water and then discharging it through the pumps occurred several more times over the next few hours. It was obvious the ship's new water-jet propulsion system was being tested by someone. Lee happened to be back at container hold five's hatch when he heard the pumps come on again. He waited several minutes for the hold to fill. It hadn't filled more than perhaps three feet yet the boat had accelerated at an even faster rate than during previous tests.

CHAPTER 36

Kesheh Research Facility

It was a big day on level six (Hot Wind) at the facility. Major Harem Fallahi was to test his software in the most advanced simulation to date and he was like a young boy unwrapping a gift. He could see on his monitors that the testing of the drone ship's software had begun. He watched the gauges on his screen rise and fall as each test was carried out and for the most part had been very happy with the results. The pump's temperatures had remained within the required parameters and the stability control that compensated for the increased speed was also functioning within parameters. At the speed the ship would be traveling, turning would be controlled with the maneuvering propellers and with very light rudder inputs.

The feedback from the system confirmed his thoughts that the higher the boat was in the water the more sensitive to the slightest input the control would be. He briefly exited the program, wrote a few dozen lines of code that linked the draft, or depth, that the boat was sitting in the water to the sensitivity of the control surface that controlled the direction and stability of the ship. He hit "Save" and re-entered the program.

With the final test completed, the ship was at only fifteen feet of draft. His subroutine was working flawlessly and his model was performing perfectly. At this point of the program the ship should be accurately reflecting the weight of its manifested cargo. He opened a tab, selected the manifest for this exercise, and hit "Enter."

Several thousand miles away, about 150 miles off the California coast, the pumps in container hold #3 and #7 turned on pulling seawater into the ship. The pumps ran for exactly 10 minutes then stopped. The *Shooting Star*, the ship that had successfully transited the entire Pacific Ocean masquerading as the *Oceans Queen*, was now sitting in the water at exactly the right height above the waves to give the impression she was fully and correctly loaded with her manifest for Los Angeles.

Major Harem Fallahi exited the program after returning ship operations to "Normal" and thought this was possibly the best day of his life.

CHAPTER 37

Shooting Star

It had been two days since Lee's last excursion on his ship. He had spent the previous day reading and sitting in his wheel house. The ship was obviously being controlled by someone or something, perhaps it was all automated. He didn't know and at this point didn't really care that much. Lee felt powerless to do anything. He was used to being controlled and under control.

Somehow this time it was different. He felt he was being used.

Captain Lee was pretty sure whatever he was bringing to the port of Los Angeles wasn't something expected. He was thinking about his options when he realized he probably had less than six hours to get this thing figured out. He was only three hours from the turn to starboard that all the ships made near San Francisco. At his current course, it seemed the illusion of normalcy was going to be maintained as long as possible.

Lee went down to the machine shop and found a pair of bolt cutters. He carefully wrapped them in a towel so as to eliminate the possibility someone could see him on the cameras carrying bolt cutters up to the deck. At least he no longer had to wonder about the cameras? That was the one thing about today he knew for sure.

Once on deck, Lee went all the way forward to a row of containers just aft of and above the new secure hold he had discovered on an earlier excursion. He cut the lock and swung open the right door. As his eyes adjusted to the light he quickly came to the realization that the container appeared empty. The floor of the container seemed almost new. He tripped stepping up into the container, fumbled for a hand hold, and while changing hands with his flashlight, succeeded in dropping the bolt cutters.

Interestingly enough, the bolt cutters made a thump when they landed instead of the usual bone jarring clang he'd become accustomed to over years of working around these containers.

Lee crouched down and examined the floor more closely. Not only did the floor appear seamless; as he swept his hand across the floor, it was almost perfectly smooth. He looked at his hand in the light. It was an almost shiny gray color. It couldn't be... He pulled out his pocket knife and scratched the floor. A thin ribbon of dull material curled up behind his knife. To his astonishment it appeared the floor of the container was covered with at least a quarter inch of lead from one end to the other. In order for it to fit the way it did in the container, it had to have been poured into the container at a foundry. It was all starting to come together now. The secrecy of the visit to the Dalian drydock, the ship modifications for speed and now what appeared to be lead shielding. All Lee hadn't seen was the device itself.

As Lee left the container, he glanced upwards to the ceiling of the container and could see some type of thick material had been affixed to the ceiling. It was wired to a small box in the corner of the container. Like so many of the devices he had seen on the ship, this one had a red LED. He didn't want to believe what he was thinking but after checking all the other containers and finding the same flooring and materials on the ceilings, he had reached his conclusion. Something was in the new secure forward hold that somebody didn't want anybody to find.

It was getting late and Lee needed some tea. He had dragged most of the ship's company into the freezer the day after he'd found them. It had been bugging him for a day now but he couldn't help but feel that somewhere on the ship he'd missed someone. It was weak but there was definitely the smell of death coming from somewhere below deck.

One of the significant benefits to being the captain on the same ship for as many years as he had been on the *Shooting Star*, was that you knew all, or at least most, of the ship's secrets. Due to the nature of his usual illegal cargo, he had always been curious as to where he would hide in the event of a search by either a United Nation's vessel enforcing the embargo or perhaps a situation such as pirates.

On one particularly boring evening, just over a year ago, Lee had been out walking the forward deck and found a hatch at the very front part of the deck. It was apparent it hadn't been used for many years and had been painted shut. He presumed that at one point it had been used for a bow chain or rope. Nobody else on the crew had anything pressing to do so they agreed to make an evening of it and set upon opening the hatch.

It had taken just over an hour of scraping and prying and even some heat from a propane torch but with a rusty groan the mystery hatch opened. It was not the storage locker Lee and the crew had anticipated. Much to his surprise it was an access hatch to a maintenance space directly behind the bow of the ship. It made sense. If the ship was underway and sustained damage to her bow that penetrated the hull, a damage control team would need to get into that part of the ship to fix the breech. The ladder went down to a small triangular section of deck that extended aft approximately six feet. At that point, it was the forward most bulkhead of the ship. Looking up and aft he saw another smaller access hatch at chest height that seemed to allow access into the unused void in front of cargo hold two.

Enough traveling down memory lane, Lee had a plan. Before they had ripped the heart out of his ship he would often inspect all the hatches on the ship. He remembered distinctly a hatch that led from container hold two forward to the void. Assuming the workers hadn't welded it shut he should be able to access the forward deck hatch, crawl through the access hatch to the void, and then open the hatch to the new secure storage from the back side. With the time pressure that the shipwrights at Dalian were under, he figured he had a 60/40 chance of finding the hatch in good working order.

Lee grabbed two flashlights and a small breaker bar and headed forward.

He waited until 10:00 p.m. when he usually made his evening inspections and headed out. Lee mumbled to himself as he walked, "Pay no attention to me cameras, nothing to see here. Every member of my crew is dead except me and I'm still making my rounds like nothing's changed." He tried smiling. He couldn't.

Lee arrived at the forward deck hatch. After its initial discovery he'd had the crew lubricate the hinge mechanism and clean the watertight seal. From all appearances at least, it still looked like it hadn't been opened in many years.

He opened the hatch and climbed down the ladder to the small triangular deck. Using the breaker bar he was able to open the small access hatch to the void area forward of the cargo hold. Lee could hear the blood pounding in his ears and was thinking that for the first time in his life he was feeling a touch claustrophobic. The second hatch opened much easier than he had anticipated. Now he smiled. All those lonely nights of working out in the small gym onboard were going to pay off in the next five minutes. He hoisted himself up and through the small hatch landing with relative ease in the void.

With his first flashlight growing dim, he switched on his second and walked slowly and cautiously toward the forward bulkhead of container hold number two. As Lee approached the hatch leading into the hold, he paused. His mind was racing now. Whatever was on the other side of this hatch his government had taken great pains to hide from the world. He knew he would never rest until he found out what had been so great a secret that it required the murder of his entire crew.

Lee easily turned the wheel in the center of the hatch. When he heard the latch's release, he gave the hatch a pull and it began to move. Captain Lee felt he'd seen almost everything in his short life. Lee had witnessed piles of decaying bodies in villages, video of his own family's torture, and other heinous visions and acts he had long tried to push down in his memories.

With the hatch yet barely open an inch, the horribly nauseous smell of death and decomposing flesh whooshed out. The smell enveloped him, immediately filling the entire hold. The overwhelming stench drove the air from his lungs. He struggled to take a breath under his pea coat but the smell was already there. He took a long slow breath and peered into the hold.

The first thing he noticed was that lights were on in the hold, illuminating everything before him. What he saw made him recoil in abject horror. Beyond the edge of the hatch, and out of line of sight of the hold, he began heaving and didn't stop for several minutes. He hated vomiting. It was made worse by the fact that after each painful wretch he was forced to inhale more of the putrid air surrounding him. With his eyes watering proportionately from the horrendous smell and the tears that were filling his eyes from grief, he looked back into the hold and tried to take in what he was seeing.

Before Lee were two standard size cargo containers, one a rusty red and the other a light blue. The two containers sat about six feet apart and were connected to each other by three large bundles of cable. Surrounding and on top of the containers were what had to be over two hundred dead workmen from the Dalian shipyard. These poor men hadn't had a chance. They had most likely been herded, probably at gun point, into the secure hold and locked in. Lee briefly hoped they had died quickly. Glancing at the various positions of the bodies, it wasn't likely. Their faces, although now somewhat bloated, all appeared to have the same characteristics of the dead men on his crew. Many seemed to have known or suspected what was happening and tried to get away from whatever had dispensed the gas.

This must be why they hadn't wanted Lee or his crew, anywhere near the ship while it was in drydock. Lee had seen pictures of nuclear weapons in school. Seven or so of them could fit on one missile. Whatever this device was, it took up two shipping containers to make it work. Lee was no expert, but this had to be a very large device.

Lee had seen enough; it was time to go. He glanced forward, as he was closing the hatch, what he saw made his heart skip a beat. On the far wall, pointing straight at him was a camera. The light on the camera was a solid green. He knew he needed to somehow gather his strength and move quickly. His life would depend on it.

Pyongyang, North Korea

Although working literally in the next calendar day, two intelligence officers were watching the live feed coming from the *Shooting Star*. It was time. They picked up the phone and called General Yŏng in the room across from them in the command center.

"Yes?" The general's aid curtly answered the line.

"Please tell the general we need to meet with him very soon." "And the reason for this meeting?" asked the generals aid. "Please tell him that our friend has seen the containers."

15 miles off the Coast of California

Captain Lee realized he had to act quickly. As he'd investigated his suspicions, it was clear this was not his ship any longer. He ran up the stairs to the bridge and as he rounded the corner he could see the hatch to the bridge swinging closed. He dove forward with the bar but missed. As he lay there he heard the loud click of the newly installed automatic locks. He was locked off his own bridge.

Lee calculated he had only minutes to get himself off the ship. As he made his plans he came to the realization that whoever was behind this might still have someone on board or be watching him on the cameras.

Lee could see the ship had made the turn south and was currently cruising parallel to the coast. He estimated he was still a good twenty miles off the coast but knew the time had come. He ran back to his cabin and filled his pockets with several personal items and ran back up to the starboard side lifeboat. His brain was screaming at him to not risk lowering the lifeboat with the ship still traveling at over 22 knots. He could just make out some of the outer islands off the California coast. Now was the time. He climbed up the ladder, pulled off the cover and climbed into the lifeboat. He hit the electric winch control and waited, nothing happened. He hit the button again with the same result. Lee unlocked the manual release and started winding as fast as he could. He needed to switch arms twice but sooner than he'd expected he was perched just a foot above the waves. This was it. He braced for what he knew was going to be a very rough ride and hit the release.

Immediately the bow of the lifeboat tried to dive beneath the waves. The sudden jolt pitched Captain Lee forward in the boat, momentarily knocking the wind out of him. He knew he had seconds to jam the rudder hard over to port so he wouldn't be caught by the edge of the freighter as it passed high above him. After a few bumps he was adrift in the bubbling wake of his former ship.

Captain Lee started the motor on the lifeboat and pointed it toward shore. He reached into the chart cabinet and found it empty. Typical. Not a serious issue at the moment, he could see the coast of California and what should be the coastline of Los Angeles. Due in part to the morning fog in the area and his considerable distance from land, he could not make out the islands he knew were there. He pointed his lifeboat toward the rising sun and turned the boat's throttle up full. The wind was at his back so he was making good progress for about five minutes. Then the motor quit. He glanced down in a panic and saw the fuel gauge was indicating less than zero. He was adrift and heading toward the California coast.

Lee had been putting some thought into how to get the American Navy's attention. He had been in his lifeboat for over three hours and had a pretty good idea where he was, but didn't have a radio or anything else to signal with. Someone had apparently anticipated his abandon ship plan and removed all of the emergency provisions, radios, and signaling equipment from the lifeboat. They had also poked a good size hole in the boat. Luckily it was above the water line and although the boat was slowly taking on water he had been able to slow it considerably with some cloth he found under a bench seat.

Lee had a passing thought and then dismissed it. The waters in this part of the Pacific were renowned for their great white shark population. Setting the lifeboat on fire wasn't in the cards. What would an American do? He closed his eyes and imagined himself in America. No way. It couldn't be that easy. Lee reached into his pocket and pulled out his cell phone. He thought, what the hell, and dialed 9-1-1, and waited. It was ringing, that was a good sign, right? A man picked up the line and in the most bored voice imaginable said, "Los Angeles County 911, what's the nature of your emergency?"

Captain Lee didn't think the operator would believe his story about the container ship with the nuclear weapon on board so he went with: "I'm approximately one mile off the coast of the Farallon Islands and my lifeboat is sinking." He thought for a moment and added, "Operator, there are large sharks circling around my boat." He thought it better to go with the more plausible, yet slightly more dramatic, story at this point.

Kesheh Research Facility

On his computer screen the major could see the blinking update from the *Shooting Star* as she made the turn to starboard after passing waypoint #11 at 22 knots, Major Harem Fallahi entered the last two sets of GPS coordinates into his system. First for waypoint #12 he entered:

32°28'1.12" N
117°25'55.59" W
For the next and final waypoint he entered:
32°39'30.36" N
117° 9'32.21" W

He pressed the Enter key. He entered the coded cipher that he had committed to memory over twenty years before for just something this important.

He very carefully typed:
1 t 5 M Y 5 T 1 (k M @ h M 0 0 d
He had told no one his passkey:

I-T-S * M-Y * S-T-I-C-K * M-A-H-M-O-O-D.

Harem had created the computer that sat before him now from parts in a box. He'd taught the computer its very own special language. He'd designed this system, his "son" as he saw it, to do specific tasks in a specific order. He imagined that someday it would feel this way watching his human son at his first soccer match. His "son" was a super star. His "son" then asked him two very succinct questions. The first was:

ARE YOU SURE?

Harem grinned. He had written the program himself and decided at the time, "Why not have some fun?" He had written the code to give him two prompts. He stared at the screen for a moment. He glanced up at General ShahAb Tehrani who was beaming down at him like a proud father. The selections he had written reflected the youth he never had:

ABORT! / MOST DEFINITELY!!!

He moved the cursor over to the box that read, MOST DEFINITELY!!! He highlighted the box.

With an approving nod from the general, he clicked the right mouse key.

He had so carefully written the code that even pressing the incorrect mouse key would abort the task. LOCK? was his next prompt. The general nodded in the affirmative. The major noticed the general seemed to have a look in his eye that Harem hadn't seen since his childhood. Was it the man from Hamas who had smiled that smile? No, it couldn't be.

He clicked YES with the left mouse key.

As Harem had written the program to do, the monitor screens in front of him became awash in meaningless code. Seconds later, just as he had programmed, he could hear the hard drive scramming itself.

Harem was very proud of himself. He smiled; he'd done it just as he had promised all those months ago. Uncle Mahmood would be so very proud of him! His test of the new drone system had been a complete success. The simulation was complete. To be perfectly honest, Harem had anticipated some cheering. He heard nothing except the computer's hard drive spinning itself uselessly in its case. Then he realized something was wrong. Suddenly, he remembered where and when he'd seen that look. Major Harem Fallahi looked up into the eyes of a grinning madman. The bullet entered Major Harem Fallahi's brain through his left eye.

Six thousand six hundred and eight nautical miles away, the *Shooting Star*, still successfully masquerading as the *Oceans Queen*, turned south at waypoint #12 to her new course and waypoint #13. She was now only sixty miles from the California coast. Her fully automated systems were performing flawlessly. The two pumps in her belly slowly came to life again and with each passing minute the *Shooting Star* settled slightly lower into the water.

CHAPTER 38

USS Connecticut

"ARSENAL OF THE NATION"

Below the cold water of the Pacific, Commander Trent Briggs, Commanding Officer of the *USS Connecticut*, was thrilled to be back at sea. They had made it back from their last cruise in mid-December. Unlike the larger, but fewer in number ballistic missile boats, attack subs like the *Connecticut* had a one crew, one boat rotation. With budget cutbacks, the *Connecticut* headed back to sea after only three months in port instead of the usual six. The shorter time in port was hard on the crew and even harder on their families. The new three-month rotation cycles would be the new normal until money could be freed up to fund what crews were now rather sarcastically calling "currency tours."

Most skills on a submarine are considered perishable in that they need to be used frequently or they will diminish. Starting last budget cycle, ships and subs were going out to sea just long enough to keep their crews' skills current in their various crew positions. It wasn't just Trent's base, Naval Base Kitsap; the entire navy was trying to operate with significantly diminished funding.

Over the past few years, Trent kept in touch with several colleagues at Naval Base San Diego. According to his friends in San Diego, as of last month, only one carrier group, the Reagan Battle Group, was at sea. The Reagan was on maneuvers with her six ship group in the southern Pacific and the two cruisers were up north patrolling the waters off the Aleutians. Instead of being on deployment in various areas of the Pacific, all the other ships that normally took turns home porting at San Diego were all in port at the same time. In real numbers it meant that 75% of the combat vessels normally assigned to Naval Base San Diego were all now competing for space in the crowded Port of San Diego.

While in port, both the *Connecticut*'s crew and the boat itself caught up on needed maintenance tasks. This time it had been more mundane things, such as doctor and dentist appointments for the crew and scheduled software upgrades and reactor maintenance for the boat.

Trent had been fortunate this year in that he'd actually been able to spend the Christmas holidays with his family. It was a rare event and he had savored every moment. Since the first of the year, He'd spent the majority of his time ashore catching up on one of the always dreaded administrational duties required of every senior officer in the armed forces, attending PowerPoint briefings. The briefings covered everything from upcoming deployment schedules, budgetary concerns, crew morale and welfare, health and safety, boat and weapon upgrades, communication issues, and his personal favorites: writing the *Connecticut*'s post operational cruise report, reviewing his officers' fitness reports and enlisted crew members' evaluations. Briggs' favorite task, which he took a lot of good natured ribbing about, was his crew's annual performance evaluations. In his opinion, his entire boat was filled with top notch personnel. It had been several years since he'd approved the firewalling of all of their ratings. This time ashore, he was able to attend a briefing he'd been both looking forward to and dreading at the same time, his first of several retirement briefings.

Captain Trent W. Briggs was the commanding officer of one of the deadliest class of submarines on the planet. The Seawolf class submarine was designed specifically to combat the threat of large numbers of advanced

Soviet ballistic missile submarines such as the Typhoon-class which had the ability to launch nuclear capable ICBMs into targets of its choosing anywhere in the world and attack submarines such as the Akula class which were a particular threat to any ship in the oceans of the world, including his.

Briggs' crew took some comfort in the fact that the Seawolf class submarines were built both for lethality and survivability. Seawolf hulls were constructed from HY-100 steel, which is stronger than the HY-80 steel employed in the construction of previous classes of submarines. The benefit was twofold; they could withstand not only the tremendous water pressure at greater depths while either hunting or lying in wait for their prey, but also better survive the pressures brought to bear in underwater explosions. Although the exact diving depth of the Connecticut was a closely guarded secret, Briggs had taken the boat down past 2000 feet on several occasions to avoid detection from several ships that had been actively looking for them.

This submarine was larger, faster, and significantly quieter than any other class of American submarine and also carried more weapons and twice as many torpedo tubes, for a total of 8. When the mission called for it, the *Connecticut* could be equipped to carry as many as 50 UGM-109 Tomahawk cruise missiles for attacking land and sea surface targets. The *Connecticut*, as was the case of all submarines, was affected by the load out of equipment placed onboard. The amount of weapons and crew affected the buoyancy and thus operational parameters of any mission. To ensure the Seawolf class subs were the most lethal hunters in the sea, the ship had been outfitted with the more advanced ARCI Modified AN/BSY-2 combat system, which included a new, larger sonar array, a wide aperture array (WAA), and a new towed-array sonar. Briggs was quite confident that if he could find it, he could kill it.

As the *Connecticut's* commander, Briggs knew his boat was one of the four stealthiest submarines in the US Navy. The navy considered stealthiness the Seawolf class sub's greatest asset. Briggs personally felt *Connecticut's* true ace in the hole was its tremendous power. The *Connecticut* was powered by a S6W nuclear reactor which gave him almost instantaneous control over 52,000 horse power (HP). All that power was connected to an almost silent pump jet propulsion system that pushed water out of a nozzle assembly at the back of his boat. He often simplified it for his non-submarine friends by describing the *Connecticut* as a 52,000 HP Jet Ski that carried 150 passengers, made almost no sound, traveled underwater at over 25 miles per hour, never had to come up for food or fuel, and could shoot torpedoes and missiles at his command. He was a frequent winner in the "Cool Job" category.

Briggs split his time ashore at his apartment in Bremerton, Washington, near Naval Base Kitsap and visiting his wife in San Diego. Naval Base Kitsap is the US Navy base located on the Kitsap Peninsula in Washington State. It was created in 2004 by merging the former Naval Station Bremerton with Naval Submarine Base Bangor. The Mission of Naval Base Kitsap is to serve as the home base for the navy's fleet throughout West Puget Sound and to provide base operating services, including support for both surface ships and Fleet Ballistic Missile and other nuclear submarines having their home ports at Bremerton and Bangor.

The time spent on leave visiting his wife of just over ten years now, the former Stacy Katherine Anderson, had been amazing. They met at a fund raising event in the spring of 2004 for the then still fledgling Wounded Warriors Project. She was bright, passionate about helping others, and a side benefit, apparently cared a great deal for the then young Lieutenant Commander Briggs. They got married six months later, again squeezing the event between cruises. Two years after they were married and somewhere in between deployments and cruises in 2008, Stacy got pregnant with his now almost eight-year-old, Grace. Two years later, Trent decided to surprise the girls and come home for a week of leave in the middle of his deployment. With little planning and throwing caution to the wind, the two set in motion Trent's son, Alex, being born nine months later.

As was typical in the life of a career navy man, Briggs only caught snippets of their first years of life when he wasn't at sea. He had used every technology available to stay in touch with Stacy and had been there for his wife and children as often as he could if not physically, virtually. Trent was certainly very appreciative of the incredible changes in technology from when he first joined the navy. Back in the early 90's on his first cruise there hadn't been video conferencing, chat, cell phones, or Skype. Many of his shipmates would, depending on their missions, be out of touch with loved ones for many weeks or even months.

Stacey had just finished up her Master's degree in Counseling at San Diego State and been working for the past three months to sell the couple's home in the town of La Mesa just east of San Diego. They purchased the home back in 2005 before the housing market imploded. At the time, Trent had been assigned to the Naval Warfare Center at Naval Base San Diego. In the four years he'd been assigned there, Trent had taken two deployments to the Persian Gulf to get that out of the way. With the housing market the way it was, when the assignment came up to Kitsap they agreed to keep the house as a rental.

Two years ago, when Stacy decided to get her Master's degree, she was still a California resident for tuition purposes and with Trent's deployments and lengthy cruises, returning to San Diego sure beat the rain and clouds of the Northwest. After sprucing up the house from several years of renters, it had almost been like being home again. Stacy's friend and neighbor, Diane, watched the kids while she was at school and for a couple hours here and there if Stacy needed some kid free time to study or just take a deep breath.

After almost two years of separation and her Master's degree safely packed in a moving box, Stacy was thrilled. She closed on the house, by herself, three weeks ago and had been renting it back from the owners until Trent had gone back to sea.

It was Captain Briggs' last tour of his twenty-three-year career. He had mixed feelings as most career military folks do. He hoped he would find something purposeful to do with his time. When he talked like that to Stacy she would always do her best valley girl impersonation and say, "OMG! Hello? Kids that think you're like the center of the universe, duh."

At the end of this tour, Trent planned to return to Naval Base Kitsap, meet up with Stacy, the kids, and both sets of parents, retire with all the pomp and circumstance he rightly deserved, and then join his family outside of Sand Point, Idaho. He would miss the sea but their newly built 2800 square foot log home north of Sand Point was on sixty-three acres of hunters' paradise and less than five miles from Stacy's parents' house. He decided he would find something he liked, kids notwithstanding, declare it "purposeful," and enjoy the rest of his life.

Captain Briggs had always been an avid hunter. He learned his hunting skills from his father who was a third generation rancher and skilled hunter. Briggs could track almost anything and had been able to lend his skills to various State Park Rangers when they were involved in a real life search and rescue or just doing some weekend training. His skills and abilities had transitioned well to the fast attack boats. He always had to be ahead of his prey mentally and anticipate their next move. He had a reputation, over the years, for making the right calls at the right time.

The *USS Connecticut* was in its final week of assisting the Columbian government with some drug interdiction and surveillance missions of their north western coast when all the craziness started up north in the Aleutians. The newest phase of the cartels' relentless efforts to ship cocaine north was the use of miniature submersibles. These boats, which remained below the surface, were the cartel's answer to the coast guard and other agencies finding them on the surface. Each of the submersibles cost over a million dollars to build but carried enough cocaine in one trip to pay off the initial investment.

Three weeks ago, the *Connecticut* received Intel from the Columbian government about three new high-tech submersibles that were to be launched in the next few weeks. They found one of them so far and after unsuccessfully trying to force it to the surface had, with the permission of the Columbians, sunk the vessel. They had been hiding offshore for two days waiting for the other two vessels to pass by them when they received their recall notification to proceed up north as quickly as possible.

It had been just over three days ago when the *Connecticut's* orders were changed. Their new patrol sector was designated "X-ray 6" which was a box shaped area extending from just off the Northern California coast to just below the northern border of Washington state. Their patrol range extended out to the west approximately 1000 miles. Captain Briggs had been told to get there without delay. He knew several good folks on the SBX-1 platform and hoped they had not been in the wrong place at the wrong time.

The *Connecticut*, travelling at periscope depth, had just passed the Coronado Canyon. The canyon was just south of the entrance to San Diego Harbor. Briggs had requested the sub's navigation officer set up their route north so he could peek at San Diego one last time. Briggs requested that he be here at 6:30 a.m. and his navigator had nailed it. It was 6:30 a.m. exactly. Briggs asked his executive officer if he wanted a peek. They traded places and small talk. Briggs called out, "Sonar watch for traffic."

"Aye, sir," was the clipped response.

Briggs resumed his conversation with his executive officer, "Stacy, Grace, Alex, and Boomer should be packed up and on the road by 9:00 this morning."

The two senior officers had known each other's wives for years and they knew from experience the chances of Stacy leaving the house by herself, on-time, were remote. The thought of the circus that would probably be going on at the Brigg's house this morning made them both laugh. They tried to picture a frazzled emotional Stacy, overly caring neighbors, crying kids, and a dog with bowel troubles getting on the road on time. There was just no way that was going to happen. They just both wished they could catch the moment on tape.

Briggs was nothing if not a perfectionist. At 6:40 a.m. his boat was travelling submerged at two hundred and fifty feet, 27 knots, on a heading of 320°. An hour passed and the *Connecticut* was just sliding up past 29 knots, due west of San Clemente Island, when the encrypted message came in over the Very Low Frequency (VLF) secure communications link. It notified him to standby for a message.

"Helm, reduce speed to 10 knots. Diving officer, periscope depth."

"Aye, sir, periscope depth."

"Exec, check the surface."

His executive officer gave the periscope a swing of 360° around their position. "Negative surface contacts."

"Very good, send up the communications mast."

"Aye sir, communications mast up."

"Sonar, watch for surface traffic," Briggs knew this was a dangerous area to have any part of his submarine above the surface-day sailors, jet skiers and drunken fishermen coming in from a nighttime of fishing, drinking beer, and telling stories.

"Aye sir, checking for surface contacts."

"Chief, I don't want any screw ups on my last cruise."

The Chief of the Boat (COB) couldn't resist and parroted, "No screw ups, aye sir." They were muted, but he did hear some laughs on that one. Briggs shot the COB a smile.

The next message in was longer, more detailed, and informed him that some analysts at the newly established BOATSS group would like him to check out a ship in his patrol area. Apparently, no surface ships were available due to all the attention being placed up north in the Aleutians. Briggs ordered the helmsman to hold course and speed.

"Sonar, continue your watch for surface contacts."

"Aye sir, still negative for surface contacts."

Unfortunately, ever since the collision of the Los Angeles class submarine *USS Greenville* and a Japanese fishing boat *Ehime Maru* off Oahu in February 2001, submarine commanders were under strict orders to use all caution necessary when even approaching the surface.

"Sonar reports negative traffic."

The COB had the communication folks make the connection to BOATSS. These days, this type of link was like a really good Skype or FaceTime setup. There were several minor exceptions of course. His link was above "Top Secret" and unlike Skype; your contacts were very limited and preselected. The connection was as clear as a bell. The captain heard a soft voice and then on his monitor was one of the prettiest women he'd seen in quite some time; with the exception of his wife of course. Sailors were still sailors and he could hear some much muted whistles. He patiently waited for the pretty lady's boss to come into view.

Jewels greeted the captain once and yet he was just sitting there looking at her. Not bored, not busy, just sitting there. She tried again, "Captain Briggs, this is senior systems analyst Julie Folk; can you hear me?"

His eyes locked on hers and she could tell that she now had his full attention. Jewels explained who she was and exchanged the briefest of pleasantries. She got right into the meat of the matter.

She explained a ship the naval intelligence folks had thought was in a drydock in Dalian, China had been spotted by an overhead asset passing north of Hawaii in the shipping lanes two days ago and was now rapidly approaching the California coast.

What Jewels needed was a visual confirmation of the ship to compare it with the engine and propeller sounds on file. She had checked and the captain had been briefed on the BOATSS program. She might have worked in the basement of one of the most bureaucratic towns on the planet, but even Jewels understood her request was probably not going to be received well. Briefed or not, these folks did not see themselves as "errand boys."

Jewels could only hope for the best. Gina was sitting right next to her for moral support. Jewels looked at her best friend, crossed her fingers and just as Jewels thought Gina was going to say something profound she whispered, "Good luck."

"Captain Briggs," Jewels started, "We would like you to visually inspect a ship we anticipate will intersect your assigned course sometime later today. I will have my assistant send you the wave file we have on that vessel."

Gina slapped a hand over her own mouth and dramatically fell out of her chair laughing.

"Assistant," she hissed, "What assistant?"

Jewels hesitated briefly, looked at her friend on the floor, and continued, "We anticipate the vessel *Oceans Queen* to arrive in your projected patrol area in approximately five hours. She is manifested to arrive in the port of Los Angeles this afternoon." Jewels took a deep breath and waited. She was way out on a limb and knew it. This submarine captain had a saw sharp enough to not only cut off the limb she was precariously perched on, but potentially cut down the whole damned tree. Jewels took a deep breath and waited for the captain's response.

On board the *Connecticut*, Captain Briggs hit the transmission "mute" button just in time. Despite the decorum legendary on submarines, as soon as the signal light turned red the bridge crew erupted in laughter. His XO quickly regained the normal tone of the bridge and whispered to the captain, "She can't be serious."

The captain paused for a moment and thought of all the calls he had made in his career. This girl really had some spine to ask this of him and obviously some connections through CINCPAC to have even been able to make the call. Forget making the call, the girl knew what his Top Secret patrol area was. Captain Briggs un-muted the transmit key and said, "Send us the wave file, *Connecticut* out."

The connection went dead. Onboard the *Connecticut* there was only one question on everyone's mind: Who was that super-hot chick?

Jewels' "assistant" had regained her composure and was formatting the wave file for transmission to the *Connecticut* when Ramón walked in and demanded to know what they were doing. He could see the open BOATSS files on one of the monitors and noticed that on the other monitor, she still had the secure video program up on her screen. Gina and Jewels exchanged a look, and without saying a word, agreed on a plan of action. While Jewels talked to their boss, Gina quickly uploaded the file and sent it to the *Connecticut*. Ramón had had enough. He demanded to know what they were up to. They tried to explain. Jewels quickly explained to him the significance of the wave file they had sent to the submarine. It was no use. Ramón was writing them up and told them, "I'm in charge and what you've done is not in this Center's Operation Plan. We're not even an operational unit, in one week's time you've partnered up with some lone wolf agents, of the NSA and CIA, concocted some cock and bull story about an Iranian submarine, and now you're making unauthorized requests of a United States nuclear attack submarine? I wouldn't be surprised if they close our doors by week's end because of you!" Ramón grabbed the crypto key from Gina's phone as well as several other keys from surrounding phones and stormed off.

Without the key, the girls had no way to get back in touch with the sub.

More importantly, the sub had no way to get back in touch with them. The girls realized they'd taken an enormous risk and decided to do what they always did when they were in trouble. They went for coffee.

CIA

Mitch finally got to see Rick's office but didn't have the time to absorb the atmosphere before he needed to sit down and get to work. He logged onto his system and looked for the rogue signal he'd been watching for the past few weeks. Last night the signal had been on and off for about three hours. What was most significant was that for the first time since he had been tracking the signal it had been on and off for significant amounts of time. He believed he might actually have enough to run a signal comparison. He hit one of his favorite tabs on the *Confero* software; it dropped down all the customized search's that he had put in that were particularly helpful to his mission. He selected "Map." That's when the proverbial fan got turned up to high speed and all manner of smelly materials began flying into it.

"Rick, I think you've got a serious problem here."

Rick came over and looked over his shoulder. "What's up?"

Mitch was typing furiously "Give me a second and I'll tell you just how bad a day you're about to have." His voice had risen a level or two.

"Mitch, chill out, you're drawing a crowd."

He was right; several people had begun to walk toward Rick's desk.

Mitch had placed a three-minute run of the mystery signal into the signature data base search program and been waiting for its answer.

"Oh Shit, Oh Shit, Oh Shit."

"Mitch, relax, please..."

"Rick, I figured out what the signal is that I've been tracking across the Pacific." "That's good, right?" asked Rick, hoping that Mitch would calm down.

"No, dude, it's really, really bad. Do you remember when the Iranians captured our drone a year or so back?"

Rick nodded. So did several of his co-workers.

"This is that drone's electronic signature," shouted Mitch.

"Mitch, please keep your voice down, I gotta tell you buddy, I don't understand what the big deal is."

Mitch changed screens to the map. "The big deal, my spook friends, is that I have been tracking this signal all the way across the Pacific Ocean."

"And?" asked Rick, still not putting it together.

"Rick, damn it, this is bad, you've got a large container ship being controlled by our drone program closing in on the west coast of California."

And that's when everyone ran back to their desks and picked up their phones. Mitch called Jewels and told her the news.

"Without your software, we wouldn't have figured this out."

"Mitch, I need to talk to Rick right now."

"Jewels did you hear what I said?"

"Yes, and now I need to talk to Rick."

Mitch could sense something besides what he was working on was up and he got Rick over to the phone.

"Hey, Jewels, we're a little busy over here can this wait?"

"No, it can't Rick, I need you to have your boss immediately suspend Ramón and put me in charge over here. He had a hissy fit and swiped all the crypto keys. We don't have any way to securely communicate with the *Connecticut,* or for that matter, even you guys."

Rick gripped the phone tighter and clenched his teeth. "I'll handle that right now." Pausing just long enough to briefly place his finger on the disconnect button, Rick quickly selected another extension…

The woman's voice that answered was curt but pleasant enough. "Roger Batsly's office."

CHAPTER 39

Pedro Miguel Locks

PANAMA

On the north and south shorelines of the Panama Canal, two hundred yards away from the Pedro Miguel Locks, four men, two on each bank, sat in the shade of the trees watching their targets. Each pair of men had a man with what appeared to be a large remote controller for an RC aircraft. The other man was glued to a pair of very high powered Zeiss binoculars.

The man on the south shore, remarkably enough, was fixated on a floating empty bottle of orange juice. The man on the northern bank had his binoculars focused on a floating bottle of Pepsi Cola.

Every few moments, the man on the south would shift his gaze to the Pacific bound panamax freighter entering the locks. She was empty, riding high, and returning to South Korea for another load of cars. He was intently watching the distance between the floating bottle of OJ and the bow of the empty car carrier.

The man on the opposite bank, watching the empty Pepsi bottle was also watching a vessel. He was intently watching the stern of a vessel heading east through the locks, on its way to the Atlantic.

Thirty feet beneath the slow moving muddy water, two battery powered submersibles were following the commands of unseen hands on the north and south banks of the canal.

Purchased from the Columbian cartel in a sort of quid pro quo arrangement, the submersibles had been originally designed to carry upwards of one thousand pounds of cocaine north to feed the hungry veins and brains of America.

This morning, however, the submersibles were carrying a volatile mixed load of plastic explosives and ammonium nitrate. The navigation control signal was being cleverly passed down a whip antenna whose end was capped with floating liter bottles.

Both of the submersibles had almost been nabbed two days ago in the waters just outside the Columbian town of Jurado. No more than twenty minutes before they had been put in the water, the people running the operation had received word from their Columbian government sources that an American submarine was assisting the government in their quest to find the submersibles. They decided to delay launching the submersibles for a day when they received word that the American bases in Alaska had been attacked and the American submarine had been ordered north.

For the mission to be successful, the men high up on the banks above the canal would need to have almost perfect timing. The man on the southern bank guiding the west bound submersible had entered the middle stage of Lake Miraflores earlier in the morning and had waited for his target to come to him. Now he needed to keep his floating bottle 1000 feet in front of his vessel. His goal was to place the submersible against the locks western doors while the eastern doors were still open. The resulting explosion would blow both sets of doors of the northernmost lock allowing for the water from Lake Miraflores to rush through the lock and like a canoe in the rapids, push the empty car carrier through the set of doors on the western end of the lock.

The other man's job was virtually the same with the exception that he was placing his submersible at the eastern base of the other set of locks. His submersible would follow his vessel into the locks but remain when the vessel left. When his device was detonated, the doors of the southernmost lock doors would be removed allowing water to flow from the high eastern half of the lock out to the sea.

With the controls of the locks so regimented in their design, any doors open at the time of the explosions would permanently remain open.

Over the entire length of the canal, any ships in the canal at the time of the explosion would begin to run aground as the water from the lakes drained freely through the western locks and into the Pacific Ocean.

It was an ambitious plan but would shut down traffic through the Panama Canal for at least a year, or with any luck, longer.

From an international trade and environmental aspect, it would be an unparalleled disaster. From a terrorist's perspective it would be a greater blow to the Americans than even September 11, 2001. The men could only hope.

—∞—

José had done as he'd been told and gone to his uncle's house for a visit last week and then dutifully gone to work with him for the past nine days. On each day he had accompanied his uncle to the locks and followed him around. One of his uncle's duties was to walk the stretch of the facility that divided the locks that lifted the large ships heading to the Atlantic up to Lago Miraflores from the set of locks normally used to lower ships down to the sea level of the Pacific.

Three days ago José had received a text on the phone they had given him, instructing him where to go to pick up the items he would need for his task at the locks. He had picked up six identical very heavy black backpacks. For the past six days he had done as he was directed and dropped four of the backpacks over the side of the concrete walls of the locks into the water by the massive doors. He had tried to get them to land as close to the base of each of the heavy western lock doors as possible. He had also placed one backpack under a desk in the control room and another below the control rooms where the actual control mechanisms where located.

When he originally received his instructions, he had expressed some concerns about a couple parts of the operation. José's first concern dealt with the potential of the current sweeping the bags away when the massive doors swung open.

The odd man of many languages from Seattle had explained to him that half the weight of the backpack was made up of very strong rare earth magnets. As he explained it, the very first time the lock doors opened they would make contact with the backpacks and the magnets in the packs would adhere to the large metal door. José's second concern was how the device would get a signal to detonate if it was underwater. That too had been explained. As a matter of fact the man had laughed. "That was my own personal contribution to the effort."

José had just looked at the man not fully grasping what he was saying.

"I received my Master's degree for the idea of how you can make a cell phone call reach underwater."

José wasn't sure what a "Master's degree" was, but the man from Seattle sure seemed impressed by his accomplishment.

José could only hope they were right. The "no failure" part of the deal was worrisome. José had just pushed the last backpack into the water no more than an hour ago when he received his final text. It was only two words; it read, "Be ready."

José needed to convince his uncle to get away from the locks as quickly as possible. Both sets of locks had a vessel in them. José and his uncle had just walked to the maintenance building on the north side of the locks when he received his last text. It said, "NOW."

José glanced toward the locks that his uncle had worked on for so many years and felt ashamed at what he was about to do. He could see that one ship had just departed the locks and another was just starting the entry sequence. He thought about his brother and the thought of his own wife and two daughters being hoisted up a flag pole was too much for him to bear. José placed the call.

Three hundred yards to the east, on the southern bank of the canal, three cell phones rang. On one of them, close to the water, the third ring energized a circuit that was attached to a hydrophone. A hydrophone was a communication device that took advantage of the fact that sound travels very efficiently underwater. The technology had been around for many years. The hydrophone had been dropped over the side of a canoe several nights ago and sat on the bottom of the canal. A coded set of low frequency tones pulsed through the water of the canal. At the base of the two sets of lock doors a receiver inside the backpacks heard the tones and immediately started a fifteen second timer. On the two other phones, farther up the banks of the canal, a message was displayed. It said: 15 SEC.

High up the canal's banks, and partially hidden from view, the two men had needed some last minute high speed maneuvering to get the submersibles into position. Both the Pepsi bottle and the empty bottle of OJ were no longer moving and were right where they were supposed to be.

At first José was relieved when nothing happened. He remembered they had told him he would have thirty seconds to prepare. He began to count in his head. As he had been instructed, he removed the Subscriber Identity Module (SIM) card from his phone, put it into his pop can, crushed it and threw it into a pile of garbage. He wiped off his phone and placed it in the other garbage can. He had just asked his uncle what they were having for dinner when he reached thirty.

As four enormous, but strangely muffled, explosions shook the ground under their feet, four enormous geysers of water erupted from each corner of the western locks and the entire front half of the control building blew forward toward the locks. No one near José moved. Just as it seemed the geysers of water had stopped and the smoke was beginning to lift from the control building, two more massive explosions ripped through the locks. The debris from these explosions included sections of lock doors and chunks of concrete and, sadly, several people.

As the initial shock of the explosions wore off, nothing appeared wrong for a moment. Suddenly, although his ears were still ringing from the blasts, José could hear men screaming "the water." At first it was difficult to realize exactly what was happening. The light weight panamax car carrier that had just entered the locks seemed to be gaining forward speed. Soon, the lightweight car carrier began to groan as the level of water from the lake increased behind it. With the force of the water rushing into the lock, and beginning to pile up behind it, the ship was being pushed through the lock. With little room to spare, the ship was getting turned slightly in the current and becoming jammed in the locks. The small tugs that were used to guide the enormous ships through the locks had never been designed to hold back that much force and were ripped from their respective tracks.

The freighter, with the water running out of the lock in front of it and the ever increasing force being applied to its stern, had nowhere to go except forward, and down. Its keel was now scrapping along the concrete bottom of the lock. As it reached the area where the lock doors were formally attached, the bottom of the freighter hit the six-foot concrete lip that was used to support the doors.

For several seconds it looked as if it had become stuck. With a sudden sickening screech of steel against concrete, the bottom of the ship was peeled open like a can of sardines. Free of the bottom, and very much like a cork coming out of a bottle, the ship lurched forward out of the lock into the lower section of Lake Miraflores.

To the west of the locks, the first ship to sense the danger was the eastern bound freighter that had just five minutes before passed through the locks. The sudden current change caught its captain completely by surprise and turned his ship sideways in the narrow neck of the canal. With no room to maneuver the captain tried to drop anchor. It was a good idea but he wasn't fast enough. Faced with an insurmountable amount of pressure from the current hitting the ship amidships the freighter simply rolled over on its side and sank.

Farther east in the canal, ships that were monitoring their radios heard about the disaster and began dropping anchor so as to not be dragged toward the locks. Within two hours, seven ships were sitting on even keel but deep in the mucky bottom of Lake Miraflores. Four other ships had not been as fortunate and had rolled over as the water level in the lake had dropped.

CHAPTER 40

USS Connecticut

The sonar team on the sub received the transmitted wave file from the BOATSS folks. That was the good news. The bad news was the ship that the signature belonged to wasn't where it was supposed to be. They had passed the *Oceans Queen* an hour ago heading south toward San Diego. That didn't track with Ms. Folk's story. Something was wrong and the girl with the green eyes and real pretty face wasn't answering her secure line.

Sonar briefed the captain on the change of events. The captain didn't like the way this was starting to spin. He had an "on station" order that he had to comply with or at least have permission to deviate from. He made the call. While his XO got San Diego COMSUBPAC on the secure line he ordered right full rudder and told sonar to give him an intercept course. It was a long shot. Captain Briggs thought about it and realized that his chances of catching the *Oceans Queen* were about sixty percent. Against. Then he got more bad news.

Mike Long, *Connecticut's* chief sonar man was on his last cruise as well. He'd made it twenty-two years but had other things he wanted to do besides sub hunt. He was listening to the sounds coming from the *Oceans Queen* when his face went pale. Petty Officer Long got a fix on the *Oceans Queen* and the numbers that came back were alarming. The vessel was on heading of 180° and travelling at 20 knots. These container vessels didn't stop on a dime. What was the skipper on the *Oceans Queen* thinking?

BOATSS

Ken Shortman's job wasn't very exciting. He worked the day shift at the front desk of the new office called BOATSS. Some of his friends worked security at other federal offices across town and everyone knew they had important jobs. Ken wasn't so sure. While two of his friends worked over at the FBI, another one worked at the Justice Department. They were recognizable Washington offices. Ken figured he was suffering from "cool job envy." He'd coined that expression to make himself smile half way through a long day on his feet. Nobody "cool" ever came in here to visit. The name of the office was never in the news. None of his friends had ever heard of BOATSS. On the plus side, almost everyone in the new mystery office was very kind to him, greeting him in the morning and several would occasionally bring him coffee. He especially liked the tall brunette. From the looks she got as she walked by, apparently a lot of people did. Only one guy in the building treated him like he was invisible.

What Ken did know for sure was that when he received the call that he needed to remove someone from the building for a security issue he was oddly apprehensive. Not for the reason many people would be apprehensive. Ken had the training and stood at six foot three and weighted an honest 235 pounds. Ken really didn't want to hurt anyone. He was dutifully starting to fill out the information on the required bureaucratic paper work when he got to line three.

"Sir, can I get the name of the individual you wish me to escort out of the building?" "Let me read that back to you, R-a-m-ó-n R-o-d-r-i-q-u-e-z, is that correct?

"Anything else I can do for you, sir?"

"I need you to get all the crypto keys from him before you take him out of the building; I need you to give them all to Ms. Julie Folk. She's in charge down there now."

"Sir, do you mean Jewels?"

The CIA Deputy Director of personnel looked over at his friend and colleague of fifteen years, Roger Batsly, and received a thumbs up.

"Yes Ken, that's correct."

"Thank you, sir, that's the best news I've heard all week."

"You're very welcome Ken, goodbye."

Ken grinned, things were looking up. He headed down the hall and keyed his walkie-talkie, "Tony, I need some backup in the BOATSS shop."

"On my way buddy, are you expecting trouble?"

Ken could tell from his breathing that Tony was already running his way. Ken smiled, "No, I just want to make the right impression."

USS Connecticut
25 miles off Point Loma, CA

"Chief, are we getting any emergency traffic regarding this boat we're chasing? Because, I swear to you, I'm hearing pumps onboard."

"Sonar, tell me what you're hearing." Briggs needed some answers quickly.

"Communications reports no distress calls in the vicinity."

Petty Officer Long was now truly puzzled. He ran some software profiles against the sounds and what he got made absolutely no sense what so ever. The computer came back and said that the signature they were listening to were mining pumps. "Sir, the computer says we're chasing a ship with mining pumps running."

"Chief, what kind of boat do *you* think we're chasing?"

"Could those pumps be driving a jet pump set-up?"

"Sir, all we know is that it's supposedly a container ship from South Korea. Until two hours ago, it was supposedly heading for the port of Los Angeles."

Something was very wrong with almost everything about this ship. First, it wasn't where it was supposed to be and now it had added a significant change to its acoustic profile. Why was he hearing mining pumps? They needed to hail that ship, and right now.

North Korean Special Operations

Six thousand miles away, in Pyongyang, North Korea, a junior officer who really would have preferred to remain invisible couldn't stay that way any longer. 1st Lieutenant Hyo Phen was the satellite resource officer and had been given only one task today. The lieutenant was to alert his superiors when the cargo vessel *Shooting Star* dropped anchor inside Los Angeles harbor. He had so desperately wanted to be the guy with the good news. It just wasn't working out that way.

On her scheduled course the ship should have been seen on the overhead satellite pass two hours ago. The lieutenant doubled his efforts and contacted the owners of the satellite. They assured him that they were not masking his data. On the satellite's pass last hour it wasn't even close to Los Angeles. On the pass just completed this hour he had broadened the viewing angle and found the *Shooting Star*. He was relieved. The ship appeared fine.

In hindsight, he probably could have presented the news in a better fashion. He had tried; it just hadn't worked its way from his brain to his mouth correctly. What he ended up saying was, "Good news sir, I found the missing ship *Shooting Star* and it's heading straight toward the Port of San Diego."

Everything in the room seemed to stop for a moment before it exploded in chaos. The lieutenant was suddenly invisible. All he could hear was the senior staff officers screaming at the tops of their lungs, "Get the captain of the *Shooting Star* on the radio at once! He must stop his ship immediately!"

In what was probably only several moments, word came over from the communications center that they were unable to raise anyone on the *Shooting Star*. He hadn't thought it could be possible for the room to get any louder. He was mistaken. When asked the ship's exact location, 1st Lieutenant Hyo Phen snapped to attention and promptly told them that the ship was 13 miles due west of Encinitas, California and only thirty miles northwest of the port of San Diego. Apparently, the senior staff didn't like that answer either. Chaos turned to complete bedlam.

BOATSS

"Mr. Rodriquez, a word sir?"

Ramón didn't even respect them enough to raise his head.

"What do you two need? I'm busy."

"Yes, sir, we understand, we're here for a couple of reasons. First, sir, today is crypto key inventory day and we need to match all of your department's keys against their respective phones, and then test them." It was a lie, but Ken had been told to retrieve the crypto before removing him from his office.

"Well, what a coincidence," sneered Ramón. "I have all of the keys here in my safe."

Ramon, carefully shielding the combination from the two security personnel, opened the safe, removed the keys and handed them to Ken.

"That's great, Mr. Rodriquez, that will help us a lot with the second thing we need to do today."

Ken took the five keys from Ramón, checked them against the log, and handed them to Tony with a wink.

"Mr. Rodriquez, the second thing we're here to do today is to remove you from the building. Please come with me."

Ramon considered his options. There were relatively few and resisting the two large men wasn't even on the table.

Ken nodded to Tony where to take the keys. Tony waited a moment the walked them over to Jewels. Once they were in the hallway, Ken bent down to Ramón Rodriquez's ear and very softly whispered, "I'm not so invisible now, huh, prick."

CHAPTER 41

Dry Land

Captain Lee was picked up by a Coast Guard MH-65C "Dolphin" helicopter less than fifteen minutes after his call to 911. The helicopter was assigned to Air Station Los Angeles and stationed out of Los Angeles International Airport. Lee had indeed been very fortunate this morning. As Lee entered the cabin and took a seat on the floor, one of the crewmen put a set of headphones on him.

As Lee watched the receding waves below, out the helicopter's window, the Coast Guard pilot swung around in the helicopter to get an accurate fix on the now mostly submerged lifeboat. The pilot needed to send a message out to small craft in the area to watch for the submerged lifeboat. As the nose on the chopper dropped and they made their way toward the lifeboat, Lee noticed the crewman on the far side of the cabin staring at him. He heard, "Sir, can you hear me?" in his headset. He gave the young man the thumbs up.

"Sir, it's the luckiest day of your life." He went on, "Sir, this helicopter, Hotel 7, was already in the air and on its way to another call when we received your distress call. It would have taken at least another thirty minutes for another bird to come get you."

Both men were looking out the port side door window together. Lee's lifeboat was nowhere to be seen.

As the helicopter was bringing them back to base, Captain Lee informed the first officer, over the headset, that he would need to talk to the most senior ranking officer available as soon as they touched down.

Lt. Commander Leon Trask, USCG was still at the gym when his cell phone rang. It was 8:00 a.m. Monday morning. Had he not recognized the especially annoying ringtone he had set for calls from his watch officer, he would not have taken the call. The duty officer tried to explain that it was his understanding that they had picked up a North Korean freighter captain that had abandoned a North Korean container ship masquerading as a South Korean container ship. The commander stopped him at that point and told him he'd be right in. Ten minutes later, he was.

Trask ran a tight ship and his mornings were normally very structured events. At 7:30 a.m. he started his workout. At 8:00 a.m., after showering and putting on his uniform, he received his morning operation's briefing. At 8:30 a.m., he had his second cup of coffee and settled into his day. That wasn't to say that in a crisis he wasn't the man you wanted in a crisis. Lt. Commander Trask was excellent in a crisis management situation. Trask just liked being the guy to determine whether something was, in fact, a crisis.

From where he was standing, still perspiring, in his workout clothes and smelling more than a little ripe, this didn't appear to be a crisis. The little man from North Korea wasn't hurt; he wasn't posing a danger to himself or anyone else, and was drinking a cup of fresh hot coffee. The duty officer over at the State Department had been notified and would be here in twenty to thirty minutes depending on traffic. With LA morning traffic, Trask was betting on thirty minutes and headed for the showers.

It was now exactly 8:30 a.m. and Trask had finished up his morning routine. He was heading down the hall when he could hear several elevated voices coming from the conference room. The North Korean captain was apparently demanding that he, Trask, speak to him immediately. Trask really wasn't sure where he stood legally at the moment and really wanted the North Korean freighter captain to just have another cup of coffee and wait for someone from the State Department to show up. It appeared the captain was having none of that.

Captain Lee was a patient man but was very aware that he was running out of time. He hadn't wanted to rush the conversation with Trask, but the delay in speaking with him had changed his plans.

Trask approached Lee with an outstretched hand. Lee didn't take it. "Commander Trask," he began, "I'll be right up front with you; I wouldn't believe the story I'm going to tell you either but I'm afraid you must."

Trask looked at the little man with the wrinkled uniform standing before him and wondered just how long it was going to be before the State Department representative got there.

Trask smiled, "Well, Captain Lee, is it? What's your story?" and motioned for the captain to take a seat.

Lee had had enough. In his very best command voice he said, "Commander, you must listen to what I'm telling you and act immediately!" Trask didn't think he liked the little man's tone and started to interrupt. The seaman who was at the door acting as security took a step into the room and looked to Trask for guidance. Trask backed him off with a glance.

Lee had been patient but he was running out of time. "Commander, I believe there is a large nuclear device heading for the west coast of your country. It is due to arrive today on my container ship." There, he'd said it.

In a different situation, Lee would have had to describe Lt. Commander Trask's face as hilarious. His mouth moved but no words were coming out. His eyes were so wide open; Captain Lee could see the whites of his eyes all the way around the iris. After a moment the commander's brain connected with his mouth. Sadly, he could only muster up one word, "What?"

Captain Lee was exhausted and knew it was now or it would be too late. He turned to one of the seaman closest to him who was still digesting what Lee had said. As officiously as possible, Lee said, "Get me a map of your California coast."

Stunned, the seaman looked at Trask for approval; Trask nodded. Lee spread out the map and tried to describe what he knew for sure and what he speculated. He knew the approximate speed of his vessel, when it had sailed past San Francisco harbor and the fact that, in its forward cargo hold number 2, section 2, level 1, to be exact, was a very large nuclear weapon. What he did not know was where it was headed. He told Trask that he believed the intended target must be San Diego. And he believed his ship should be arriving there later this morning.

Trask had started to leave when Lee spoke up. "Commander, before you think you're just going to go hunt down and destroy my ship, I should tell you; this isn't just any container ship."

Trask stared at him not really sure what his comment inferred. Trask asked him smugly, "And why do you think your ship's so special, captain?"

Captain Lee stared back at him incredulously. Was this guy for real? "Well, besides having what I believe is a rather large nuclear weapon on board, and that it has no captain or crew, it has a rather unique propulsion system that propels it through the water at about 35 knots."

Now Trask had all his mind and body parts synced and he became the picture of effective leadership his cadre of sailors was hoping for. "Get me the Navy Command Center at San Diego on a secure line, right now." While he waited, he tried to remember the name of that new intelligence group in D.C., the one with the name he should never forget. The phone rang. It was the San Diego Navy Command Center Combat operations group on a secure line. Then Trask remembered, BOATSS. As his aid looked up and dialed the number, Trask asked, "Is there anything else you think I need to know about your former ship, captain?"

Lee thought. "I think it may have some kind of protective countermeasures." An incredulous Trask sighed, "Like what, guns, missiles?"

"No, I think it has some kind of armor or something."

"And what makes you think that?"

"All the containers on the upper deck have some kind of material stuck to their ceilings."

Trask had started to move quickly for his phone when his guest added, "Oh commander, one last thing, I think it might also have sonar."

One of the many things that had been added to the *Shooting Star* while in drydock was a relatively new, barely used TSM 2233 ELEDONE / DSUV-22 sonar suite imported from France in the early 1990's. It was one of the things that Captain Lee had noticed while inspecting its hull in the Dalian yard. The addition of the sonar was seemingly so insignificant compared to the cutting of the holes in the bottom of his ship for the water jets he hadn't given it much thought; it had simply slipped his mind.

CHAPTER 42

CIA
LANGLEY, VIRGINIA

When it rained, it poured. Rick was just walking in the door when he'd received the word about the freighter off the California coast. A nuclear weapon on a freighter? Years ago, he'd run into a guy who'd told him something like that. It had seemed silly at the time. Then the bad guys had used civilian airliners to attack the Twin Towers and it suddenly wasn't so funny anymore.

The command center was in full conference mode with multiple agencies. It was lunchtime in Washington and very few of the key offices had a full staff. Of those offices that had personnel, all eyes, ears, and brains were focused on the evolving situation in San Diego.

When at 12:10 p.m., local D.C. time, the message came in about "an incident" at the Pedro Miguel locks on the Panama Canal, no one really paid too close attention. When the Pentagon called over and said one of its ships was sinking into Lake Miraflores several people put two and two together.

Rick called over to BOATSS on the secure line hoping they hadn't gone to lunch.

"BOATSS, Gina Hughes."

"Gina, thank God you're there."

"Rick? This better be good we're up to our ears in alligators and we're out of coffee."

"Gina listen, I need you to pull up anything you have from the past hour either off the coast of Panama or in the Canal Zone."

"What's this all about, Rick?"

"Gina, we've got no time now, I'll explain later, please just do it quickly."

Gina entered the data request screen, selected Pacific/Panama and entered a time range of one hour. The results were almost immediate.

"Rick?"

"Go ahead, Gina."

"The system has reports of four medium size subsurface explosions followed almost immediately by two massive explosions."

"Thanks, Gina, I gotta go." The line went dead.

Rick hung up from Gina and immediately picked up the secure phone to the CIA operations watch officer.

"Watch officer."

"It's Rick Wagner down in Operations. It's our belief, down here, that we are under attack on several fronts and I need to get the word out to all agencies ASAP to immediately increase our readiness posture."

"Mr. Wagner, I'll make the calls. I don't know whether to hope you're right or wrong, sir. I sure hope you know what you're doing."

Off the California Coast

The *USS Connecticut* had not ever practiced chasing a civilian container ship. It wasn't that it was a dumb idea. It was more likely along the lines of why? For that reason alone, the "Rules of Engagement" when chasing a civilian owned and operated vessel that was not responding to hails, were not on the forefront of anyone's thoughts. They were gaining on the *Shooting Star* but

Captain Briggs wasn't sure he was going to win this race.

—⁂—

The computer onboard the *Shooting Star* calculated the distance to the target as thirty-five miles. The software program that controlled the pumps and the jet nozzles in the aft of the boat was designed, barring any unforeseen change in the plan or programming, to kick in at eighty-five percent of maximum power at the five-mile mark. They were then to go to maximum power for ten minutes or the conclusion of the voyage, whichever came first.

The ship had slowed to 20 knots and was sitting low in the water. If the seas had been a few feet higher she would have rolled over and gone to the bottom. Deep in the ship, as pre-programmed, the "anti-pirating system" had been activated. Lights all over the ship turned from red to green. All over the ship the new automatic hatch systems closed and locked any hatch that was still open.

Above each door a small steel box dropped a deadbolt down over the lip of the hatch and showed secure with an LED light that glowed bright red. The ship was sealed. Any attempt to breech any hatch or cargo hold door would send a scrambled code to the device sitting in the red container hold #2, section 2, level 1.

—⁂—

The *Shooting Star* was just passing the southern tip of Point Loma when the secure satellite link on the *Connecticut* hummed and the communication officer took the message to Captain Briggs. The message had come in a message format called "Flash." A flash message preempted every other message in the system. The message read:

Commander USS Connecticut //Exec Officers
Engage and immediately sink target identified as "Oceans Queen" by any means

necessary
Weapons release code: Bravo-Yankee-9-Sierra-Alpha-6
Commander US Navy Fleet//Pentagon

Unfortunately for the captain, this was going to be much easier said than done. Had he received the order a half hour ago or maybe even fifteen minutes ago, it would have been an easy shot. Now the ship was near the end of Loma Point and getting surrounded by other ocean going traffic. If he waited too long the *Oceans Queen,* or whatever ship it was, would make an expected turn to port any second.

It was an impossible request. The *Connecticut* was still fifteen miles away from the *Shooting Star*. The *Connecticut* was gaining but a tremendous amount of traffic was leaving the port this morning. Briggs didn't have the angle to take the shot and he sure as hell wasn't going to send a spread of torpedoes screaming around the end of Loma Point into one of the most active ports on the west coast looking for a ship that was now radiating one of the most confusing acoustic signals his sonar team had ever heard.

Briggs figured he had no more than two minutes to figure out a firing solution and less than three to send the torpedoes to their target. He simultaneously ordered the *Connecticut* to come to a course of 180° and accelerate to maximum speed. As the *Connecticut* quickly slid past 35 knots he ordered the helm to hold that course for three minutes then snap to a heading of 150°. Then the captain made his first bad decision since getting out of bed this morning. He ordered his forward torpedo doors to be opened.

The computer aboard the *Shooting Star* had no memory problems and had turned the system from stand-by to active twenty minutes ago. It heard the *Connecticut*, even as quiet as she was, go past her some thirty minutes ago and had recorded her signature. The sonar aboard the *Shooting Star* also heard the sub turn around and accelerate after it. It waited until it heard the submarine open its torpedo doors before it began to take appropriate measures to defend itself.

On the deck of the *Shooting Star,* all of the containers on the upper deck had been wirelessly hooked up to the defensive systems on board. The ceiling of each container contained several inches of reactive armor. Essentially the containers were designed to explode when hit by a missile. The shock of the reactive explosion would significantly disrupt the incoming missiles.

—~—

As soon as Briggs had ordered the torpedo doors opened, he regretted it. "No do over on that one dad," as his young son Alex used to say. This was going to be a tricky shot. The container ship was travelling at 22 knots with a draft of forty feet. Sonar said the engines were running at an estimated eighty-five percent capacity. Even if the vessel increased its speed by one or two knots this was going to be over in five minutes. The firing solution had the torpedoes in one and two set for thirty feet so they would hopefully pass under any other ships exiting the harbor. This required a change to the normal programming of the Mark 84 ADCAP.

In an open ocean battle, the Mark 84 torpedo was given its target and it would find it in any number of ways including coming around again in the event of a miss. The port was entirely too crowded at this time of the morning. They would shoot low and break her back. The Mark 48 had a speed of just over 48 knots and the current firing control solution had the torpedoes finding their mark in 23 minutes.

Captain Briggs ordered, "Ready tubes one and two."

"Tubes one and two ready."

"Fire tubes one and two."

"Tubes one and two fired, sir."

Less than one second later two Mark 48 torpedoes were on their way. At four seconds, Petty Officer Williams yelled something about pumps. Moments later he hollered that the target had increased speed to 25 knots and that engines were still only running at eighty-five percent but did not appear to be straining. The weapons officer reported that the firing solution was becoming corrupted. The speed had changed so significantly that he was concerned that...he never finished his explanation.

"Sonar reports vessel's draft now only at thirty feet.

"Impossible!"

"No, sir, now twenty-five feet." They needed another firing solution.

"Ready tubes three, four, and five." "Mark those pumps, zero depth!"

"Tubes three, four, and five ready."

"Fire tubes three, four, and five."

"Firing three, four, and five," replied the weapons officer.

"Initiate self-destruct on torpedoes one and two," called Briggs. The last thing Briggs needed was two 650-pound seeker warheads looking for something to kill in the waters off San Diego.

"Torpedoes one and two aborted."

The *Connecticut's* sonar man had just started to call off the vessel's speed. At 27 knots the chief swore. At twenty-nine, even the captain swore.

"Weapons officer, put a targeting solution into three Tomahawks." The weapons officer quickly placed all the information they had from the fire control computer into the three Tomahawk missiles.

"Tomahawks ready."

"Launch the missiles," shouted Briggs.

"Launching three Tomahawks."

The ship shuddered slightly as the three twenty foot missiles raced out of their respective silos, broke the surface and headed toward their targets.

"Time to impact?" inquired Briggs. The weapons officer quickly glanced at the fire control computer.

"At our current distance from target, missile time to impact is four minutes, ten seconds."

CHAPTER 43

BOATSS

Jewels walked to her desk, inserted the recovered key and tried to make a connection with the *Connecticut.* She had been able to speak briefly to the *Connecticut's* communications officer and relay all of the latest Intel she had, including the little gem about there being the distinct possibility of a nuclear weapon onboard. She included their most recent discovery that this was not, in fact, the South Korean freighter *Oceans Queen* but the North Korean vessel *Shooting Star.* That now being the case, it significantly increased the likelihood that they should expect the unexpected. Jewels was groping for something upbeat to tell the communications officer and ended up with, "Cautious hunting, sir, BOATSS out."

USS Connecticut

"Captain!"

"Yes, COB!"

"We have an update from the pretty lady over at BOATSS."

"Read it. And COB, just the things I need to know right now."

"Yes sir, first, the CIA believes that this ship is a drone ship with no captain or crew, they apparently have multiple sources on that." "Great," mumbled Briggs.

"Not done, sir, they say it's a North Korean not South Korean vessel. Second, they believe that the ship may be carrying a large nuclear weapon in its hold." "A what?" Briggs was livid.

The COB could sense that his captain was starting to lose his temper so he read even faster.

"Sir, it apparently has a massive pump jet system that rapidly accelerates the ship up to, but this can't be correct, 38 knots."

"That's all?" Briggs tried sarcasm to lighten the mood.

"No, sir, according to the captain of the vessel that literally jumped ship several hours ago, the ship is equipped with a sophisticated sonar system and is protected by a layer of reactive armor across the top of the ship."

"COB!"

"Sir."

"How the hell do you put reactive armor on the deck of a..." his voice trailed off as he answered his own question. "The containers..."

The normally very calm Captain Briggs was getting angry. "People, we have been behind in this race since we started. Let's get our heads up right now! Time to impact?" inquired Briggs. "Tomahawk time to target, two minutes." Captain Briggs ordered all ahead full, again.

"Periscope depth!! Right damn now!!!!"

"Weapons officer, I need at least one, if not all, of the Tomahawks reprogrammed to hit the side of that ship."

"Reprogramming the missiles now, sir."

When sonar called, "Draft now twenty feet, speed 38 knots," they knew this race was all but over.

—∾—

The sonar system tied to the computer system so ingeniously built by Major Harem Fallahi heard the second group of torpedoes leave their respective tubes and their screws spinning madly in the water trying to catch her. It was too late.

At 9:21:58 a.m., the *Shooting Star's* sonar indicated that, although the ship has riding higher and increasing speed every second, the bottom was coming up even faster. The computer calculated the speed of the boat, the depth of the water, the distance to the target, calculated that it would take fourteen seconds to be on target, waited those fourteen seconds, and sent the coded signal to the forward cargo hold.

At 9:22:01 a.m. Charlie and Kenny Hudson were sitting on the stern of their little fishing boat *Dawn Curfew* in Fiddlers Cove Marina when they saw the *Shooting Star* approaching the Silver Strand Blvd. straight on at almost 40 knots. As Charlie cracked open their third beer of the morning he turned to his brother and said, "Dude, that captain's so not gonna make the channel." He was right of course.

At 9:22:04 a.m., San Diego local time, two out of three launched Tomahawk missiles made contact with the containers on top of the aft deck of the *Shooting Star*. The reactive armor did a superb job of deflecting most of the blast up and away from the ship's engine room. The third Tomahawk, that the *Connecticut's* weapon officer had been able to reprogram, tore into what was normally empty cargo space above and behind the engine room.

All things being equal, the resulting explosion should have torn through the containers and aft bulkhead of the ship. Today, however, the *Shooting Star's* rear hold was completely full of water. The warhead detonated in a tremendous explosion of water rupturing the upper two decks of the containership's hold.

At 9:22:10 a.m., the first nuclear strike carried out against America occurred on a little spit of land just less than two miles from the largest concentration of navy ships and personnel on the Pacific Ocean.

The flash blocker system on the periscope was all that spared the captain's eyes. From four miles away, the entire horizon exploded and began to lift toward the heavens.

"EMERGENCY DIVE! EMERGENCY DIVE! DOWN SCOPE!
ALL BACK EMERGENCY!!!
NOW!"

The sea within one mile of the detonation evaporated when the weapon had momentarily created temperatures in the region of over 20 million degrees. As the seawater rushed back toward the coast, the *Connecticut* was caught up in the sudden surge of water and began to be pushed to the bottom of the channel.

"SOUND COLLISION ALARM!"

"BRACE FOR IMPACT!!"

The *Connecticut's* pump jet caught quickly and began pulling the boat backward from the temporary abyss created when the weapon detonated.

The *Connecticut* was a mere one hundred feet from the bottom when the boat's rearward thrust of the screw overcame her headlong dive to the bottom. The sea had rushed back in and saved her from certain destruction. The effect of the sudden stop was compounded by the forward rush of the water trying to pitch the *Connecticut* down by her bow.

"Right full rudder! Bring us to course 275°! Flank speed!"

Distance would be their best friend. "Maintain flank speed, Mr. Fox."

Only the captain had seen what had happened. The rest of the crew was in physical shock. Captain Briggs couldn't get his head wrapped around what he had seen. What in the name of God *had* happened? "DAMAGE CONTROL CENTRAL REPORT!!"

All stations reported in with bumps and bruises. Captain Briggs was in shock. What had he done?

Northbound I-15

Mrs. Stacy Briggs had gotten a late start this morning and just knew that if Trent was home he'd have given her an earful, laughing the whole time, but certainly an earful. She had taken a few more pictures of the home she had raised her babies in. She hugged her neighbor, Diane McElroy, and said that of course they'd keep in touch. Their dog, a black lab named "Boomer" had needed to pee and do his business just one more time. Her daughter Grace made her drive past her elementary school, "Just one more time mommy."

An hour after they planned to leave, they were on highway I-15N on the uphill stretch to Escondido just coming up to the Ted Williams Freeway exit ramp when Stacy Briggs heard what she thought was the loudest clap of thunder she had ever heard. She looked in her rear view mirror. Her two children heard the sound and looked out the rear window. Although they were already almost fifteen miles away the effect of the blast was tremendous. The shock wave shook the car violently enough that she found herself on the rumble strips.

In the southbound lane of I-15 the drivers had not been so lucky. Many of the drivers coming down the hill were apparently gazing toward the sea when the blast, brighter than many suns, lit up the port of San Diego. They were instantly blinded by the flash and many of them crashed through the barrier along the southbound lane of I-15 at 70 mph.

Mrs. Briggs had been married to a man involved with nuclear weapons long enough to know what she needed to do next; Drive!

Homeward Bound

The *Yunes* was currently almost 1310 miles southwest of Shemya. She had proceeded down the coast of Kamchatka in the Kuril-Kamchatka Trench and was now cruising south past the Japanese island of Hokkaido. In about six hours, just south of Tokyo, she was scheduled to execute a slight turn to starboard and transit the Nankai trough.

The submarine was just below the surface when the sonar man yelled something and removed his headsets. "Captain, I just heard a tremendous explosion. If my bearing is correct it initiated on the west coast of the United States. I've never heard anything like it."

Mr. Feng didn't seem surprised, at all, by the news. He casually looked at his watch and smiled.

"Captain, can we raise the communications mast? Perhaps there is something on the cable news?"

"Sonar, do we have any surface contacts?"

"No, sir."

"Periscope depth."

"Periscope depth, now, sir."

"Raise the periscope and the communications antenna."

The first thing received by the boat was a coded message from the Iranian Navy high command.

It was only seven words long but they told the captain of the *Yunes* everything he needed to know. The message read; Captain Babakan, job well done, Allah Akbar.

BOATSS

It was 12:22:11 p.m. on the east coast and everyone in America would remember, for the rest of their lives, where they were when the city of San Diego was destroyed in less time than it took to blink. Jewels and Gina had skipped lunch and were plotting a possible projected course for the Iranian submarine *Yunes* when a small window opened up on their computer screens indicating that the entire SOSUS network for the west coast had rebooted. The next instant someone down the hall was wailing, "No, Noo, Noooo!"

Someone turned on the cable news. It was live coverage from KTTV the Fox affiliate out of Los Angeles. They had received a report of a large explosion on the San Diego waterfront. They were transmitting a live feed via their station's helicopter. It was an image of a tremendous mushroom cloud ascending over what should have been the city of San Diego. Jewels broke herself away from the television and called Jack.

"Jack, Jewels here, I know a terrible sight. Your agency must issue an immediate order to the FAA and ground all aircraft on the west coast until we know where this cloud is going. One pass through that cloud and everyone on the aircraft will be dead."

No, she'd heard nothing from the *Connecticut*.

USS Connecticut

The crew of the *Connecticut* escaped with their lives but not much else. When the submarine was ten miles off the coast, Captain Briggs ordered all stop. He needed to address the crew shortly but was unsure as to what he should tell them.

They knew that the boat had been rocked by a massive explosive force but most of the crew who were not in the control room had little idea, if any, what the submarine had been doing when the concussive force hit the submarine.

"Helm periscope depth."

"Periscope depth in ten seconds, sir."

Briggs looked around him. Everyone had the same mixed expression of both curiosity and dread. "Periscope depth, sir."

"Up scope."

Captain Briggs carefully walked the periscope around until he found what he didn't want to see. Five minutes had passed and the enormous mushroom cloud was still there but the base had dissipated significantly enough for him to see what had formally been the city of San Diego. It was immediately obvious that the Port of San Diego was completely gone. The harbor essentially no longer existed. Adjusting the magnification, he could see that the immediate blast radius had to have been close to four miles. He could see fires as far away as the 805 freeway. There was no traffic on I-5. He hit record on the HD video link.

"COB, you need to see this. Somebody get me D.C. on the line, right now." He let the COB look through the periscope. No words were exchanged between the two men. "Send this flash precedence."

Navy Base San Diego and Naval Air Station Coronado destroyed. No survivors possible. Catastrophic damage extends at least four miles out from anticipated ground zero of Silver Strand Highway 75, possibly Fiddlers Cove area. Connecticut assessing damages but underway. Live video feed established.

"Pete, read that back to me."

"Yes, sir, read back as follows: Navy Base San Diego and Naval Air Station Coronado destroyed. No survivors possible. Catastrophic damage extends at least four miles out from anticipated ground zero of Silver Strand Highway 75, possibly Fiddlers Cove area. *Connecticut* assessing damages but underway. Live video feed established."

Captain Briggs chose his next words very carefully. "Add that the city of San Diego would seem to no longer..." Briggs's voice cracked... "exist."

"Do you need me to read that last part back, sir?"

"No, just hurry up and send it."

"COB, I want all personnel not on critical systems to please assemble in the galley. I want a full ship assessment after I meet with the crew."

Captain Briggs went to his quarters. He needed to think. He went into the head grabbed a washcloth and ran it under cold water. He dragged it over his face a few times, checked his hair, squared up his shirt, and headed out to brief his crew. He paused by his desk and looked at his montage of family photos, so many of the memories of his family were in pictures. He reached down and touched each of the kid's pictures and their drawings from school. Boomer being Boomer licking his kids faces clean of smeared ice-cream. Over on the less crazy side of his desk were the pictures of he and Stacy, "chillaxing" as the kids called it these days. He picked up the picture of Stacy holding the kids and while getting a lump in his throat so big it felt he couldn't take another breath he looked at the picture and said, "For the love of God, Stacy, tell me you got out of town on time."

CHAPTER 44

Highway I-15 N

Stacy Briggs and her kids were travelling north at eighty miles per hour and were being passed by cars full of people. The only person in the cars looking forward was the driver. In every car that passed the passengers were glued to the back or side windows straining to get a glimpse at the city they used to call home. After several miles' people began to get other cell phone towers that hadn't been affected by the blast. With the explosion being at ground level the majority of the EMP affect had been absorbed by the ground and surrounding hills.

More cars and emergency vehicles were now screaming past them in the south bound lanes. Those vehicles were being passed as well by family or friends trying desperately to get to loved ones, not wanting to believe what had happened.

Stacy had Grace, who desperately needed a distraction, turn on the radio and find a station.

Every station they came to had switched over to the Emergency Broadcasting System.

Authorities had closed all the roads into the San Diego area and had begun reading off the names of the towns they and the National Weather

Service had projected would be in the most danger of receiving fallout from the explosion. They were telling everyone to gather as much water as possible as quickly as possible. They repeatedly emphasized not to drive east as that was the direction the cloud containing the fallout was heading.

Despite all the information available in the state about disaster preparedness, very few people heeded the advice. Stacy could see that the feeder roads coming up to the highway were starting to fill up and that the lines at gas stations were already forming. Stacy tried to focus on the positive things. One of which was that although for the most part a prince, Trent was an absolute ass about preparedness. Here she was on her way to Idaho with two kids, a dog, three suitcases, fifteen gallons of gasoline, and two gallons of water. Every time they went on a trip it was the same thing. An extra suitcase of clothes or a five gallon can of gas. If everyone survived the day, she knew that Trent would only have one thing to say: "I told you so."

The traffic was picking up and Stacy switched to the left lane just as a car that was trying to get on the freeway was rammed from behind. The ensuing melee took out at least seven cars and had the kids crying again. Boomer did what he could to comfort Alex, and after a few minutes of almost suffocating Alex with his tongue, her son was laughing again at the big stinky dog.

In all the excitement Boomer had apparently ripped one and the kids had another problem on their hands-trying to breathe. Stacy opened the windows of the car in an attempt to get some better smelling air. Even Boomer seemed to be looking for some fresh air. His head was out the window, his eyes all puffy in the wind and his ears flat back against his head.

Stacy laughed out loud with her kids. Suddenly her tears of laughter turned to tears of grief as she thought of all the neighbors, friends, and strangers alike who would never again experience the simple joy she was having right now.

She was snapped out of her pity party by her cell phone ringing. Her caller ID said "Nana." On a day like today her hands free device would be a godsend but she needed to make sure her mom knew she was on speaker phone.

"Hi Mom, you're on speaker phone. Do you want to talk to the kids?" "Hi kids!" Her mom had apparently broken the code. From the back seat Alex piped up, "Hi, Nana!"

"Hi Alex sweetie, how's your trip going so far?"

"Nana, Mommy's driving really fast and cars are crashing all around us."

"Good heavens, honey, are you okay?"

Alex apparently thought that his Nana was still talking to him and said, "Sure, Nana, I'm fine, I just hope that Boomer doesn't fart again."

After a long pause, and at a complete loss for words, Stacy's mom said, "Me too, sweetie, me too."

Stacy tried to spare her mom from any further embarrassment, "Hi Mom."

"Hi Honey, is everything okay?"

"Everything's okay at the moment, Mom. The roads are really getting crowded. Everyone's panicking because nobody can tell if it was an attack or an accident at the base."

"Stacy, your dad wants me to tell you that you shouldn't stop unless you absolutely have to. There are rumors that it was just the first bomb and that there's more bombs in the other major cities.

No food stops, nothing. He's already hearing stories of looting in Los Angeles."

"Okay, Mom, we'll be careful."

"Honey, do you have Trent's..."

"What was that Mom?"

She was gone. The wireless systems were swamped and had either shut themselves down or her provider had suspended service. Stacy checked her gas gauge, she still had almost a full tank of gas.

In addition, she had a pretty good head start on anyone else trying to leave California.

Stacy thought about her route to Idaho. She knew that with all the craziness going on the last thing she needed was to appear like the frazzled mom. The kids would make her an easy mark for robbery, carjacking or worse. Stopping at a highway rest stop for a bathroom break, or gas, would make her even more vulnerable. She had four hours to think about it.

She smiled grimly to herself; maybe having Boomer in the car would finally be an asset.

Several hours later, Stacy and her very hungry and tired troop of travelers had made it just over the state line into Nevada before Nevada, like Arizona, had closed its state line access to vehicular traffic.

They had just pulled off the freeway into the Primm Outlet Mall when the National Guard started to set up a road block on Interstate 15. Stacy and the kids could see the checkpoint from the Taco Bell parking lot where they had stopped to feed Boomer, take a pee break and grab some tacos. From what she could tell, the checkpoint was made up of several National Guard Humvee's with mounted gunners in HAZMAT suits, lots of Nevada State Police cars, and about two dozen people in HAZMAT suits walking up to the cars in line with some kind of gadget in their hands. The workers would check out the vehicle then either wave it to the right or to the left. People waved to the left usually mashed the gas and came up to the mall and got in line for gas. Vehicles waived to the right had a red slash spray painted on the back window and were apparently instructed to drive over to the right of the checkpoint where several automobile transport trailers sat idling.

Just about fifty yards east of the trailers were what appeared to be several military busses. In between the trailers and the busses was a growing line of people hauling only what they could carry in their hands.

Stacy tuned into a Las Vegas radio station that was broadcasting emergency information regarding "The Event." According to the radio, the National Guard were conducting tests for radioactivity on the surface of the cars before letting them pass into the state. "Tell me something I don't know," mumbled Stacy.

"I know something," piped in Grace.

"What sweetie?"

"I know something that you don't know." Apparently Grace had taken her literally. "What's that Grace?"

"You don't know where daddy is."

"You're right sweetie, and I sure wish I did!"

They were just finishing up at Taco Bell when Stacy thought she could hear gunshots. They had been watching what appeared to be a rather orderly process when all hell broke loose. To their left they could see two pickup trucks hauling butt away from the checkpoint out into the desert. The National Guard was apparently not taking that action lightly and was in the process of stopping them, by force.

It was time to go. As Stacy was backing up the car, she could hear more gunfire coming from the direction of the checkpoint as well as the desert behind the shopping center. She had stopped just briefly at a stop sign near the exit of the mall parking lot when Boomer started to bark. Three men with hoodies and baggy pants were charging her car and they didn't look like they were coming for anything Stacy wanted any part of. She floored it out of the parking lot, narrowly missing a car flying into the gas station.

Fortunately, Stacy had not needed to use her spare gas from the trunk on the way up to Vegas. She had filled up at the mall gas station before eating. It had been a wise decision. The station now had orange traffic cones out and the line was at least twenty-five cars long.

Stacy gunned it back onto I-15 and took a deep breath. The Garmin said it was twelve hundred miles to home. She felt like crying. She was tired and scared for herself and her kids and worried about what the worrying was doing to her folks. She needed a sign, something to give her hope. "Mommy?" Alex's little boy voice came floating over the seat.

"Yes, sweetheart?"

"I was just talking to Grace and Boomer."

Alex often had "conversations" with Grace and Boomer; she moved the rearview mirror and smiled at her little guy, "And what did they say honey?"

"They said you're doing a great job getting us to Nana's house."

That's when Stacy Briggs started to cry. Grace was right; she had no idea where her daughter's daddy was, and she sure wished she did.

CHAPTER 45

BOATSS

It had been several hours now since the *Shooting Star* detonated on the narrow spit of land separating the Port of San Diego from the sea. Each report coming out of California was worse than the last. Even for a state that took pride in its readiness for disasters, the situation in several other California cities was already out of hand. Store shelves were being cleaned out and in the more routinely dangerous cities like Oakland and several sections of Los Angeles, had in the span of several hours, become warzones.

Mitch met Jewels at her office at 3:00 p.m. and they had done some work on plotting the *Yunes'* course but had spent most of the afternoon watching the news out of California. Everyone finally called it a day around 9:00 p.m. Jewels and Mitch had taken the train back to DuPont Circle and were standing on the corner of Connecticut and DuPont Circle. They were mentally and physically spent. Mitch really didn't want to go back to his hotel and Jewels, despite being exhausted, did not want to be alone. They both started talking at the same time and Mitch yielded to Jewels.

Jewels smiled and took both his hands in hers, asking, "How do you feel about Dim Sum?"

Mitch's mind raced but couldn't come up with an answer. So with one question Mitch revealed one of his true and secret weaknesses to Jewels; he wasn't a foodie, "Who's Dim Sum?"

Jewels laughed so hard she had tears running down her face. "It's not a who, it's a what!" Still laughing, Jewels was trying hard to catch her breath.

"It's food?"

Just the physical release of laughter had picked up her spirits. "Listen, there is a Dim Sum restaurant directly across from my apartment where we can sit and talk and try to forget about today."

They sat and talked for almost two hours and just kept ordering food. The food was delicious, the company extraordinary, but not only was the place closing, they both agreed tomorrow was going to come early and be a very, very long day.

Mitch walked Jewels across the street to her place. After a long embrace that was more reassuring in nature than romantic, Jewels went inside. Mitch had waited until he saw her actually step onto the elevator before he left and continued the four blocks to his hotel. As he passed the desk, two men in suits he'd either never seen or never noticed gave him the once over. He gave them as casual a nod as he could and went up to his room.

When he opened his door and stepped in he saw a folded piece of paper on the floor. He picked it up, tossed his jacket over the chair and tossed what he thought was a bill onto his nightstand.

As he got ready for bed he thought about the day's events. Mitch realized this afternoon that everyone had started to "what if" themselves to death. He knew that type of thinking was toxic but it was tough to avoid after a day like today.

Mitch flopped down on the bed and was just about to call Jewels when something about the note struck him odd. It had opened slightly as he had tossed it onto the nightstand and he could clearly see it wasn't a bill. It was a letter from the hotel, specifically the management. It read:

Dear Valued Hotel Guest,

It is with upmost regret that we must inform you, effective at midnight tonight, each room will be assessed a twenty-five dollar per night building security surcharge.

In light of current events in California, and other cities across the nation, we feel that it is in the best interest of all our guests that we increase the presence of security at our hotel.

In addition, we would request that you make an effort to return to the hotel as early in the evening as possible. We, as I'm sure you do, hope that these measures are only temporary in nature. Thank you for your understanding in this matter.

~ The Management

The town's going mad was Mitch's first thought. He called Jewels to say goodnight and tell her about the crazy letter. Surprisingly, she had a note under her door as well. They apparently weren't going to hit her up for any money at this time but they had developed a new building security plan. The plan included locking the outer doors of the building at 9:00 p.m. as opposed to midnight and there was a new visitor sign-in procedure. Until further notice, all visitors needed to be on both a visitor list and sign in when they arrived at the building.

It had been a long night for Jewels and she felt tomorrow would be one of those days where coffee would never be far out of reach.

The news out of California, the next morning, was very bad. The situation had deteriorated rapidly and was getting worse by the hour. Airports were jammed and traffic leaving California was solid all the way to the Nevada border. Sadly, many people thought they knew best and had fled east to Arizona on I-8 or I-10. Both of those routes were directly in line with the predicted highest concentrations of radioactive debris and fallout.

They weren't dead yet, but history was not on their side. Many of them would be getting sick in a few days' time and not even know why. This had been a very large dirty bomb and had lifted several hundred tons of San Diego waterfront three miles up into the air. All of that radioactive debris, mostly dust at this point was heading east at about fifteen miles per hour.

Gina was very solemn this morning. The girls both knew people that were from the San Diego area or that still had family there. What everyone was having trouble getting their heads wrapped around was that this wasn't like the conflagration in Oakland, California in 1991. Those folks were rebuilding six months later. You could rebuild after a fire. The city of San Diego was finished.

At 10:00 a.m., Rick called on the secure line and asked if they had been watching the news. Jewels said they had, but only intermittently. "What's up?"

Rick explained, "The Arizona National Guard is not letting anyone pass any farther east than the Winterhaven/Yuma pass in the south and the Ehrenberg area in the north. They are telling them to leave their cars and possessions and get on busses. Apparently the people don't understand that they, as well as their cars, are covered with radioactive contaminants. About thirty minutes ago some folks tried to shoot their way through the road blocks. The press is going crazy because the FAA still has all the press helicopters grounded. Jewels, bring up your High Side computer, and follow the link I sent to your inbox."

Jewels logged on, opened her email and accessed the link. It was the video feed, obviously from an aircraft, and what it was showing was beyond description.

"Rick, what am I looking at?" Jewels asked without taking her eyes off the monitor.

"That's a live High Side only feed from the Air Force's Constant Phoenix aircraft. It's in a racetrack pattern over what's left of San Diego Harbor."

"Aren't they afraid of being contaminated?"

"There's always a risk, but they have all kinds of protective gear onboard to limit the crew's exposure. We've had this type of mission aircraft around since the late forties. There used to be seven of these big OC-135 variants back in the early nineties until their funding got cut." Rick went on, "The aircraft were used for all kinds of stuff, now they're down to one maybe two birds. The plane's only real modifications are primarily related to the on-board atmospheric collection suite, which allows the crew to detect radioactive clouds in real time. It will collect gaseous and particulate samples over the city and then probably track the debris cloud downwind. I imagine fairly soon we'll have a pretty good idea what we're dealing with, radiologically, both there in the port area and east of the city. The most important job for those operators is protecting themselves and the rest of the crew from potential over-exposure to the radiation."

Jewels was mesmerized by the scenes coming over the monitor. It was like watching an epic disaster movie that just wouldn't end. Every moment the camera would capture something more horrific than the last.

Rick told her, "We used these planes, and others, after Chernobyl to warn folks on the ground as well as notifying commercial air traffic where the cloud of debris was heading. They certainly don't want anyone to unintentionally fly through the debris cloud. I'd imagine they'll probably be doing the same thing here."

From the angle of the shot, Jewels could tell the plane was flying south. At the bottom of her screen was a little information window that gave the aircraft's speed, altitude and GPS location.

"Jewels, they just opened up the audio link."

She could hear a man speaking, "They were looking at what used to be Naval Air Station North Island." The camera zoomed in at what used to be Naval Air Station Coronado. It was now just a smooth section of land at the end of an island.

Jewels was just about to ask what island it was when the man zoomed his camera in on what, even at this altitude, appeared to be an enormous crater in the middle of the bay.

"That's ground zero," she heard the man say.

He panned the camera back briefly to give some perspective of what he was looking at then zoomed into the former navy base. Jewels could discern nothing recognizable. No ships remained at the port. The camera man zoomed in on the bow or the stern of some kind of ship. It was hundreds of yards inland and other than its general shape not matching its surroundings didn't look much like a ship.

"SE, Pilot"

"Go, SE"

"We've got ten, maybe fifteen, more minutes then we need to RTB (return to base)."

"Roger that SE, can we get one more turn to the north?"

"Yes, sir, and then you need to find us some cool rain over the ocean." They had chopped the audio feed so Jewels talked to Rick.

"Rick, can I ask you a couple of questions?"

"I might not know the answers, but sure."

"Who's 'SE' and why are they trying to find some rain?"

"On an aircraft, every crew position has a shortened title for talking on the radio. For example, you have the Pilot, CO-pilot, NAV-igator. Well, the crew that works the radiological detection stuff in the back of the jet are called Special Equipment Operators or SEO's. That's still a bit too long for the radio so they shortened it down to "SE." The second question is easy. They've been flying through all this hot radiological crap for a while and there's probably a good chance some of it is stuck to the outside of the plane. They'll head out to sea and find a good storm to get off what they can before they fly back to whatever base they are operating out of. No sense contaminating the ground crew where they land."

Jewels was rather impressed. While perhaps the high-tech nerd stuff wasn't necessarily Rick's area of expertise, he certainly knew a lot of other stuff. She had to know, "Rick, how did you get so smart about this plane, its crew, and its mission?"

Rick laughed. "It's a long story, Jewels. It involves an air show, two old crew dogs, three pretty girls and a couple of cases of ice cold beer." Rick tipped back in his chair, placed his hands behind his head, closed his eyes and smiled. Those were definitely better days.

—⁓—

Mitch was a man on a mission. Prior to "The Event" as everyone was now calling it, he was strictly in charge of finding, monitoring, and keeping records of drone related signals. He had a new job now and was currently on semi-permanent loan from the NSA to the CIA's Signals Analysis Division. As long as he didn't focus on his division's acronym (SAD) he was okay with the temporary duty. Mitch had only one job to do now, and that was to find the source of the ship's drone signal. Now that he knew what he was looking for his job was somewhat easier. He had also been granted access to somewhat better resources and a much faster, more robust computer network.

What the CIA and all its subordinate agencies had determined so far was that this had definitely been a North Korean device. The science wasn't even in yet from the national labs where the samples had been sent, but Washington had already received, at first through channels, then directly from the North Koreans, an acknowledgement of it being their weapon. It was their apparent attempt to get out ahead of what was sure to become a high level retaliation and they were trying to mitigate the damage.

According to the generals they had spoken to, the plan was to just park the freighter in Los Angeles Harbor as a show of strength and to get the west to lift the various trade embargos against their country. According to the diplomats, their plan had obviously gone awry and they were working on what could have possibly happened. In essence they were trying to tell D.C. this was an accident. Washington was skeptical and not amused.

With more access, a larger metaphoric hammer and some uncharacteristic help from the French government, Mitch was able to identify the private party owner of that particular frequency. Sadly, yet quite characteristically for the French government, they had not been as helpful when they were asked for his location.

Apparently, although maligned recently in the press for several supposed failures, the CIA still had significant sway when it came to dealing with this type of stumbling block. Rick figured it was a pretty good bet that when the CIA, MI6, and the Mossad were all looking for you, you will be found.

The man was identified, located, and grabbed within hours of Mitch pointing out what satellite had transmitted the drone signal. He was currently being questioned at an undisclosed facility.

CHAPTER 46

USS Connecticut

Ten miles out at sea, Captain Trent Briggs and the crew of the *USS Connecticut* had completed the battle damage assessment by lunchtime yesterday and were currently at station keeping. Essentially the *Connecticut* was maintaining their position, monitoring the wind direction and still sending HD video back to the various agencies in D.C. At about 7:00 a.m., they had seen the OC-135 Constant Phoenix jet go by and waved. The jet waggled its wings in a universally known greeting and acknowledgement, "We see you." The *Connecticut's* communications officer raised them on the secure VHF and the boat's radiation control officer and the operations officer from the Constant Phoenix OC-135 talked for a few moments on what the harbor looked like from the air.

The operations officer onboard the jet reported they had completed two out of three orbits around the metropolitan area and it was devastated. The jet's southbound legs were along the coast each time and they had subsequently extended their track to the north and south and widened their track inland by two miles with each orbit. According to observers on board, after the first two passes, they had not seen any signs of life until well past Interstate 805 to the east, Imperial Beach on the south end of the track, and Point Loma to the northwest.

The operations officer reported that huge fires were raging unabated and with no one to turn off the commercial and residential natural gas supply, they were spreading rapidly. Periodically they had seen secondary explosions as propane tanks or other highly volatile mixtures caught fire. In many other parts of the town, the piles of rubble and debris of buildings left partially standing after the initial blast had turned into raging pillars of fire.

The tank farm at the Defense Fuel Supply Point (DFSP) Point Loma to the north had exploded immediately when the initial heat wave ruptured the tanks. Twenty-eight million gallons of aviation gas and diesel fuel ignited simultaneously. The primary and secondary blast waves from the exploding tanks had blown burning debris past the facility and into the La Playa residential area. These fires spread rapidly north and were now consuming the residential areas of Roseville-Fleet Ridge and Sunset Cliffs.

It had almost been twenty-four hours since the explosion, and still remnants of what used to be thousands of private boats moored at the marinas had become nothing more than large Molotov cocktails, each with its own unique length of fuse. Occasionally, a solitary exploding boat would start a chain of explosions where the incoming tide had bunched a group of shattered boats together in a pile. Much of the former downtown area had been instantly consumed by the weapon's initial fireball, with flame heights in several areas, still exceeding 400 feet.

The fire's intensity continued to grow and created its own weather pattern or "fire storm" drawing in surface winds with destructively violent surface in-drafts. In the distance the aircrew had seen several tornado like whirls from exploding fuel trucks or other sources of accelerant. These fires were far beyond human intervention and would die out only when they became starved of anything combustible.

The chief concern of the plane's crew, from a radiation standpoint, was a combination of two things they could do nothing about: the onshore breeze and the height of the super-heated debris plume. The strong onshore breeze had continued unabated since early morning and continued to feed several firestorms on the outskirts of town. Flames in many of these areas were several hundred feet high. As the fires continued to grow, their relative distance to each other got smaller. Several of the massive fires had already merged and were heading east consuming blocks of homes at a time and presumably their residents as they went. The wind was not only affecting the fires but the radioactive dust and debris deposited after the initial explosion. Any material that was contaminated, was being superheated by the fires, turned to radioactive ash and smoke, then carried high aloft and blown due east.

At this point, the Air Force was recommending to FEMA that anyone able to evacuate should travel either due north on I-15 or south on I-5, I-805 or SR 125 to Mexico. Evacuations to the east were not advised. The Constant Phoenix aircraft had first detected the radioactive debris plume on their way to San Diego over three hours ago. They had been only 25 miles west of Phoenix, Arizona. By now, the plume had reached well past downtown Phoenix. The OC-135 had flown past them one last time, wig-wagged its wings and headed out to sea in search of some storm clouds.

Captain Briggs was at his desk reading the *Connecticut's* damage report. Other than some blistering of the anechoic tiles on the front third of the boat, it had made it through the explosion relatively unscathed. They had been very fortunate not to have been any closer to the explosion or resulting shockwave. None of the radiation detectors on board had even chirped. This indicated that the submarine had been shielded from the initial burst of gamma radiation by the amount of water above her at the time of the blast.

Other than several crewmen being injured, bumps and bruises mostly, by the sudden and unexpected movement of the boat, nobody was requiring assistance from anyone other than the ship's medical officer. Captain Briggs had the feeling the news that no one on his crew needed outside assistance may be the best news he would receive today. During the last hour, as he peered at the California coastline, he wasn't sure where any help would have come from.

According to the report Briggs received from the Pentagon, the navy lost all of the ships that had been at port when the bomb detonated. It was widely believed that, due to the magnitude of the explosion and the overall effect of the weapon, they did not anticipate any survivors. It was a grim assessment, but it made sense. When you took into account that nobody had the capability to get into the port and look for survivors, their estimates were probably spot on.

Of the larger ships lost, the list included the aircraft carrier USS Carl Vinson, five Los Angeles class fast attack submarines, twelve destroyers, four frigates, four cruisers, three amphibious assault ships, and the hospital ship Mercy. This was not the entire list but the summation of the report was the navy did not expect any vessel or crew in port at the time of the explosion to have survived.

Captain Trent Briggs, a navy man on the last cruise of his career, a man with a wife and two wonderful children waiting for him somewhere, called the office of the Chief of Naval Operations at the Pentagon and asked what any American serviceman would ask at a time like this: How can we help?

Elmendorf /Richardson Base Hospital

Jonah was glad to have the tube out of his throat but it unfortunately meant more questions. He was still very sore in several locations but making progress. The neck wound, which had the doctors so concerned when he was first brought into the ER, wasn't giving him much pain to speak of. Talking and swallowing were still a painful challenge. His shoulder was another story. The damage to that area had been significant.

The bullet entered high in his back, passed over his shoulder blade but found and fractured his collarbone. After the initial surgery, to staunch the bleeding, the orthopedic surgeons made the determination he needed a titanium plate for the collarbone. The wound site around his collarbone seemed to hurt each time Jonah took a breath.

The rest of the guys were in various states of recovery. Terrance and Roy were both doing well in their physical therapy regimens. The hospital's orthopedist was pretty sure the wound in Terrance's calf would leave him with a limp. That was okay with Terrance. His new limp came with one hell of a story.

Skip's shoulder was mending slowly. The bullet entered high on his back, creased his shoulder blade then exited just above his collarbone. It hurt like hell to move it, but like Terrance, he had one heck of a story to go with it.

With the healing process came more and more questions about the *Dreamer* and its now deceased captain, Mark Lamb.

Sadly, there wasn't much Jonah or the other guys could tell them about the man they'd known as Mark Lamb.

Over the past few days, every three letter agency you could think of had paid him at least three visits. Everyone wanted to know pretty much the same thing. Where they had met Mark, when, or did they ever, get suspicious and did any of them know who the other men attached to the cages were.

The only "aha" moment was when they said the men might have been Middle Eastern but were definitely sailors.

"Why can you be sure they were sailors?" asked an FBI agent from Seattle. Skip had chuckled and chimed in about the goofy looking sailor suits.

Now the big boys were interested. The man in the dark suit asked Jonah if he thought he'd be able to identify the uniform if he saw it again?

"Do you know who I am and what I used to do for a living?" asked a tired and very sore Jonah West.

"Yes, you're retired Navy Seal Jonah West."

"Do you think I would have made it through to retirement if I was unable to identify people and uniforms of various armed services around the world?"

"Probably not, sir."

"These guys were Iranian Navy Special Forces."

The man was busy scribbling on his notepad for several moments before he finally said, "I see."

Jonah, who felt he had been asked one too many silly questions was growing tired of the whole questioning thing, looked at the nurse and croaked his voice just for effect said, “Enough for today.” Less than ten minutes had passed when a knock came at the door. Jonah really wasn’t in the mood for any more questions. From his perspective he’d done his part. He rolled his head toward the door and was ready to verbally confront whoever was trying to bother him now.

Jonah had to blink a few times to clear his eyes to make sure of what he was seeing. Had the nurse given him something for pain? He recognized the pattern of the LL Bean jacket right away.

His mind was still working on the rest.

Any doubts of who was coming in the door were erased by a booming voice he’d heard many times before, “JW, if I’d wanted to travel thirteen hours to come visit you, I would have come to see you in Afghanistan. It might have actually been closer.”

Jonah closed his eyes and smiled. With those words Jonah knew his dad was there and everything would be okay.

The Yunes

The *Yunes* had been traveling south southwest for almost two days and was just about to pass through the Babuyan channel between Taiwan and the Philippines. In just over two hours the boat was going to turn south and travel through the Palawan trench.

Kilo-class submarine captains are always trying to find the perfect balance between speed and endurance, the sweet spot so to speak, where they could get the most out of their boat and their crew without compromising the mission. The slower the boat traveled, the longer it could stay fully submerged. The *Yunes* had been traveling at only 3 knots submerged which had increased its range to 400 nautical miles. They had not fully charged their batteries since Thursday afternoon.

It was hard to keep a secret for very long on a submarine and eventually everyone on board the *Yunes* had heard about the devastating explosion in

San Diego. Naturally, Allah was to be praised for assisting with the killing of over 2.3 million Americans. What perhaps the crew didn't know was that very few times in naval history had anyone been looking for a vessel as ardently as the world was probably looking for them.

Fortunately for the crew of the *Yunes*, the Americans wouldn't appear to know exactly *who* they were looking for or *where* to look. Captain Babakan expected them to solve that mystery soon enough. Unfortunately, from a tactical perspective, the *Yunes* needed to surface and refuel. They had been in contact with their supply vessel and had surfaced only about 50 yards away from her stern.

After maneuvering closer to the other ship's stern, they connected the fuel lines and began the fuel transfer. In addition to fuel, the ship brought fresh fruit and vegetables to the *Yunes* to restock their now almost empty food lockers. All manner of food stuff was sent onboard and the crew's spirits were definitely on the rise.

Within five minutes of the quartermaster telling him they were ready to untether from the supply ship, the supply ship's captain called over that there were two planes on his ship's radar coming in very low. Babakan would have only minutes to get away.

"Secure the boat for emergency dive," shouted Captain Babakan.

"Boat is secured for emergency dive, sir."

Babakan had not come all this way to die like this. "Dive the boat and give me a firing solution on that supply ship."

"Sir?"

"Get me a firing solution on that resupply ship right now!"

"Firing solution locked."

"Fire the torpedo!"

Mr. Feng was over in the shadows of the bridge watching the captain. He smiled as he watched the young submarine captain come of age.

"Distance to target?"

The range between the vessels had been so short that, before his sonar man could answer, everyone on board heard the tremendous explosion. A quick check through the *Yune's* periscope confirmed that the vessel was gone and only a burning sea remained.

Captain Babakan checked with his exec and navigation officers and adjusted their course away from the coast through the deepest water of the Babuyan channel. If they were lucky, the two aircraft weren't sub hunters and hadn't put any sonobouys in the water to find them or torpedoes to kill them. Babakan took comfort in thinking on the positive side. In reality he knew that with any mission, the longer it takes to accomplish that mission, the more likely you were to run out of luck. As he ducked his head and left the bridge, he caught a glimpse of a smiling Mr. Feng. Feng had gestured good job and shouted, "Good job, Babakan, no loose ends."

As the captain of the *Yunes* walked to his quarters he wondered at what point he and his crew would be considered loose ends.

Great Wall

One of several items of interest that Captain Lee, of the *Shooting Star*, had delivered to the port of Shanghai on his way back from the Iranian port of Bandar Abbas was a pair of type 53 Russian made torpedoes. It had taken a bit of engineering but the crew of the *Great Wall* and some engineers from the Bohai Shipyard had figured out how to shoot the Russian torpedo out of the Chinese submarine. Their latest orders were very clear; they were to shoot two inert torpedoes into the side of the *Bien Hoa*, disable it, and then recue the crew. The captain had to read that part of the message twice. The next part of the message was also clear. When they were next contacted, they were to locate and sink the Iranian submarine *Yunes* with two Yu-8 torpedoes. Any recognized survivor should be rescued from the sea.

The *Bien Hoa* had continued its mapping of the sea floor without let up and had been working their way north of the position worrisome to the Chinese.

Every few hours, the *Great Wall* would move very slowly to the north, following the *Bien Hoa*.

Provo Utah
Highway I-15 N

Stacy and her intrepid family set out from Primm, Nevada almost six hours ago and desperately needed some gas. She had stopped twice and quickly put 5 gallons of gas from one of the cans into the car. It was late evening and she was exhausted. The kids were asleep and she desperately needed to close her eyes.

According to Garmin there was a gas station about a mile away. Stacy planned to stop, get gas, and then find a place to sleep. Trent always told her to fill the cans first. It was definitely a hassle but she would do as he had instructed. Stacy pulled into the station and had just got out when two men came out of the office with long guns and angry faces.

"Where are you from pretty lady?"

Stacy thought fast. She knew why they were asking and knew that saying "California" wasn't going to go over well. It was time to tap her tired side. Stacy began to cry, "We're returning from a trip to Denver and just found out our home in San Diego got blown up. Now we're homeless and trying to make it to my parent's house in Sand Point."

The men looked mortified and quickly placed their guns back in the office. Both men took turns trying to apologize. As they explained it, the authorities were warning that many cars had made it out of California that were carrying both radioactivity on the outside of the cars and on the passengers as well. They had been asked to stop cars with California tags and call the authorities.

The larger of the two asked if he could help her pump her gas. Stacy agreed and the two men filled both the tank in her car and the gas cans.

Stacy asked the men if they knew of a safe place for her to stay and they agreed the best place was at their home on the north side of town. Although tempting, Stacy was leaning toward a hotel where they wouldn't impose on anyone.

The men told her there was an exit about 15 miles north on I-15 that had everything she was looking for. Stacy had no intentions of leaving her car tonight and planned on parking in the back lot of a hotel right across the street from perhaps a McDonalds. Like most towns near the highway these days, it was not a difficult combination to find a hotel across the lot from a fast food joint.

Everyone cycled through the bathrooms and got some burgers. Even after he'd been fed, Boomer worked on the kids. The whining was bad enough. It was only because Stacy couldn't stand the drooling; she relented and let the kids feed Boomer a cheeseburger. She had a good idea what that decision would lead to, but the kids were worried about Boomer starving to death.

At around 2:00 a.m. everyone in the car regretted serving Boomer the cheeseburger, except maybe Boomer, who slept through the entire, particularly smelly, event.

At 6:00 a.m., Stacy's mom called and woke everyone up. Apparently both her mom and dad were coming south down Highway 15 to rescue them and had no idea she was so close.

"Honey, Dad's Garmin says the 265 West University Parkway exit is only 20 minutes away from us, is that true?"

Although Stacy was proud of her mom for making an attempt to embrace the technology of this century, apparently how the little black box worked was lost on her. "Mom, I don't know where I am right now let alone you."

"Well Dear, I know exactly where you are. The thingy says you're 18 minutes away from us."

Stacy hadn't had any coffee and maybe tomorrow this whole exercise would be cute. Right now, though, she needed it to stop.

"Mom? Do you want to talk to the kids?"

Stacy's mom, God love her, sometimes couldn't think that perhaps the other person had something else to do at 6:00 in the morning, like for instance…pee, and kept on talking. "Do the kids want to drive with Nana or Papa? Have they eaten yet? Can you wait for us and we can all eat together?"

By now, Boomer was pawing out the door to be let out. Stacy couldn't blame him, she felt the same way. Lord knows what he would do if he didn't get out and do his business.

"Mom? Talk to the kids while I walk Boomer, whatever you work out is fine with me. See you soon."

Stacy handed the phone to Alex and hooked Boomer to his leash. Apparently Boomer couldn't wait for her to open his door and came up and over her seat. She had learned years earlier to not try and stop an eighty-five-pound Black Lab in mid-flight, and out he came. When Boomer was done with what he needed to do, Stacy cycled the kids through the bathrooms and then locked the kids in the car with the dog while she walked briskly down to the McDonald's ladies room.

It wasn't homemade coffee, but it was working well enough. Stacy grabbed the last newspaper out of the rack and learned about not only the complete and utter devastation of San Diego but the bombing and destruction of the Panama Canal lock system. According to the news, the west coast of the United States was on its own.

USS Connecticut
Off the Coast of San Diego

The *Connecticut* had been sitting off the coast for two days now and her usefulness as an observation platform had been usurped by other assets more suitable for remaining on the surface. The *USS Chafee*, an Arleigh Burke Class Aegis Destroyer was due to arrive on station tomorrow morning and relieve the *Connecticut*. The Burke Class Destroyer class is one of the US Navy's most advanced and powerful ships. Its normal mission is to conduct prompt, sustained combat operations at sea in support of national policy. Coupled with the vessel's size, crew compliment, and advanced communications systems, it was by far the better vessel for remaining on the surface in a crisis management and monitoring mode.

The crew of the *Connecticut* was bone weary and suffering the effects of being on the surface. The submarine's crew was unaccustomed to the constant rolling of the boat and some of the crew had even resorted to Dramamine to calm their seasickness. For pride's sake, the doctor had written it up as "temporary inner ear instability." They had dutifully completed their mission of monitoring and videoing the remnants of the harbor and as much of the downtown as possible. The crew had kept a live video feed to D.C. up and manned for their entire time on station. Although they received permission to leave station several hours ago, they postponed their departure until nightfall when the forecasters had predicted the wind would change direction and bring the still falling radioactive debris in their direction. Then with some reluctance and an overwhelming sense of hopelessness, it was time to go. They buttoned up the hatches, dove the boat, and headed north.

Their new orders were to report to her home port of Bremerton at best possible and safest speed. What Captain Briggs really wanted to do was park the *Connecticut* on the bottom and let the crew sleep for a day. He had gone to minimal manning as they proceeded north up the coast. When they were about an hour out of Los Angeles they had been asked to report on what they could see in the Port of Los Angeles area.

The *Connecticut* had just come abreast of Los Angeles when, from just over 15 miles off the coast of the city, the watch officer on the *Connecticut* could see the fires. They were big, spreading and illuminated large areas of the downtown. The towns of Long Beach, Seal Beach, and San Pedro all had large multi structure fires burning. Several downtown high rises were completely engulfed. Briggs shook his head, what a waste.

Captain Briggs had the communications officer tune into the National Guard (NG) frequency and quickly learned that several cities had been virtually abandoned by anyone who could leave and the towns left for the looters. Even the police had fallen back to regroup. According to several reports, the rioting and looting was on a scale unprecedented in recent history. They picked up a short wave operator's broadcast who was reporting that the riots over the past two days made the Watts riots of 1965 look like an out of control birthday party. He reported that from his location he could see at least thirteen of his neighbors dead in the streets. They'd had no way to protect themselves and had been dragged out of their homes and killed. The 911/EMS system was completely swamped and was no longer responding to calls. The NG frequency was reporting that thousands of calls were not even being answered.

When the National Guard was called up by the governor up in Sacramento, who after two days still hadn't made it down south to witness the carnage, the troops opted to follow the orders of the on scene commanders. When the governor had again ordered them to deploy to the downtown areas, the on scene commanders halted their deployment until they received their promised additional air support. They sent scouts forward and their reports were that they had almost immediately come under small arms fire. They would apparently be doing more than directing traffic.

Most of these troops were returning combat veterans from either Iraq or Afghanistan and they recognized they were heading into the same urban warfare environment they had recently left. These troops weren't waiting for the California Highway Patrol to show up. They were waiting for Apache gunships.

Captain Briggs met with his officers and it was agreed the crew should begin the process of trying to contact their families. By 11:00 p.m. PST, five of his crew from the San Diego area, who were trying to call home, did not speak to their loved ones. Instead, they had received a recorded message that explained circuits were disrupted in that area and that technicians were working on the problem and hoped to restore service soon. The men knew better and were bearing up to the news far better than the captain anticipated. The captain asked the men where their families lived. Their answers were disturbing. Three of the men's families lived one block farther away from the port than Stacy and the kids. A true naval officer, Commander Trent W. Briggs, Captain, USS Connecticut, would be making his call… last.

CHAPTER 47

Washington D.C.

Both the folks from the BOATSS office and the CIA, as well as Mitch's folks from the NSA, had been working very hard to convince the State Department and the Pentagon they not only knew for certain what vessel had delivered the explosives to destroy the SBX, they knew where it was in real time. They made presentations at the Pentagon as well as over at the State Department all to no avail. No one in Washington wanted to give a go order until they knew in their minds, it was the right time.

The other fly in the ointment was the situation in Panama. They found the audio file of the two submersibles entering the lower half of the Panama Canal one day prior to the destruction of the locks and knew they had come from Columbia yet, as with the Yunes, according to the State Department they were still gathering "pertinent data."

Although the locks were owned, operated, and maintained by Panama, the Panamanian government formally requested the United States Army Corps of Engineers look at the situation. The Engineers report was bleak. According to the Corps, whose estimates always tended to be on the optimistic side, the locks at Pedro Miguel would not be functioning for at least eighteen months. By their estimates, the new locks to the north had the potential of opening sooner. Of greater concern to the people of Panama was the developing potential for environmental and economic disaster from the grounded freighters spilling fuel or other toxins into the lakebed.

Washington had several more significant problems on their hands, chief among them being the loss of the Panama Canal. In their last briefing at the Pentagon, it was briefed that the navy, from both a tactical and strategic point of view, would be limited to whatever surface ships were currently in the Pacific. Instead of the average 28 days to get from Naval Air Station Mayport or Naval Submarine Base Kings Bay on America's southeast coast or the slightly longer 30-day voyage from Naval Station Norfolk in Virginia, the navy was now looking at 63 days and 64 respectively. In addition, the trip would require passage around the southern tip of South America which was never a pleasant trip even in the best of weather. With the past several year's drawdown of the US Navy's surface fleet, it was generally hoped by all those in attendance at the briefing that the navy would not be called upon for anything more than routine patrol duties.

As of this morning, the greatest and most immediate concern for the nation was the rapidly unfolding humanitarian disaster on the west coast. San Diego was gone and even the experts were in agreement there was little hope for survivors inside an eight-mile ring of the city. Every community northeast, east, and southeast of San Diego for two hundred miles was now or was rapidly becoming, a ghost town. The fears, both known and unknown, of radioactive fallout was the initial driving force for leaving but for many, the mass exodus of the population of the coast had been the tipping point. Store shelves were empty and the usual resupply chain for their region originated in San Diego, a city that no longer existed or Los Angeles, where Marshall Law had been declared last night.

Several brave truckers tried to bring in much needed supplies and had been rewarded for their efforts by having their loads high jacked, with several of the drivers being killed. FEMA tried to get stuff brought in on trains but even with National Guard troops riding shotgun, they were still unable to find crews willing to risk heading into the hell that the southwestern states had become.

Great Wall

The captain of the *Great Wall* could hear the engines of the *Bien Hoa* very clearly now and they finalized their preparations.

"Weapons officer, are you sure the weapons are inert?"

"Yes, captain, I've checked it myself," replied a nervous weapons officer. He wasn't privy to the whole plan and found it curious they were shooting two inert Russian torpedoes in the first place. That curiosity was compounded, of course, by their target. The *Bien Hoa* was no longer anywhere near the Chinese drilling sites.

"Torpedo room check torpedo guidance controls," ordered the *Great Wall's* executive officer. He ran the automated diagnostic of all the interfaces between the submarine and the torpedoes.

"Torpedoes guidance system test complete, sir."

"Very good, I will need a firing solution on the stern of the *Bien Hoa* in about five minutes."

"Communications, send the message in this envelope to the address I gave you earlier." The captain handed his communications officer a sealed red envelope.

"Should I wait for a response, sir?"

The captain thought for a moment. "No, not this time, carry on."

Yunes

The *Yunes* had been traveling submerged now for just over 26 hours and were just east of Payne Shoal in the northern half of the South China Sea. Although crew morale was higher now than over the past few weeks, Captain Babakan was worried. His motivation behind blowing up the supply ship last night had been purely one of survival. Maybe if time had permitted he could have warned them to abandon ship. His decision was based on his belief that if someone boarded the ship and interrogated the crew, he felt confident they would have given him up fairly quickly.

It felt odd to believe in Holy Jihad and feel little or no empathy for innocent people killed in suicide bombings, but strangely, somehow, feel badly for the family and friends of the strangers in the supply ship he had essentially murdered in cold blood. The expression, "no loose ends" was really starting to bother him.

Before turning in at 9:30 p.m. Babakan ordered his executive officer to bring the boat to radio mast height at 2:00 a.m., when they anticipated the least amount of moonlight, and check for message traffic. He was also curious to see what was going on in the world. His communications officer had complied and received only one message. The message wasn't from the Iranian High Council or anyone in Iran's Department of Defense or Government. The message headers were from an unknown source. It simply read "Attention Mr. Feng" in Farsi and the rest of the message was a series of Chinese characters.

The communications officer knocked on Mr. Feng's door. It was just after 2:00 a.m. He hoped the Chinese man wouldn't be upset. Needless to say, the officer was rather startled when Feng opened the door completely dressed and put out his hand. Feng hadn't seen the envelope because it was behind the officer's back yet somehow this man, at 2:00 a.m., knew he had brought him something.

Mr. Feng opened the envelope quickly and read the short message. It was in his native tongue. Loosely translated to English it read, "Hide little rabbit, knock, knock, knock."

"Very good, thank you. Might I ask when you received this?" The communications officer glanced at his watch.

"About four minutes ago, sir."

"Excellent, could you step into my cabin a moment while I dictate my response?" "Yes, sir."

As the communications officer crossed the threshold of Mr. Feng's cabin the seven inch Special Forces knife Feng had concealed behind his back had come around with lightning speed and was in and out of the younger man's chest three times before he hit the floor. He wasn't dead yet and stared up at Feng.

Mr. Feng looked down at the communications officer's face as the life slowly ebbed from his body and whispered to him, "No loose ends."

Wiping off the blade on the man's shirt, Feng gathered his duffle bag and headed toward the bow of the boat. He had less than five minutes now and he couldn't afford to be late. Two crewmen passed him, giving him as wide a berth as possible in the narrow confines of a submarine's passageway.

Feng opened the dive trunk, sat down quickly on the floor and opened his duffle bag. In the bag was a survival suit and a small breathing device. He changed quickly and, with one minute to spare, stood on the small seat of the dive trunk. With a small hammer, Feng produced from his bag, he pounded on the steel frame of the hatch three times.

Great Wall

"Sonar reports three metal on metal sounds bearing 035°."

"Very good, I need that solution on the *Bien Hoa* right now."

"Firing solution for two inert torpedoes locked on target one, sir."

"I also need a firing solution on the second target reported at 035°."

"Fire both inert torpedoes at target one and monitor for their impact."

"Firing two inert torpedoes at target one."

With only a slight motion to the rest of the boat, two Russian built Type 53 torpedoes closed in on the stern of the *Bien Hoa* at almost 52 miles per hour. They estimated the run time at 45 seconds.

"Weapons officer! Where are we on the second target?"

"They are very quiet sir, I cannot be sure of the firing solution."

As if his voice and thought had traveled through the 2 miles of water to the Yunes, three bangs once again came over the sonar man's speaker.

"I've got him!"

"Put two torpedoes into that target as fast as you can."

"Firing tubes three and four."

These torpedoes had several methods of tracking a target and the captain had little doubt that at least one was going to impact the Yunes in less than three minutes.

"Sir, I have two confirmed hits on the *Bien Hoa*. No explosion, but from all the noise, she's taking on water."

So far, so good. The captain of the *Great Wall* impatiently waited for the rest of his little ruse to play out.

Yunes

"Sir, I've got two sets of torpedo screws in the water, two bearing away and two closing on our position."

"Get the captain, come right 090° and increase to flank speed."

After almost colliding with the man sent to retrieve him, Captain Babakan literally flew onto the bridge, "Report!"

The *Yunes* sonar man, with some question in his voice, said, "Sir, a moment ago I had two types of torpedoes in the water. Then I distinctly heard two direct hits from the first two torpedoes on their target but no, I repeat *no* explosion. Maybe they didn't arm themselves? The other two torpedoes are headed toward us."

"Launch countermeasures."

"Launching countermeasures, sir."

"This pair has a much higher screw speed. They are locked on us and closing very quickly."

In the partially filled divers' trunk, Mr. Feng was growing impatient when he suddenly heard the collision alarm. It was almost time to go. All over the ship every hatch was being sealed in a vain attempt to postpone the inevitable. Feng knew he needed to patiently stay inside until the torpedoes had detonated so as not to be killed by the pressure wave from the two explosions.

The first torpedo detonated ten feet forward of the stern with the second breeching the hull and detonating another fifteen feet forward of that. The ship was mortally wounded and started its slow fall to the bottom.

It was time to go. Feng put on his breathing apparatus and flooded the remainder of the escape trunk. In one mighty shove he pushed the hatch open and slowly kicked his way to the surface far above him. He was far deeper than he thought they were.

On the bridge, the crew knew they were dead. The question was who and why? Captain Babakan, in the midst of all the chaos around him, noticed two things. First, there was no sign of Mr. Feng and second, as he glanced over at his gauges, he saw that the light for the dive trunk was illuminated. That one observation answered both of his last two questions. Mr. Feng had tied up yet another loose end.

Babakan had just issued the order to emergency surface when the diesel fuel compartment was breeched and the whole rear end of the boat exploded and came apart. As the bulkheads burst, and the crippled ship slowly spiraled backward to the depths of the South China Sea, as the men around him screamed, Captain Babakan had one final sad thought: We were always a loose end.....

BOATSS

The intrepid team of Jewels, Gina, Mitch, and Rick tried hard for the past two days to convince the powers that be at the State Department and the Pentagon that they knew for a fact it was the Iranian submarine *Yunes* that had delivered the explosives up to the *Dreamer*. They were even able to supply evidence that it had been the *Yunes* who had blown up her very own resupply ship four days ago. They heard every excuse in the book, some so lame they had walked away embarrassed for the person who'd made the statement. Even the US Navy, who for years had sworn to the accuracy of tracking down submarines by their signatures alone, had been pressured to back down by the handwringing bureaucrats at the State Department.

As of this morning's news cycle, the White House was addressing only the results of the attack and not making any comments on the possible persons or country involved in perpetrating the attack. The scope of the emerging humanitarian disaster was allowing the White House press secretary to successfully dodge the 'who' and the 'why' without very much pushback from the main stream press. The message from Washington was they were doing everything in their power to help those people in the stricken areas.

On this morning's overnight news from the BBC's Far East desk came the news story that the People's Republic of China's submarine *Great Wall,* on a routine training mission in the South China Sea, had picked up a distress call by the Vietnamese research vessel *Bien Hoa* moments after it had been attacked without provocation and struck by two torpedoes. Although the torpedoes had not detonated, the alert crew of the *Great Wall* had detected the other submarine's presence and fired twice to prevent any further potential loss of life. The submarine, believed to be the rogue Iranian Kilo-class submarine *Yunes* had been destroyed. Moments after the terrified Vietnamese crew had been rescued and were safe on board the *Great Wall* the two torpedoes stuck in her stern detonated. Munitions experts from the *Great Wall,* while conducting rescue operations, had identified the torpedoes as Russian type 53's which were routinely carried by Kilo-class submarines.

What only a handful of people in the CIA knew, and even they had been told not to divulge, was that the BOATSS system had determined that all four torpedoes had come from the Chinese submarine *Great Wall.* With that knowledge sticking in her gum like a caraway seed, when asked her opinion at this morning's staff meeting, Julie Folk, the holder of a Bachelor's degree from Stanford, a Master's and Doctoral degrees from MIT, with her hands on her hips, had only one thing to say, "What a bunch of crap."

A small group consisting of Jewels, Rick, Mitch, Gina, and some BOATSS support staff, left the conference room and rode the elevator down to the BOATSS offices on sub level three in complete silence. As they rounded the corner of the hallway past the security desk, Ken Shortman gave them a big smile, left his security desk, and fell in behind the little group as they walked down the hall. Ken was still smiling about tossing Ramón out of the building and high-fived his buddy taking his place at the security desk. As they were about to pass Ramón's old office, Roger Batsly stepped out from the dark office, smiled broadly at Jewels and motioned her over. Roger, in a display of showmanship, dramatically flipped on the lights of the office. To no one's surprise, except perhaps Jewels, the new name on the desk said ***Julie Folk***. Mitch waved her deeper into her new office. On the credenza was a very large bouquet of flowers and something covered in a light blue bed sheet. Smiling wickedly, Mitch pulled back the sheet revealing a large commercial grade coffee maker and a five pound can of Columbian roast.

"Speech, Speech," chanted several perverse individuals.

Jewels blushed slightly at all the attention.

Roger spoke first and he was brief, "Jewels, your crew here has done some exceptional work."

"Thank you, sir."

"Don't thank me too quickly; we expect great things from you. Do you have anything to say to your new team, Jewels?"

"Yes, sir, I do."

"Then, by all means, you have the floor."

Jewels looked around her office at the people who were now going to count on her for guidance and realized this had the potential to be one of those defining moments people would probably talk about for a long time. Despite realizing all the significance of the moment and with Gina recognizing the look in Jewels' eye and desperately shaking her head no. Jewels looked in the direction of her new boss. "Mr. Batsly, we all know those Chinese bastards are lying and somehow we're going to prove it." The applause from her small dedicated staff said it all.

Epilogue

For the next several weeks, the nation struggled to come to grips with what happened and continued to evolve on America's west coast. Not only had the death toll from the attack in San Diego continued to rise, the ensuing anarchy in Los Angeles all but destroyed that city as well. For the first time since the American Civil War, federal troops planned and executed coordinated attacks on a population center of the United States. Supported by helicopter gunships and up-armored Humvees, the California National Guard and a division of Marines had retaken the city of Los Angeles. Many former residents of the city's wealthier areas simply left the state. A mass panicked populace was now heading north and east to not only escape the horrific event in San Diego but to flee in front of the exiting population of Los Angeles as well. The western states bordering California, Arizona, Nevada, and even Mexico were resisting the panicked migration of people.

On a small island in the eastern Caribbean, Atash settled into another day of relaxing in the shade near the beach slowly drinking seventy-year-old scotch. He was always in the company of no less than six fair maidens from around the world. Each worked very hard every day to convince him they loved him the most. Some days, Atash took a lot of convincing. Always present in the shadows was his security detail. Every night just before Atash closed his eyes he had the same vision of his friends being murdered in Taiwan. He knew someday the money from his Chinese partners would stop and they would come for him. By his accounting, he was one of the last loose ends.

In the Spratly Islands, two new steel monoliths of Chinese technology and industrial might now loomed 375 feet above the waves. Around the two new drilling platforms, the "Jing qi" and the "Qi Wang," a five-mile security cordon of Chinese naval vessels had been established and patrolled the waters twenty-four hours a day. Under the waves, the Chinese submarine *Great Wall* now patrolled the approach routes to the two drilling rigs. After only three short weeks of drilling, the "Qi Wang" successfully tapped a large pocket of natural gas which the Chinese estimated to be three billion cubic feet. They began lining up trade deals to offload directly from the platform within a week of the discovery. Two formal protests had already been lodged with the United Nations on behalf of Vietnam and the Philippine governments. It was generally understood that without the help of the US Navy, nothing would be done or even be brought up for discussion on the floor of the United Nations.

The next few weeks also saw changes at the BOATSS office. The office itself, having proven its capabilities was now, even in the financially austere environment, fully funded. For Jewels and her crew this meant they finally had heat in their offices, just in time for summer.

Acknowledgements

I would like to thank the following individuals without whom this book would have sat at the edge of my consciousness forever and never been written. First and foremost, my wife, family and friends who had the patience to read the paragraphs, pages and chapters for as long as it took.

Arnie Patterson (US Navy Retired), who kept me straight on my nautical terms.

Alyssa Burkholder, Unalaska CVB for her information on daily life in Dutch Harbor.

Russell Newberry (Deadliest Catch) for his insights on crab fishing and life on the water.

Jack McCormick, Carolina Container Connection, LLC.

Greg Rice, World Wide Equipment.

www.ingramcontent.com/pod-product-compliance
Lightning Source LLC
Chambersburg PA
CBHW022102280326
41933CB00007B/224

* 9 7 8 1 9 4 4 3 1 3 5 1 7 *